Praise for *Revolutionary Moth*

"*Revolutionary Mothering: Love on the Front Lines* is juicy, gutsy, vulnerable, and very brave. These women insist on having their children in a society that does not welcome them, in a world that is rapidly falling apart. Their dream for their children, based on their love of them, encompasses the sorrow and the joy that mothers everywhere, whether human, animal, or plant, feel at this time. A radical vision, many radical visions of how to mother in a time of resistance and of pain."
—Alice Walker

"For women of color, the art of mothering has been framed by the most virulent systems, historically: enslavement, colonialism, capitalism, imperialism. We have had few opportunities to define mothering not only as an aspect of individual lives and choices, but as the processes of love and as a way of structuring community. *Revolutionary Mothering: Love on the Front Lines* arrives as a needed balm. As Toni Cade Bambara once said, we need to 'make revolution irresistible.'"
—Alexis De Veaux, author of *Warrior Poet: A Biography of Audre Lorde* and *Yabo*

"*Revolutionary Mothering* is a love offering from diverse women of color around the globe—queer, immigrant, activist, feminist, poets, workers. An urgent call for radical, transgressive, political, defiant mothering, co-editors Alexis Pauline Gumbs, China Martens, and Mai'a Williams provide an antidote to obligatory, compulsory motherhood which is pioneering and liberating."
—Beverly Guy-Sheftall, Anna Julia Cooper Professor of Women's Studies at Spelman College

"Since i am a 'non-bio/mothering' female, who finds the idea of something growing in, then popping out of my body repugnant, nauseating, and depressing to even contemplate, it comes as a great and refreshing surprise that i honestly enjoyed this intense, vibrantly inspiring collection about 'radical mothering.' Not just enjoyed but learned and totally admired the range of eclectic essays and approaches, as well as the brave, wonderful, trailblazing writers. Recommended for any passionately thinking person who cares about the quality of life in the near or distant future. For people who want to make a major, serious difference; for revolutionaries on a most profound and basic level."
—doris davenport, poet/writer/educator and one of the original contributors to *This Bridge Called My Back*

"There are some books that are considered to be necessary and needed because they speak to the issues that guide our heart and situate our world. *Revolutionary Mothering: Love on the Front Lines* is one of those books. Although it is primarily written for mothers of all ages, the issues that are raised—about family, love, struggle, sacrifice, and acceptance—are universal as they speak to the revolutionary that exists within all of us. It is the book that you will turn to again and again, the one that will become a lifestyle handbook in your home, and the one that you will recommend as a lifeline when folks feel that they have nothing left to give either to themselves or to others. It is the book that mothers have been waiting for."

—Karsonya Wise Whitehead, PhD, author *Notes from a Colored Girl: The Civil War Pocket Diaries of Emilie Frances Davis* and *Letters to My Black Sons: Raising Boys in a Post-Racial America*

"there is an artform in the nurturing of life. when we think of the word 'revolutionary,' what often comes to mind is a warrior with a roar of 'NO' on their lips, moving against the forces of oppression. and there is this other force, the soil for the seed, the water for the green and fragile form, the wisdom to listen, the question that climbs under the cover where you cower away from the psychological and socioeconomic monsters, the shoulder with a collarbone cup for tears. the soft voice whispering, and believing, that who you are is marvelous and miraculous and irreplaceable. this collection offers us voices from those living into and redefining the act of mothering—in your hands is gift after gift of lessons learned on an intergenerational front line. listen to those who hold hands with the future—herein lies everything."

—adrienne maree brown, co-editor of *Octavia's Brood: Science Fiction Stories from Social Justice Movements*

"*Revolutionary Mothering: Love on the Front Lines* is the revolutionary Black and Brown, queer and trans, disabled, non and many partnered parenting manual manifesto we have been waiting for. I am so grateful to see this book in the world, collecting pieces of work I have soaked up eagerly when I read them online, in zines, as handouts in workshops and in now out of print magazines. 'Love is lifeforce' is a line June Jordan said, presented in an essay of hers published here for the first time. That phrase has been on my lips since I read it. This book is revolutionary, marginalized, resisting mama/parenting love lifeforce magic."

—Leah Lakshmi Piepzna-Samarasinha, author of *Dirty River, Love Cake,* and *Consensual Genocide*

"Through *Revolutionary Mothering: Love on the Front Lines*, Alexis Pauline Gumbs, China Martens, and Mai'a Williams have acted as parteras comunitarias, midwifes of words and experiences. This collection reflects, documents, and carries on an ancient and living legacy of practicing and defining motherhood beyond the constraints of the biological. As someone who has been living and writing about mami'hood, the intersection of race, class, gender, sexuality and activism through the lens of mothering, this book reads and feels like a shared collective deep breath, a shared chant/cancion of affirmation, reclamation, and transformation."
    —Maegan "la Mamita Mala" Ortiz, NYRican mami media maker

"This is the book for readers who know mothering is not just about a baby and a mother or parents in an isolated suburban nursery, but that mothering happens in a context of generations, a context of racial history, and in a spiritual context; that it takes place from the shoreline to the front line, in times of scarcity and abundance; that it is queer and love-filled. Here, revolution, love, and mothering are an inseparable unity. Here, the voices of women of color feminists—mothers, daughters, childcare workers—carry on the conversation begun in the 1970s and 1980s, pick up the threads of the reproductive justice movement which has been in the struggle for 20 years.

    "These writings are grounded in the force of transgressive love. It is an act of love by the editors and a gift for readers that June Jordan's 'The Creative Spirit: Children's Literature' is anthologized here for the first time. Jordan says, 'Love is lifeforce. . . . I see love as the essential nature of all that supports life.'

    "The book's first sentence opens in the 'complex matrix of domination and oppression . . . under Ronald Reagan's cowboy capitalism.' The dozens of essays which follow illuminate the complexity of radical 21st-century mothering. The book ends in the home, close up, with one mother and her children: for a year, the mother has drawn a coffee cup a day to remind herself to mind her own needs and desires. On her birthday, her children give her a coffee cup paper sculpture which they have made. After her children have gone to bed, she writes, 'I savor how much there is to celebrate during this time of transformation.' And transformation is what this collection of inspiring essays is about."
    —Faith Holsaert, co-editor of *Hands on the Freedom Plow: Personal Accounts of Women in SNCC*

Revolutionary Mothering

Revolutionary Mothering

Love on the Front Lines

Alexis Pauline Gumbs
China Martens
Mai'a Williams

PM Press

BTL

2016

This edition first published in Canada in 2016 by Between the Lines
401 Richmond Street West, Studio 277, Toronto, Ontario, M5V 3A8, Canada
1-800-718-7201
www.btlbooks.com

Every reasonable effort has been made to identify copyright holders. Between the Lines
would be pleased to have any errors or omissions brought to its attention.

Library and Archives Canada Cataloguing in Publication

　　Revolutionary mothering : love on the front lines / Alexis Pauline Gumbs,
China Martens, and Mai'a Williams, eds.

Between the Lines ISBN 978-1-77113-254-1 (paperback)

　　1. Mothers--Social conditions. 2. Minority women--Social conditions.
3. Motherhood--Social aspects. 4. Motherhood--Political aspects. I. Gumbs,
Alexis Pauline, 1982-, editor II. Martens, China, 1966-, editor III. Williams,
Mai'a, editor

HQ759.R49 2016　　　　　　　　306.874'3　　　　　　　C2015-907923-3

Revolutionary Mothering: Love on the Front Lines
Edited by Alexis Pauline Gumbs, China Martens, and Mai'a Williams
© 2016 by PM Press

ISBN: 9781629631103
Library of Congress Control Number: 2015930906

Cover: John Yates/Stealworks.com
Cover print, Heartbeat City by Favianna Rodriguez (Favianna.com)
Layout: Jonathan Rowland

PM Press
P.O. Box 23912
Oakland, CA 94623

10 9 8 7 6

Printed in the USA

dedicated to all the revolutionary mothers and all the revolutions they've created, because **mothering is love by any means necessary**

Contents

Preface

Loretta J. Ross

Imagine feminists of color in 1981 seeking to explain the complex matrix of domination and oppression we faced under Ronald Reagan's cowboy capitalism, yet feeling invalidated in our communities of color because our militant feminism called attention to sexism, homophobia, and violence. Simultaneously, we were devalued in majority-white feminist circles because we confronted racism, xenophobia, and colonialism in feminist thought and practices. The term "women of color" itself was only four years old, and we were eight years away from Kimberlé Crenshaw's introduction of the word "intersectionality."

As a young feminist in my twenties, I felt like we were frontline warriors without an articulated visual depiction of our nascent understandings about our ambiguous and interwoven positions. I needed a modern-day word cloud to represent my inchoate need for intesectionalized radical feminist theory, despite reading Toni Cade's brilliant *Black Woman* in 1970, which included Francis Beal's groundbreaking essay "Double Jeopardy" on the twin demons of racism and sexism. Audre Lorde and Angela Davis mercilessly attacked the underlying racism within feminism, describing it as reinforcing the patriarchal white supremacist system. Dolores Huerta was organizing farmworkers in the 1960s in California; Geraldine Miller was organizing domestic workers in New York City in the 1970s; and Sandra Camacho also organized violence survivors in the 1970s, but I only learned about these women (and many others) much later, after we had a sufficiently large critical mass of widely accessible feminist scholarship and activism.

Based on the fierce achievements of the women of color on whose shoulders we stood, as young feminists we knew we had to prepare ourselves for when history needed us. We needed to find each other and, beyond that, find each other *in* each other. We usually caucused at the conferences of white women to overcome the huge geographical, political, and cultural gulfs between women of color, and to try "to make a speech that is heard." Infrequently, we had the resources to sponsor our own conferences, such as the 1980 Third World Women and Violence conference at Howard University in Washington, DC. But still, an illustration, a metaphor was needed for the project of coming together.

Now re-imagine 1981 when two remarkable books, *This Bridge Called My Back* by Cherríe Moraga and Gloria Anzaldúa, and *Ain't I a Woman* by bell hooks, erupted in our lives at nearly the same time! It is impossible to overstate their catalyzing impact. Feeling unmoored from the white feminist movement, women of color—especially Black women—anguished that we were constantly throwing the realities of our experiences up against their disbelief. It was as if we personally commissioned the writing of these particular books to affirm our lives and politics. These writers addressed the denial, fear, and self-delusion of some white women seeking power who saw feminism as an equal opportunity to oppress. Now I think it's called *Leaning In*.

For me, *This Bridge Called My Back* in particular created a stunning visual of a bridge that connects from one place to the "other" in the literal and metaphorical sense of the word. The choice to be a bridge is a dangerous, often trod-upon, and frequently invisibilizing decision. People seldom pay attention to the bridges they walk across because destinations, not means, are their priority. Yet without these bridges, they couldn't go anywhere new.

The bridge metaphor in the literatures of women of color speaks to our never-ending compulsion to connect people, spaces and places to emphasize the intersectionality of oppressions, and offer transformative libratory practices. When I teach about the importance of *This Bridge* today, I draw a visual picture of how women of color may either choose or refuse to be bridges between their realities and white feminists, or between men and women of color, or between trans and cis people etc. Just as Kimberlé Crenshaw illustrated our realities when she drew a traffic intersection on a blackboard with the race, gender, sexuality, and class streets intersecting, *This Bridge Called My Back* offered the powerful testimony of women offering to be a bridge to new understandings among women of color, with also nearly an inadvertent impact on white feminists. Their purpose was to help build the movement(s) of feminists of color for our strength and succor. Transforming white feminism was not their immediate goal, but was a welcome unintended consequence.

Now thirty-three years later, along comes *Revolutionary Mothering: Love on the Front Lines* edited, by Alexis Pauline Gumbs, China Martens, and Mai'a Williams, an anthology on radical mothering that is directly informed by *This Bridge Called My Back* and the tradition of women of color feminism. This extraordinary book is not only radical in its redefinition of "mothering," but also addresses the fact that humanity is interdependent, and we need each other to survive, in a way that Carol Gilligan has described. This is in direct opposition to the demonization of human inter-dependence used to justify dismantling of the welfare state. How do we get from a conservative definition of mothering as a biological destiny to mothering as a liberating practice that can thwart runaway capitalism? This book builds that particular bridge while also providing a bridge from the women of color testimonies of the 1980s and '90s to today's imperatives.

This radical redefining of mothering as investing in others' existence moves far beyond biological determinism of the far right, or the libertarian dog-eat-dog individualism from Ayn Rand so eagerly embraced by the thinly disguised racist movement rebranding itself as the Tea Party, or the classic moral degeneracy tropes around motherhood embraced by most Republicans and Blue Dog and centrist Democrats. Their coalition gave us welfare reform, remember?

In contrast, the introduction to *Revolutionary Mothering* presents the radical concept of "mothering—creating, nurturing, affirming, and supporting life." Women are socialized (not created) to care for others and to expect others to care for them. Mothering, radically defined, is the glad gifting of one's talents, ideas, intellect, and creativity to the universe without recompense. "Radical mothering is the imperative to build bridges that allow us to relate across . . . barriers," the editors say.

It is fortuitous (but perhaps not accidental) that I was asked to write this preface in 2014 at the same time we are celebrating the twentieth anniversary of the conceptualization of the Reproductive Justice (RJ) framework. Without intending it as its primary goal, Reproductive Justice has significantly transformed the abortion-focused, pro-choice movement in a short two decades by moving far beyond a singular focus on protecting abortion rights. Frustrated by the inadequacy of this limited vision for Black women, Reproductive Justice theory was developed by African American feminists in 1994 and subsequently popularized by many women of color through the leadership of the SisterSong Women of Color Reproductive Justice Collective. The Reproductive Justice framework demanded that in addition to fighting for birth control and abortion, equal attention must be paid to the human right to become a mother, and the concomitant and enabling right to parent our children in safe and healthy environments. Said most simply, Reproductive Justice is (1) The human right to not have a child; (2) The human right to have a child; and (3) The human right to parent in safe and healthy environments. In the words of Audre Lorde, we sought to "give name to the nameless so it can be thought. . . . As they become known to and accepted by us, our feelings and the honest exploration of them become sanctuaries and spawning grounds for the most radical and daring ideas."[1]

Reproductive Justice demanded our right to become parents in the face of sub rosa race- and class-based policies of population control and manipulation. We recognize that the purpose of reproductive oppression today is to facilitate the neoliberal economic system. For example, the myth of the undeserving mother of color (or poor, or immigrant, or Black, or queer) used by the 1 percent and their puppet politicians rationalizes the austerity justifications for destroying the social safety net and the transference of industrial production to other countries as part of the neoliberal reorganization of capitalism. Because of the immoral transfer of wealth from the 99 percent to the 1 percent, current economic and demographic crises force this white supremacist system to rearrange itself. By attacking abortion, birth control, and sex education, demographic demagogues coerce young white women to have more babies as a way to save "Western Civilization" in general or Christianity in particular with the Duggars as role models (nineteen kids and counting). By manipulating scientific developments like genomics and assisted reproductive technologies, they use science in racially deterministic practices, as described by Dorothy

---

1   Sherri Taylor, "Acts of Remembering: Relationship in Feminist Therapy," *Women & Therapy* 36, no. 1–2 (2013): 23–34.

Roberts. By discrediting the motherhood of women of color, poor white women, queer mothers, immigrant mothers, etc., this turns maternal virtue on its head, as these "bad" mothers are held responsible for all the ills of society from the Wall Street mortgage crisis to environmental degradation caused by climate change. Because our children (however mothered) are the product of "morally impoverished" mothers, our children become disposable cannon fodder for U.S. imperialism around the world or neo-slaves in the prison industrial complex. Our children either protect or produce more wealth for the 1 percent.

At the time of the birth of RJ theory and practice in that Chicago hotel room, we did not discuss that the radical claim of mothering as a human right was not only the province of biologically defined women, and that mothering—like gender—is not biologically determined but socially constructed. This may have been due to our activist rather than academic backgrounds. We were focusing on the policy implications of health care reform sans reproductive justice, and how to put pressure on the Clinton Administration. In looking back over the exciting developments of the past twenty years, I am not surprised that the forward-looking RJ conversations became open source code for other tectonic shifts in many quarters, including expansion of the conceptualization of "mothering" as a queer thing. Radical mothering does not seek to deny the critical role biological mothers play in sustaining humanity. As Alexis Pauline Gumbs says, "Not just when people who do not identify as heterosexual give birth to or adopt children and parent them, but all day long and everywhere when we acknowledge the creative power of transforming ourselves, and the ways we relate to each other. Because we were never meant to survive and here we are creating a world full of love."

In *Revolutionary Mothering*, Alexis says in her framing article, "Black feminists audaciously centered an entire literary movement around . . . the rights of Black women to reproductive autonomy in the biological sense, but also the imperative to create narratives, theories, contexts, collectives, publications, political ideology and more." *Revolutionary Mothering* makes mothering theory both lyrical and lucid in the tradition of Black feminist analysis rather than the insular and specialized post-modern writing style that postures as original and radical theorizing today.

In this latest manifestation of the ongoing articulation of Reproductive Justice, the concept of "mother" is less a gendered identity than a transformative, liberating practice irrespective of historically determinist rigidities. Children are not individual private property, but they are also not objects through which we seek to achieve our political goals or address our emotional needs. To do so would violate children's human rights.

This calls to mind the white anti-abortion protesters who frequent our feminist marches and abortion clinics, while they feverishly thrust forward their adopted Black children to establish their anti-racist credentials. They love to shout at Black women that they, as white pro-life women, are the true saviors of the Black race from the "genocide of abortion." I am so tempted to remind them that mothering is for the sake of the child, not for the sake of their political goals; but I refrain, thinking about how difficult that's child's life already is when parented by an unconsciously racist mother.

This anthology asks if we can use our powers as radical mothers to responsibly uplift and sometimes represent others, or conversely, to smother or diminish others for our own purposes. It is a radical act to nurture the lives of those who are not supposed to exist. Not supposed to grow old (Oscar Grant). Not supposed to speak up (Mumia). Not supposed to survive domestic violence (Marissa Alexander). Not supposed to walk across streets (Michael Brown). Not supposed to wear hoodies (Trayvon Martin). Not supposed to ask for help (Renisha McBride). Not supposed to play loud music (Jordan Davis). Not supposed to be old (Kenneth Chamberlain). Not supposed to be inside our homes (Kathryn Johnson). Not supposed to shop for toys at Walmart (John Crawford III). The tragedy of our continuing genocide is that by the time this preface is published we will have many more names to add to the list of martyred victims of white supremacy.

Our mere existence is a subversive act. Rethinking mothering from a radical point of view leads to considering survival as a form of self-love, and as a service and gift to others whose lives would be incalculably diminished without us. Sharing our strengths while honoring our weaknesses together is not a contradiction but a way to *make love powerful*, the essence of this ambitious and theoretically futuristic anthology.

August 2014

Introduction
Mai'a Williams

This book has followed me in my life as an exile, as a revolutionary, and as a mama.

When Lex first shared her idea of a book about revolutionary mothering inspired by *This Bridge Called My Back* in 2009, I had just moved to Cairo and was a community organizer with Sudanese gang boys in the Cairene ghettos. These Black boys who carried machetes, told quick stories about being ex-child soldiers, loved Tupac, played with my baby girl, and drew hearts and butterflies beside their gang signs on the pink walls of their community center. Two years later as China, Lex, and I were gathering the submissions, it was 2011 and tear gas rolled through the streets of ground zero for the Arab Spring. By this point my daughter was four years old and learning new Arabic words for "freedom," "revolution," and "army."

From Cairo to the Sinai, from Berlin to Ecuador, from my daughter in diapers to her riding a bike without training wheels, I have come back again and again to this book. From Theresa's first day of kindergarten, her first fight with her best friend, the first time I had to explain racism to her, and how babies get in mamas' bellies, I've had to learn to let go, to hold on, let her make her own lines rather than just following mine. She has learned to stand on her front lines, to read between the lines and to figure out for herself how far she can travel on this earth and swim in the Red Sea.

Even before I was a mama, it was mamas on the margins who shaped my vision of the amazing and heartbreaking possibilities of being a mama. The punk mamas who lived across the street from me in the valleys; they breast-fed in ripped T-shirts, leather cuffs and purple/blue/green hair. The Palestinian mothers I visited In the West Bank who told stories of their toddlers hiding on the far wall of the house as they listened quietly to the Israeli military bombing the neighbors' home. The Congolese mothers who sung praise songs with their babes on their laps and shared their stories of being rape survivors. Some of the babies grew in their bodies from the militias' violations. Teenage Black mamas who lived in the mostly forgotten parts of Minnesota and fought against the medical professionals for the right to give birth as they chose. Sudanese refugee mamas in the crumbling buildings and ghettos of Cairo, waiting for years for an EU visa and a new life. The Egyptian mama, on January 28, 2011, the "Day of Rage," who had one child on her shoulder, another by the hand, she waved an Egyptian flag and faced down the police's tear gas and water cannons.

No matter where I go, in this life of exile, revolution and mamas, front lines and daughters, are what feed my life. This book came from a vision I had of mamas who believe in themselves and their children, in the future and the ancestors so fiercely they will face down the ugly violence of the present time and time again.

I have spent so many nights working on this book while Theresa made her own books with paper, stapler, crayons, and glue. Both of us, in our own way, creating line after line about what is most important to us in this one delicate life.

May this book give to others what so many mothers have given me, small glimpses of the revolution.

Revolution ain't cute or tidy and neither is mothering. Mama, you know that vision you have about mothering. The one you keep holding onto, that helps you get through the pain, the sleeplessness, the disappointment, the heartbreak, the passive aggressive letters from school. Maybe your vision was of being a mama with your fist in the air, with your baby on your back as you climb mountains and paint murals. That vision you had of the three-year-old who would go to a protest, look at the line of cops, and say fuck the police. Maybe your vision is different. Maybe it was country roads and writing novels with your babe playing in the wildflowers, maybe it was communal living and hand-to-hand combat training while your kid laughs at the serious faces the grown-ups make. Maybe it was a feeling of freedom. A feeling of openness. Some place where you could really breathe. I don't know exactly what it is. What I do know is that revolution ain't cute and neither is mothering usually. But like our visions, revolutionary mothering is necessary and real and happening every day. You are necessary, we are necessary and so are our children.

On the Organization of This Book:
Roots and Branches

Roots

This collection started with the intention to center radical mothers of color and marginalized mothers' voices at its very inception, not as an afterthought, but at the heart of personal experience. Although racial diversity is more often measured by the inclusion of a few voices of color within white-dominated media, we are a diverse collection, centering on radical mothers of color with a few marginalized (queer, trans, low income, single, and disabled) white mothers in this anthology.

We are writing these words at a critical moment, as we are witnessing and participating in a resurgence of a civil rights movement led by Black youth and Black mamas, who are taking over the streets, over traditional and social media, over the national conversations and proclaiming—in the words of Alicia Garza, Patrisse Cullors, and Opal Tometi—that Black Lives Matter. We are writing these words on the anniversary of the killing of Michael Brown and in solidarity with Brown's mother, Lesley McSpadden, who says that her son did not die in vain. We write in solidarity with mothers who must send their child out into the world, knowing that the powers that be would prefer their child not exist anymore.

As writers and editors we have brought our lives to this collection, our relationships growing with each other through organic means (video chats and mango smoothies; café meetings and emails) like the mighty oak, not as old as the tree under which China sat while writing an early draft of this but grounded and connected, to the past, and to the future. To the earth, and to the sky.

We have talked of mission, discussed each essay and word, worked in a kind of natural consensus built on formal inquiry and practice, where sometimes one or another leads while one or another is busy with life, our communication still the roots growing underground to hold us tight.

We have worked to curate revolution, not perfection; love which can be afforded, truth which feels dangerous but necessary; and commitment without which nothing can grow.

Still, we lose the notes of what we wanted to say here. We lose the notes in our messy lives of increasing piles of paper and computer crashes. And then we re-member again, for each other, reflecting back to each other, as we work to edit our words together into one cognizant whole, or part of the whole, that is not whole. What brilliant thing did Alexis say about our movement building purpose? "We are accountable when we are specific," "We define mothering in a particular way as a radical and revolutionary practice," and "We connect it explicitly to the feminist of color tradition, and claim we are building knowledge for radical mothering as a transformative practice in our movements": some of the jewels found poring through old transcripts. Also, that "Our wide net, it caught its own ocean" was something that Alexis wanted to quote China on. And editing is an act of love (thanks, Jessica Hoffman), giving us parameters to guide us during that long time we discussed submissions in online chats and through computer screens. How exactly did Mai'a word that thing she said, that she says all the time about the importance of centering the more fragile/precarious within society, how this better supports each and everyone of us to make an improvement which will really make a difference? We never could find the podcast, but in an essay Mai'a wrote many years ago, she says that "Black babies matter," which seems to foreshadow this very moment. Her essays on the effect of the stress of racism on infant mortality were groundbreaking. She remains on the cutting edge of revolutionary midwifery. This is where we want to work.

Too many times we have seen what is called radical be something that not everyone could afford, not everyone was included. The underlying racism, white privilege, classism—as well as other systems of oppression—still not addressed. What has been called, in some limited but powerful circles (like mainstream media and even alternative media) "mothering," has been almost entirely white mothering, to the point where it needed not even be said. The word "white," which dominates, calls itself by no name, no color, so much so that "mothering" can be code for "white mothering" and we find this extremely dangerous. We find it important to counter that narrative in real, practical ways.

China recalls how her writing progress as a marginalized single mother on welfare in the '90s (fighting to have her own voice included, her own experiences validated, and then finding out with gains made in publishing for radical mothers that still most single mothers, especially single mothers of color were being excluded) has taught her the utmost importance of addressing white privilege and racism in publishing and that white supremacy must be confronted, systematic changes made, headfirst: named, called, and fought against in order to build the future we envision, crave, desire, and demand! White supremacy surely will not go away on its own.

Branches

We organized the pieces into sections as a way to point to the conversation that we believe mothers are already having with each other and to provide some evidence of the conversations the three of us are having about what is important to us about revolutionary mothering. We have used the organizing metaphor of lines, because we are threading something together with you, pointing out life-lines and drawing connections piece to piece.

Since this conversation has been going on for a long time, we open with an intergenerational introduction. This includes a framing piece by Alexis about how the ways feminists of color talked about mothering in the 1970s and '80s are relevant to the radical childcare and revolutionary mothering activism going on today. It starts with an essay by revolutionary ancestor June Jordan called "The Creative Spirit and Children's Literature," which has never been published in book form until now. It goes on to acknowledge our literary and theoretical "foremothers for mothering" and is followed by pieces by two women of color activists who describe being revolutionarily mothered. Malkia Cyril writes about her mother, who was member of the Black Panther Party for Self-Defense; Esteli Juarez writes about being mothered as a revolutionary by her community of struggle.

From the Shorelines to the Front Lines emphasizes mothering as the bridge work that requires confronting the very real barriers that oppression places in our way and also finding love and power by facing the barriers that divide us from each other across geopolitical divides.

The Bottom Line speaks to the economic reality of most mothers on the planet and asks if poverty is violence and children are hope, why mothering work, children, and poverty are intertwined with each other in our lived experiences.

Out (of) Lines looks at mothering as the queerest thing that human beings can do. It seeks to queer the idea of mothering and also to offer reflections from self-identified LGBTQ mothers on how their sexuality intersects with their mothering journeys.

Two Pink Lines looks at the messy breaking-apart process of becoming mothers via birth, transnational adoption and other spiritual means and offers the messy transformation of becoming a mother as a model for the messy transformation we must engage in as a species

We close the collection with Between the Lines, a section that seeks to time travel by featuring the work of contemporary collectives, manifestas, organizations, projects, and families who are seeking to bring a praxis of revolutionary mothering into the future.

We can't wait to be with you, in your in-between moments, with your crumbs and fingerprints. Bless these pages with your traces and attention. Thank you for every moment that you create. We are so glad that you are here.

—Alexis Pauline Gumbs, China Martens, and Mai'a Williams,
    August 2015

I.
Intergenerational Introduction:
Foremothers for Mothering

Introduction
Alexis Pauline Gumbs

Revolutionary Mothering is a bridging act, in this book and in the lives of all the people who practice revolutionary mothering in their daily lives. Boldly dressing ourselves in the legacy of the revolutionary anthologies *The Black Woman, Home Girls, This Bridge Called My Back*, and the women of color–led Reproductive Justice movement, we are flamboyantly activating the legacy of radical personal political testimonies and theories of women of color feminists of the 1970s and '80s in order to make the radical practice of mothering visible as a key to our collective liberation. The practice of mothering that inspired us to create this book is older than feminism; it is older and more futuristic than the category "woman." We are investigating and amplifying the nuances of practices that have existed as long as there have been people of different ages with different superpowers invested in each other's existence.

We are making a claim that should be obvious but is often overlooked. In order to collectively figure out how to sustain and support our evolving species, in order to participate in and demand a society where people help to create each other instead of too often destroying each other, we need to look at the practice of creating, nurturing, affirming, and supporting life that we call mothering.

This book cannot include all of the generations that have practiced mothering on this planet, but we find it important to honor at least the generation of work that precedes this project. Much of the intergenerational vision that we practice and celebrate in this collection can be described through June Jordan's declaration in 1977 that "Love is Lifeforce." In a previously unpublished speech that she delivered at a conference about children's literature at UC Berkley, Jordan poetically and urgently articulates the importance of intergenerational relationship to the fate of humankind. We want to start here, with June Jordan's words, with love, and follow up with some words from Alexis Pauline Gumbs's research on feminists of color conversations and practices of radical mothering. Maybe when we say "mothering" in this book, we really mean "the creative spirit" or "love" itself. We find Jordan's definitions of creation and love and life and power useful; we find her queer, utopian, hopeful and critical articulations of mothering crucial to the questions about and experiences of mothering we explore in this text. And we love you.

The Creative Spirit:
Children's Literature
June Jordan

Love is lifeforce.

I believe that the creative spirit is nothing less than love made manifest.

I see love as the essential nature of all that supports life.

Love is opposed to the death of the dream. Love is opposed to the delimiting of possibilities of experience.

When we run on love, when we move and change and build and paint and sing and write and foster the maximal fulfillment of our own lives, as well as the maximal fulfillment of other lives that look to us for help, for protection, or for usable clues to the positive excitement of just being alive, then we make manifest the creative spirit of the universe: a spirit existing within each of us and yet persisting infinitely greater than the ultimate capacities of any one of us.

I think of the amazing fact, for example, that tiger lilies in a field will bloom, wild as they grow, exactly on the same day as wild tiger lilies several miles away; there is an orderliness, a perpetual inclination to grow, to become manifest from an invisible beginning, a perpetual impulse to expand, and to transform, that seems to me the essence of being, even, perhaps, the irreducible purpose of being. By nature, whether we are children or tiger lilies, it seems that our essence, our purpose does not imply harm to other elements of the world. Neither tiger lilies nor children, by their nature, threaten the rain, or the bees, or the rivers of the world.

And it seems to me that love, that a serious and tender concern to respect the nature, and the spontaneous purpose of other things, other people, will make manifest a peaceable order among us such that fear, conflict, competition, waste, and environmental sacrifice will have no place.

Originally written in 1977. June Jordan Literary Estate Trust 2015; reprinted by permission; www.junejordan.com.

That is what I believe.

What I know is that the creative spirit is real beyond you or me. In my own life as a poet, and in the lives of many of my students, for instance, it has happened, more than once in a whole, that an entire poem will be "given" and/or that a completely formulated, fictional character will be "given" to us: This process, or this kind of an event by no means represents a mainstay of our productivity, but it does occur often enough to keep you humble, to let you realize that the creative spirit is as much a process depending on your receptivity as it is a process depending on your willful conjuring up of your willful projection of visual or aural or verbal constructs for which you would like to feel proudly responsible. If this is the function of the creative spirit, then, in my work as an artist, it seems to me that I am always about a most sobering task, the task of survival, for myself, and for those who may carry what I offer to them, into their own lives.

And because we coexist on a planet long defiled by habits opposite to love, it seems to me that the task of surviving and/or the task of providing for the survival of those who are not as strong as I am, is a political undertaking: Vast changes will have to be envisioned, and pursued, if any, let alone all, of us will survive the destructive traditions of our species. Enormous reversals and revisions of our thinking patterns will have to be achieved, somehow, and fast. And to accomplish such lifesaving alterations of society, we will have to deal with power: we will have to make love powerful. We will have to empower the people we love so that they can insist upon the validity of their peculiar coloring or gender or ethnicity or accidental economic status, so that they can bloom in their own place and time like the tiger lilies growing beautiful and free.

So far I have been looking at the creative spirit or the rational, and imaginative manifestation of love in a general way.

How should we see the function of this spirit in relationship to children?

I know of nothing more important, more difficult, and more purely loving than the nurture of children, be it as a parent, a teacher, or as an artist wishing to serve them well.

Children are the ways that the world begins again and again. If you fasten upon that concept of their promise, you will have trouble finding anything more awesome, and also anything more extraordinarily exhilarating, than the opportunity or/and the obligation to nurture a child into his or her own freedom.

At the same time, children depend on you and me, on the large women and the large men around them, for more than we can easily, or comfortably, imagine. Like it or not, we are the ones who think we know, who believe, who remember, who predict, a great part of what they will, in their turn, think they know, or remember, or believe, or expect simply because we are the ones who feed, who clothe, who train them to stay away from fire or dolls or Chinese food or the vigorous climbing of apple trees. In addition, children rely on us for their safety, for their sense of safety, for their sense of being in or out of their element, their sense of being capable of solving whatever problems come up, *or* of being *in*capable, of being helpless.

We, the larger ones, possess a degree of power over the lives of children that we would find inconceivable and unspeakably tyrannical in any other context. Yet, we mostly wear this power as some divine right not to be questioned, not to be wrestled with as one would wrestle with an angel for the sake of one's soul. Or we try to minimize and trivialize this power by limiting our concepts of our function to those of discipline, or to those of boundless hugs and kisses. Or we pretend we do not have this power; in the name of what we mistakenly call freedom, we exert ourselves as little as possible, beyond meeting a relatively middle-class notion of creative needs. Or we pretend we do not have this power because we look at ourselves, and we look at the mess, the horrendous, shameful mess that is our international legacy to our children and we think, "God. I don't know, kid; don't ask me."

And, of course, regardless of how we view the power, the responsibility that we embody, vis-à-vis the children, that power and that responsibility remain an incomparable, profound and inexorable opportunity to bless or to curse their lives, to open or to seal their willingness to trust, to explain, and to create.

One abiding characteristic of these little people, the children of our lives, is their unabashed sobriety: whether they are "playing house" or whether they are doubling up with giggle fits of laughter, of extremely felt joy, children are serious: they do not pretend to make believe or to laugh or to howl out the hurt, the discomfort of a moment: whether the feeling, the act, or the so-called game, the child is, compared to the rest of us, supremely unequivocal in her or his commitment to that moment of being. As a consequence, particularly young children are what we term *literal*: I remember when my son refused to return to school after his lunch hour at home, one afternoon, because, as I finally persuaded him to confide in me, the teacher told him that he was *adorable*: because the word was unfamiliar to him and because her manner was less than clearly, simply loving, he felt himself in limbo and only after I explained the meaning of *adorable* and also the meaning of folks who say supposedly nice things that they do not entirely feel, was he ready to re-enter her dominion, the classroom.

Another way of saying what I mean is to say that children, that what happens to someone as a child, whether that something is a beating, or a picture book, will happen without meeting defense, without encountering a barrier to its potential impact—for good or for ill. In childhood we live through days and nights of singularly direct apprehension, singularly vulnerable passage through uncensored experience.

Let me give two different illustrations of this fact, both of them personal:

Last night, thanks to the kindness of Anne Gold, I reread "The Ugly Duckling." The version in my hands was *The Complete Fairy Tales of Hans Christian Andersen*, translated by Eric C. Haugaard. I wanted to reread this story because two days ago Anne Durrell referred to it as "a great story" and, even as she made that judgment, my heart rebelled: my memory of "The Ugly Duckling" was rather different: I remember being given that story one night, as my parents prepared to go out for the evening, leaving me with an unknown adult, a babysitter of some sort. Abandoned as I felt, I took the little book into my crib, I believe I was somewhere between two and three years old at the time, and I read and I studied the words and the drawings of that story: *Infamous night!*

In the bastardized version that I held in my hands, undoubtedly the same candy store version now available for 39¢ or 49¢, the ugly duckling was ugly because he was Black, and because he was smaller than the rest of the brood: a runt.

As I was Black, or darkskinned, compared to both of my parents, and as I was smaller than most kids my age, there was no route that I could find for escape: I was the ugly duckling and, moreover, I was ugly for reasons I could neither control nor change. Reading that story

I met my doom: for the first time, I acquired a sense of myself as ugly, as not belonging, as *wrong*, you know, that even now I must struggle to overcome. That wound was severely crippling, severely intense.

Well, it was quite extraordinary to discover, last night, that the original version of "The Ugly Duckling" has nothing to do with color and that, actually, the duckling was larger than the rest of the brood because he was, indeed, a swan. And it was quite extraordinary to discover, last night, that I agree with Anne Durrell, that I think it's a great story, as she does, because now I can see a wonderful meaning to the tale, now I can see a message: that you will be beautiful when you are recognized as the person you really are, and that you will be beautiful when you do not try to be something you are not: when you are true to yourself then you will become like a swan: released in the grace of natural and spontaneous purpose.

That is the first illustration of the vulnerability of the child. Here is the second: this is a poem that my son, Christopher, wrote when he was nine years old:

All of Us a Family

The day will come
When people will come
Red, Yellow, Black and White
A family they'll be
And a family tree
Oh and the day will come
When a Black leader can stand in safety
Knowing that all others are his brothers and sisters
In the family of man.

At the last, that was his response to the assassination of Martin Luther King: a terrible wistfulness that no one would possibly deny as to its authenticity.

And here is a poem that Christopher wrote one year later:

I've Seen Enough

I've been through Africa
I was there when Solomon was claimed king

I was best man to Cleopatra
I've seen the death of millions over in Japan
When the treacherous bomb was dropped
Surely I can say I've seen enough
What more proof need I tell you?
Must I tell you that I bore the cross
On which Jesus Christ was crucified?
Jesus Christ! I tell you surely
I've seen enough

Now you have brief but factual testimony to the emotional and intellectual makeup of a two-year-old and a ten-year-old.

These are random examples of vulnerability, and of a serious character, commonplace to the children who we frequently dismiss as "cute" and "childish," by which we mean not serious, and inconsequential.

It is for little people of such possible response, that we frequently put together toys and books about nothing at all, or toys and books that, inherently, we would despise for ourselves because they are "cute," or silly, or pointless, or fiendish.

What do we have in mind when we give a little girl the three-dimensional replica of a kitchen stove that does nothing at all?

What do we have in mind when we give children a book that means absolutely nothing that we can discern, a book serving no purpose, not even the wonderful purpose of enlivening a sense of delight, as happens, for example, with that wonderful book, *The Red Balloon*?

It is with these ideas about the creative spirit, about love, about children, and about the world we need to redeem for their sake, and for our own, that I approach the subject of children's literature. I do not believe I am by myself in these views.

Accordingly it does not surprise me that when grownups encounter a special friend or a lover whom they really want to cherish, they will often enough head for the children's section of a bookstore: there they will look for still another copy of *The Little Prince* or for *Winnie the Pooh*, and why?

Not because, in our childhood we were regularly given materials of such love, of such respectful and tender and serious regard, but because we wish our childhood had been filled, indeed, by such materials, because, we know, deeply, that we wanted and that we needed to have such love abundant to our days.

And so we give these allegedly children's books to each other.

And in so doing we say I care about you: I love you and because I love you I think about you, I think about what may hurt you or what may make you happy, what may make you feel ugly or small, and what may make you feel competent, interesting, and safe.

For what both Christopher Robin and the Little Prince have in common, after all, is the depiction of those little people as serious, as capable young people, worth knowing, worth knowing about.

And in both stories, the writing, by any criteria, is superlative: it is not a Goosey Loosey/Cocky Locky garbage: it is a suitably serious and literate and lovingly inspired piece of writing that requires no apology, or explanation.

And so I trust that it will not surprise you to hear that I regard considerations of the usefulness, considerations of the craft, of children's literature as integral to the creative spirit: if there is no love between you, as St. Paul has written, then you labor in vain. And if your love is not respectful so that you will extend yourself in the manifestation of your love, to make your offering as beautiful, as perfect as you possibly can, then I believe we are lovers in vain: we cannot hope to serve well the needs and the potential of our children, otherwise.

And so it will not surprise you to hear that I celebrate the existence of *The Little Prince* and of *Winnie the Pooh*, and that I celebrate the existence of the Racism and Sexism Awareness Resolution adopted last year by the ALA and the similar resolution adopted by the National Conference of the Teachers of English. And I look at children's books from the People's Republic of China, books such as the *Red Army's Women's Detachment*, and find in these offerings an emulatable literature that takes children seriously and that takes the question of survival seriously. And when I turn to my own work, when I consider my own opportunities to serve the lives of children, and my own future life, simultaneously, when I remember that children are the ways that the world begins again and again, then I do think first about purpose: what will be the use of my work? And, secondly, I think about craft: how can I best present this offering so that my purpose may have the best chance of its achievement?

What I would like to achieve, regardless of the particular story or poem, is the offering of respect: an offering of the view that I believe you can handle it, that there is a way and a means to creatively handle whatever may be the pain or the social predicament of your young life, and that I believe that you can and will discover or else invent that way, those means.

I want to say to children that I love you and that you are beautiful and amazing regardless whether you are—and also precisely *because you are*—Black or female or poor or small or an only child or the son of parents divorced: you are beautiful and amazing: and when you love yourself truly then you will become like a swan release in the grace of natural and spontaneous purpose.

And I want to say to children let us look at hunger, at famine around the world, and let us consider together, you at five years of age, and me at forty-one, how we can, how we must eliminate this genocide, this terror.

And I want to say to children let us look at tiger lilies blooming to their own astonishment, and learn to cherish their own form and orderliness and freedom for our own.

And I want to say to children, tell me what you think and what you see and what you dream so that I may hope to honor you.

And I want these things for children, because I want these things for myself, and for all of us, because unless we embody these attitudes and precepts as the governing rules of our love, and of our political commitment to survive, we will love in vain, and we will certainly not survive.

I believe that the creative spirit is nothing less than love made manifest.

And I deeply hope that we can make love powerful because, otherwise, there will be no reason for hope.

m/other ourselves:
a Black queer feminist genealogy for radical mothering
Alexis Pauline Gumbs

The queer thing is that we were born at all.

I was born in 1982 in the middle of the first term of a president who won by demonizing "welfare queens," in the global context of "population control," a story that says poor women and women of color should not give birth. A story with a happy ending for capitalism: we do not exist. The queer thing is that we *were* born; our young and/or deviant and/or brown and/or broke and/or single mamas did the wrong thing. Therefore we exist: a population out of control, a story interrupted. We are the guerrilla poems written on walls, purveyors of a billion dangerous meanings of life.

And how unlikely that I would love you.

In 1983, Audre Lorde, Black, lesbian, poet, warrior, mother, interrupted the story of a heterosexist, capitalist, fashion and beauty magazine called *Essence* with a queer proposition. In an essay on the impact of internalized oppression between Black women, she offered: WE CAN LEARN TO MOTHER OURSELVES. I have designed multiple workshops with this title and I still don't know what it means.[1] Except that love is possible even in a world that teaches us to hate ourselves and the selves we see waiting in each other. Except that in a world that says that we should not be born, and that says "no" to our very beings everyday, I still wake up wanting you with a "yes" on my heart. Except that I believe in how we grow our bodies into place to live at the very sight of each

A version of this essay was published in *make/shift* magazine and dedicated to *Revolutionary Mothering* co-editor Mai'a Williams.

1   This is also the title of my dissertation, "We Can Learn to Mother Ourselves: The Queer Survival of Black Feminism."

other. We can learn to mother ourselves. I think it means you and me.

Another generative site for the queer potential of mothering is June Jordan's 1992 essay "A New Politics of Sexuality," in which she uses bisexuality as an intervention against predictive sexuality in order to create a space for freedom. This critical use of bisexuality prefigures the use of the word "queer" to describe a politics of sexuality that is not based on a specific sexual practice, but rather a critical relationship to existing sexual and social norms. Jordan uses a proclamation of her own bisexuality as a hinge to articulate her own contradictory multiplicity: "I am Black and I am female and I am a mother and I am bisexual and I am a nationalist and I am an antinationalist."[2]

We say that mothering, especially the mothering of children in oppressed groups, and especially mothering to end war, to end capitalism, to end homophobia and to end patriarchy is a queer thing. And that is a good thing. That is a necessary thing. That is a crucial and dangerous thing to do. Those of us who nurture the lives of those children who are not supposed to exist, who are not supposed to grow up, who are revolutionary in their very beings are doing some of the most subversive work in the world. If we don't know it, the establishment does.

In 2005, former U.S. Secretary of Education and officer of Drug Policy, William Bennett, publicly stated that aborting every Black baby would decrease crime.[3] This neo-eugenicist statement about U.S. race relations corresponds with globalized "family planning" agendas that have historically forced women in the Caribbean, Latin America, South Asia, and Africa to undergo sterilization in order to work for multinational corporations. In 1977, World Bank official Richard Rosenthal went so far as to suggest that three fourths of the women in developing nations should be sterilized to prevent economically disruptive revolutions.[4]

In the face of this genocidal attack, Black feminists from the 1970s to the 1990s appropriated motherhood as a challenge and

---

2   June Jordan, "A New Politics of Sexuality," in *Technical Difficuluties: African American Notes on the State of the Union* (New York: Pantheon Books, 1992), 132.

3   September 28 broadcast of Salem Radio Network's Bill Bennett's *Morning in America*.

4   Luz Rodriguez, "Population Control in Puerto Rico," Conference presentation at Let's Talk about Sex, the SisterSong 10th Anniversary Conference, May 2006.

a refusal to the violence that these discourses of stabilization and welfare would naturalize. While the U.S. state enacted domestic and foreign policies that required, allowed and endorsed violence against the bodies of Black women and early death for Black children, Black feminists audaciously centered an entire literary movement around the invocation of this criminal act of Black maternity, demanding not only the rights of Black women to reproductive autonomy in the biological sense, but also the imperative to create narratives, theories, contexts, collectives, publications, political ideology, and more. I read the Black feminist literary production that occurred between 1970 and 1990 as the experimental creation of a rival economy and temporality in which Black women and children would be generators of an alternative destiny. A Black feminist position became articulable and necessary not only because of the lived experiences of Black mothers but also because of the successes and failures of the Black cultural nationalist movement and the white radical lesbian/feminist movement.

To answer death with utopian futurity, to rival the social reproduction of capital on a global scale with a forward-dreaming diasporic accountability is a queer thing to do. A strange thing to do. A thing that changes the family and the future forever. To name oneself "mother" in a moment where representatives of the state conscripted "Black" and "mother" into vile epithets is a queer thing. To insist on Black motherhood despite Black cultural nationalist claims to own Black women's wombs and white feminist attempts to use the maternal labor of Black women as domestic servants to buy their own freedom (and to implicitly support the use of Black women as guinea pigs in their fight to perfect the privilege of sterilization) is an almost illegible thing, an outlawed practice, a queer thing.

You are something else.

The radical potential of the word "mother" comes after the 'm'. It is the space that "other" takes in our mouths when we say it. We are something else. We know it from how fearfully institutions wield social norms and try to shut us down. We know it from how we are transforming the planet with our every messy step toward making life possible. Mamas who unlearn domination by refusing to dominate their children, extended family and friends, community caregivers, radical childcare collectives, all of us breaking cycles of abuse by deciding what we want to replicate from the past and what we need urgently to transform, are m/othering ourselves.

Audre Lorde's essay had an older sister. In 1973, Toni Morrison wrote a novel about a dangerous, undomesticated woman, an "artist without an art form" who spurned her own mother's advice to settle down, insisting, "I don't want to make someone else. I want to make myself." *Sula*, the novel that inspired Black feminist literary critics like Barbara Smith and Mae Gwendolyn Henderson to invent Black feminist literary criticism, is a sacred text about two girls who "having long ago realized they were neither white nor male . . . went about creating something else to be." Sula herself is not a mother-type, except for how she creates herself, except for how she creates a context for other people to grow past the norms they knew, except for how in her name contemporary Black feminist literary theory was born and how she is how I know how to write these words.

Your mama is queer as hell.

What if mothering is about the *how* of it? In 1987, Hortense Spillers wrote "Mama's Baby, Papa's Maybe: A New American Grammar Book," reminding her peers that motherHOOD is a status granted by patriarchy to white middle-class women, those women whose legal rights to their children are never questioned, regardless of who does the labor (the how) of keeping them alive. MotherING is another matter, a possible action, the name for that nurturing work, that survival dance, *worked* by enslaved women who were forced to breastfeed the children *of* the status mothers while having no control over whether their birth or chosen children were sold away. Mothering is a form of labor *worked* by immigrant nannies like my grandmother who mothered wealthy white kids in order to send money to Jamaica for my mother and her brothers who could not afford the privilege of her presence. Mothering is *worked* by chosen and accidental mentors who agree to support some growing unpredictable thing called future. Mothering is *worked* by house mothers in ball culture who provide spaces of self-love and expression for/ as queer youth of color in the street. What would it mean for us to take the word "mother" less as a gendered identity and more as a possible action, a technology of transformation that those people who do the most mothering labor are teaching us right now?

The queer thing is that we are still here.

We can remember how to mother ourselves if we can remember the proto-queer of color movement that radicalized the meaning of mothering. In 1979, at the National Third World Lesbian and Gay Conference, where Audre Lorde gave the keynote speech, a caucus of lesbians agreed on the statement: "All children of lesbians are ours," a socialist context for mothering, where children are not individual property but rather reminders of the context through which community exists.[5] This means that "mothering" is a queer thing. Not just when people who do not identify as heterosexual give birth to or adopt children and parent them, but all day long and everywhere when we acknowledge the creative power of transforming ourselves and the ways we relate to each other. Because we were never meant to survive and here we are creating a world full of love.

Foremother moments in radical creativity provide the precedent for radical mothering that we can find articulated clearly in Black feminist and feminist of color legacies and offer a queer intergenerational and collective vision of mothering that we can see articulated in the late 1970s and early 1980s and use to contextualize our contemporary movement to create the world we deserve together through transformative bridgemaking acts. Here are some of the moments we want to remember in this anthology.

Foremother Moments in Radical Mothering

Love is lifeforce.

Children are the ways that the world begins again and again. If you fasten upon that concept of their promise, you will have trouble finding anything more awesome, and also anything

---

5   Doc in "First National Third World Lesbian and Gay Conference," *Off Our Backs* (November 1979): 14.

> *more extraordinarily exhilarating, than the opportunity or/*
> *and obligation to nurture a child into his or her own freedom.*
> —June Jordan, "The Creative Spirit and Children's
>   Literature," 1977

In 1977, the great Black feminist poet June Jordan was best known for her work as an author of children's books. Her very first published book was *Who Look at Me*, based on a poem that she wrote for her son Christopher to go along with an exploration of art by and about African Americans. "New energies of darkness," the poem says to contextualize the middle passage, "we disturbed a continent like seeds."

June Jordan's work as an author of children's literature was not by default, even though she lived in a time where both Black nationalist and library driven publishing models made children's books by Black mothers marketable. Jordan saw children's literature as one part of a holistic intergenerational imperative. At the 1974 Howard Conference of Afro-American Writers she explained what was at stake for her as an author accountable to youth when she encouraged fellow authors of children's literature to "write stories that correct the genocidal misinformation about reality" that she notes is being taught to children and adults through the corporate media. The basic lessons that Jordan advocates as necessary for children's literature—that sharing is vital, that the birth of Black children is a cause for celebration and that the Blackness of Black people is wonderful—are simple and profound. These messages, which Jordan continued to offer through her children's books and young adult fiction are direct attacks on capitalism, reproductive injustice, and white supremacy.

In a range of publications for audiences as wide-ranging as the *New York Times* Book Review section, the *Negro Digest*, and library newsletters Jordan stressed the importance of the terms of our conversations across generations about life, love, resources, and value. In "The Creative Spirit and Children's Literature" she explains the responsibility all adults have to "make love powerful" in the face of a dominating order that seeks to put love in opposition to power. "Love is opposed to the death of the dream," she explains and she reminds her audience of educators and authors at UC Berkeley that adults are responsible not only for "nurturing a child into his or her own freedom" but also for responding to the questions and challenges that young people bring to the conversation as opportunities to evolve as a species.

Our definition of radical mothering builds on June Jordan's futurism and the futurism of the Black Feminist moment out of which she spoke. In 1974, when Jordan spoke on the panel at Howard, she was sitting next to Lucille Clifton, who used her poetry and children's literature to break silence about child sexual and physical abuse. In 1977, when she spoke at Berkeley, it was the same year that the Combahee River Collective released their groundbreaking statement that insisted that "we are ready for the lifetime of struggle and work before us."

You can see the seeds germinating in the Parenting in/and/as Science Fiction reader and series of workshops generated at the Allied Media Conference, a gathering of visionary futuristic holistic media makers in Detroit. You can see the seeds growing in the intentionally visionary spaces crafted by the childcare collectives that designed content rich interactive tracks for children at the Critical Resistance 10th anniversary prison abolition conference, the U.S. Social Forums and the Allied Media Conference. You can see it in the ongoing work of collectives like Regeneración and Kidz City, all of which deeply inform the work in this collection.

Regeneración was founded in New York City as an organic act of love and collaboration with powerful women of color organizing collectives that emerged there. They are "committed to growing an intergenerational movement for collective liberation, in which people of all ages can participate, learn from each other, take care of each other, and dramatically reshape the conditions of their lives." They say it explicitly in their mission statement and they walk it out through their powerful programming presence at national convergences, their day-to-day collaboration with organization in NYC and their collective visioning work. They identify "child-raising as a form of resistance," clarifying the crucial role of childcare in the movement we need and the world we deserve.

Co-editor China Martens is a co-founder of Kidz City Baltimore, a collective founded after Regeneración and explicitly influenced and inspired by their vision for collective liberation. In their mission statement, Kidz City articulate the value of the labor of childcare as "vitally important, and often overlooked and undervalued" and emphasizes the importance of access to social justice spaces for children and parents. They acknowledge that our social justice movements are already intergenerational and see their work as supporting that intergenerationality so it can be "healthy and happy."

It is an act of love to participate in the resistance work of child-raising. It is an act of love to envision and actualize an intergenerationally participatory movement. We honor and acknowledge the work of raising and caring for children as lifeforce toward the world we can only transform together.

"All Children of Lesbians Are Ours": A Queer Challenge

"All third world lesbians share in the responsibility for the care of nurturing of the children of individual lesbians of color."
—Doc in "First National Third World Lesbian and Gay Conference," *Off Our Backs* (1979)

By 1979, the idea of mothering poor children and children of color was under direct attack. Ronald Reagan was running for president on a platform that criminalized the "welfare queen," a figure he invented in order to sell a neoliberal vision that insisted education, housing, and other social issues were not collective but individual issues. Eventually Reagan in the United States, like Margaret Thatcher in England, would spearhead a project of divesting from social services and loosening regulations on multi-national corporations. In the first few months of 1979, twelve Black women were murdered in Boston's Black neighborhoods and their murders were ignored until a coalition of feminists, including the members of the Combahee River Collective, began organizing around the value of Black women's lives and the need to end the multiple oppressions they faced. In November of 1979, the KKK opened fire in broad daylight on a rally organized by women of color and their allies demanding economic human rights in Greensboro, NC. The police arrested *victims* of what later became known as the Greensboro Massacre. That same fall, the Atlanta Child Murders began and authorities refused for months to take Black mothers seriously when they reported their children missing.

At the same historical moment, "troublesome" young people of color were in fact achieving revolutions in the Caribbean and

Latin America. The student-led New Jewel Movement in Grenada created the first Black Socialist Republic in the Americas and the student-led Sandinistas achieved revolution in Nicaragua in 1979. The question of uprising youth and criminalized mothers was directly in tension. That same year in New York the First National Conference of Third World Lesbians and Gays was a place for gay men and lesbians of color to articulate themselves as a group, distinctly from the largely nationalist groups representing people of color and the white-dominated groups representing lesbians and gays in the 1970s.

In her keynote address to open the gathering, Audre Lorde spoke directly to the responsibility of the people gathered to the next generation of youth, making it clear that they were collaborating on the future, not just with their own individual children, but with young people in general who deserved to be liberated not only from homophobia and racism, but from a violent, competitive, environmentally destructive society. In the Third World Lesbian Caucus, this collectivist stance was made even more explicit.

According to "Doc" (a mother who attended the caucus and wrote about it for *Off Our Backs*, a major lesbian periodical), as the women gathered wrote their official statement of the Third World Lesbian agenda, they explicitly thought about the labor of mothering as shared mothering and claimed responsibility for the children of all individual lesbians of color as a collective of third world lesbians. It is not clear how this particular group implemented this belief. In fact, Doc herself mentions that she prioritized going to this session but was late because of childcare concerns. Conceptually, collective responsibility for the labor of mothering and the well-being of the children in lesbian of color families has revolutionary implications. This concept came to life for Pat Parker, a Black lesbian poet in Oakland when she and her partner filled a courtroom with lesbian chosen family members in response to a legal challenge to her and her partner's right to adopt their daughter because they would not have sufficient "family support."[6]

Today, in a consummately neoliberal era, questions of custody have become even more nuanced. Many queer families face the reality that the state will track down sperm donors and treat them

6   Judy Grahn at the Sister Comrade gathering in honor of Parker and Audre Lorde, November 2007, at First Congregational Church in Oakland, California.

as fathers in order to avoid giving lesbian parents state assistance for raising their children, should the need arise. And there is also a precedent now for affirming lesbian and gay custody of children when it serves the state's financial interest (if it means the state will not have to provide assistance for the well-being of the children). If, as Audre Lorde wrote in *The Black Unicorn*, "our labor has become more important than our silence," when it comes to lesbian and gay custody law, money has become more important than deviance. This move by the state to affirm gay and lesbian parents with money and to violate the rights of lesbian parents without money in particular (when it comes to treating non-parent donors as parents) can be traced directly back to the criminalization of so-called welfare queens as the state divests itself from the lives of poor kids.

The fact that richer, whiter gay and lesbian parents are placed in a position to separate themselves from the wider, poorer LGBTQ population, especially the LGBTQ population of color, was anticipated in June 1979 by an interracial lesbian couple who wrote an article in a special issue of *Off Our Backs* where lesbians of color sought to address the dominating whiteness of the publication. Mary Peña and Barbara Carey wrote their critique of the conversation on lesbian motherhood, insisting that questions of race and class needed to be central to the conversation. Their call, as mothers, for a vision of lesbian mothering that was not about assimilating into existing white supremacist norms of family was instructive then and is instructive now. Their idea of parenting was not designed to get the benefits of the existing system, but rather to create something new. They celebrate the opportunity to "develop within our children the new idea that they can function without patriarchal authority." While much of the custody narrative then and now is based on patriarchal ideas that say the children are owned by (property owning) parents, they instead say emphatically:

THEY WILL NOT BELONG TO THE PATRIARCHY
THEY WILL NOT BELONG TO US EITHER
THEY WILL BELONG ONLY TO THEMSELVES.

Raising this precedent in 2016 by no means trivializes the daily struggles of queer families to support each other and to have autonomy over their lives, especially when it comes to the struggles of poor and working-class LGBTQ people to have the right to daily parent their children. However, this reminder of an earlier moment in anti-racist queer consciousness is also crucial to how we think about the question, concept, and project of family outside of the terms set by white supremacy and patriarchy—terms under which the richest, whitest, and most assimilated might get crumbs, but the majority of our communities will always lose.

Part of the project of seeing mothering as a queer collaboration with the future has to do with transforming the parenting relationship from a property relationship to a partnership in practice. This possibility is alive in our collection and in our communities in a way that not only opens up possibilities of non-dominating relationships with our children, but which also makes visible and viable meaningful relationships between children and adults who do not have the legal or biological status of parenthood.

Black lesbian feminist Diane S. Bogus wrote about the labor of mothering without the name mother performed by many non-biological mother figures including herself as the non-mom parent of her partner's biological children. Interestingly, in 1977, on the same page of the periodical *Lesbian Tide* that covers a number of custody battles by lesbian parents, Diane S. Bogus coins the term "mom de plume," searching for a term that connects her work as a mother without the status of motherhood to her intertwined creative work as a writer. This collection follows that trajectory. The writers in this collection look at mothering as a creative practice defined not by the state, but by our evolving collective relationship to each other, our moments together and a possible future.

Toward a Motherful Future

"Not fatherless . . . How about motherful?"
—Khadijah Matin, Sisterhood of Black Single Mothers, 1986

The ongoing exclusion and criminalization of people of color, poor people, and LGBTQ people from the status of motherhood in relationship to the state sets the stage for creativity around the labor, energy, and existence of the practice of mothering. As Cathy Cohen points out in her 1997 article "Punks, Bulldaggers, and Welfare Queens," the figure of the impoverished and deviant mother is a queer figure in the United States, whether that mother is part of the LGBTQ community or not. From the mid 1970s through the 1980s in Brooklyn, New York, a group called the Sisterhood of Black Single Mothers emerged through and around activist activities at Medgar Evers College with the leadership of Daphne Busby and directly took on the demonization and pathologization of Black single mothers and their children. The purpose of the Sisterhood was to provide tangible logistical support to young parents and to also reframe the practice of parenting as a single woman (and ultimately also as single men or young couples) autonomously and positively. The project consisted of a proactive youth program, Kianga House, which provided long-term housing for young mothers, logistical and legal support to help mothers and their children stay together, a mentoring program through which more experienced single mothers mentored new single mothers, and eventually a fatherhood collective for teen fathers or future fathers.

The work of the Sisterhood of Black Single Mothers was affirmed and intertwined with other Black feminists at the time. The work of the collective was featured in one of Kitchen Table: Women of Color Press's "freedom organizing pamphlets" as an important community model to be replicated. The dedication of a publication about this mothering work specifically by a women of color press founded by Black lesbian feminists and with a goal to address interlocking oppressions by publishing work by women of color with an emphasis on including work by lesbians is significant. The pamphlet itself, *It's a Family Affair: The Real Lives of Black Single Mothers* by Barbara Omolade, also directly links the demonization of Black single mothers to the demonization of Black lesbians within and outside the Black community and points out that this shared demonization is about the threat of women who live their lives in a way that shows that they do not need patriarchy or subservience to men.

The work of the Sisterhood of Black Single Mothers is a queer work in that it reframes mothering as a collective project that foregrounds the practical and intangible needs of those whose survival is most threatened in their community. Toward this end they refuse the pathologizing language placed on female-headed families. They insist that families nurtured by women are "not fatherless . . . how about motherful?" By shifting the terms, they make a poetic move that highlights the abundance of mothering, the power of mothers and the collaboration between mothers that makes the families least affirmed by the state dangerous, powerful and necessary. We can see the continuation of this work that centers poor and disenfranchised mothers in the work of Young Women United in Albuquerque, New Mexico, and Mamas Rising in Austin, Texas, which both support mothers of color, and in particular mothers who qualify for public assistance in accessing affirming support while giving birth and at every moment in the mothering process with an analysis that connects the revolutionary work of mothering poor children of color to a collaborative embodiment of the future.

Part of the role of this collection is to make visible the connections between a queer feminist of color practice and theory around mothering, intergenerationality and the future and what we see as the most crucial and challenging work of our time, the practice of mothering as an alternative building practice of valuing ourselves and each other and creating the world we deserve.

Motherhood, Media, and Building a 21st-Century Movement

Malkia A. Cyril

I love my mother.

From my birth in 1974 to her death in 2005, my mother taught me through her stories about the women of the Black Panther Party that mothers are a key vehicle for social change and critical to the fight for democratic rights. Perhaps this is why the conservative Right has so viciously and aggressively targeted their communications at mothers and motherhood within communities of color, poor communities, and young communities. Without the voices and visions of mothers, and their leadership at multiple levels, 21st-century progressive movements cannot win.

But like all systems of communication, our families can become platforms for the ruling class, or vehicles of rebellion and transformation in the face of the ruling class, depending on the degree to which the family is democratized and mothers are free. My mother has been dead now for ten years. Yet her complex legacy and struggle for her own freedom drives my leadership still.

I grew up the daughter of a woman in pain. With both sickle cell anemia and a history of abuse, my mother knew what suffering was. That pain, and my mother's lifelong attempts through childrearing, a career in education, and community organizing in the Black Panther Party to transform her own suffering into both safety and belonging, provide the context for my analysis about the critical role of motherhood in building social movements. I have no children, but the understanding of mothering wrought by my experience as some mother's child has transformed from a single person accountable primarily to myself to a nurturer of children, of leaders, and of the kind of social movements that give birth to new vision, new conditions, and new ways of governing and making change.

Like many of you, I learned about governance at home. From the constant reprise that I had to share with not only my younger sister, but any child or adult who was living with us at the time to the silent observation that my mother relied upon a network of women to care for her children and keep them safe from harm, it was clear to me from a very young age that governance was a communal affair, requiring multiple forms of leadership that ranged from hierarchical and collective and included consensus building strategies, shared infrastructure, and an economic system that supported the base needs of all equally and allowed for each to contribute according to their means and ability. It was also clear that the strain of single parenting, under-employment, and lack of consistent and reliable intimate partnership raised the level of volatility and inconsistency in my home. The lesson that emerged in my young mind was complex. On one hand, the partnership and leadership of the powerful and brilliant Black women that raised me was critical to my survival and success. On the other, every mother I knew had been victimized by the men they loved and trusted, betrayed in some way by other sisters, and was unable to show vulnerability except when the dam broke and it came pouring out— too often at home, alone with their children. Just as they were resourceful, inspiring, nurturing, and full of almost unreasonable joy, these women were also volatile, overly hostile, isolated, manipulative, and unhappy. These Black women who loved and nurtured me were unrecognized for their extraordinary gifts, unable to foster and maintain intimate relationships with men or women, and yet responsible for cultivating a next generation with little to no support.

How can a household, a community, or a nation be effectively governed when women are held disproportionately responsible for its future yet are disproportionately neglected, abused, excluded, isolated, and invisible? Two words: it can't.

Instead, empire is sustained, and mothers become one of the tools of its continuous resurrection. But just as mothers can become the ideological vehicles for hierarchy and dominance, they are uniquely positioned to lead both visionary and opposition strategies to it. With the right supports, mothers from underrepresented communities can help lead the way to new forms of governance, new approaches to the economy, and an enlightenment of civil society grounded in fundamental human rights. In fact, they always have.

Twentieth-century social movements saw the rise of foundation-supported social change sectors and within those efforts, the deliberate targeting of resources to strengthen the capacity of progressive and conservative movements to win. On the right, conservatives invested in culture wars, with women leading the way in many instances. Whether in the fight against reproductive justice and freedom, or against queer rights, or for incarceration, women (and mothers in particular) were projected into media debates as the spokespeople for a conservative vision of family, labor relations, and wages, and were often the most virulent opponents of immigrant rights or restorative justice policies.

These mothers were cast as crime victims, as victims of leftists who didn't value family, as victims of failed government policy. Conservative organizations worked hard to use that frame to cultivate a generation of anti-feminist female leaders (the Ann Coulters, the Sarah Palins) who continue to re-define feminism and the vision of motherhood in its most destructive and hierarchical forms. This culture war, with mothers as its motive force, has been too often neglected and ignored by progressive movements. By underestimating the impact of these culture wars on framing the future, and under-resourcing strategic communications and cultural strategies that center the voices and visions of progressive mothers, particularly those from underrepresented communities, progressive movements have weakened their ability to win.

This is true across all sectors of progressive movements, not just in the issue areas obviously pertaining to women, like reproductive justice or women's rights.

In the fight for true internet freedom and media equity, mothers are a neglected constituency with the potential to be powerful spokespeople and leaders for a new distribution of media rights and resources.

When I was in junior high school, my mother brought home our first computer.

We were the first house on the block to have one, and it launched a new nickname for my mother that stuck till the day she died on January 15, 2005. Our neighbors called her "Professor." It was clear, through the purchase of that computer, that she viewed her children's access to education as a core strategy for their liberation. This is a framework and belief shared by so many women with children, and people in general. And it is this core belief, translated into an increasingly digitized world, that makes mothers a key set of spokespeople for fights over internet regulation.

Before we had the computer, my mom bought the full set of *The Encyclopaedia Britannica.* It was a sight to see, neighborhood children coming over to our house after school to use our encyclopedia to do their homework. And once we got the internet, the phenomenon continued on a digital landscape. A mother chose that path. A mother bought those books. A mother brought that computer home and taught herself how to use it so that she could free her daughters of some of the untenable choices she'd had to make.

Right now, mothers across this nation, and across the world are deciding how best to educate their children, and they are increasingly using digital technologies and mobile platforms to do it. Whether they are at home, in prisons, being deported, jobless, or at work, mothers of all genders and physical types, with or deprived of their children, are shaping the beliefs and practices of the next generation of constituents and leaders. These children, of whom I was one, are learning at home from their mothers what type of democracy and economy they deserve. It is mothers who will teach the next generation to read not only books but mobile phones and computers. It is mothers who will shape the engagement strategies and activation point of the next generation of everyday Americans. Mothers will decide, whether implicitly and informally, or as explicit and prioritized leaders in our movements for change, what future a 21st-century social movement creates.

To transform racism and poverty, and the stories and media infrastructure that supports and directs that transformation, social movements must strengthen the infrastructure to support motherhood, change the story about mothers from underrepresented communities, and increase the visibility of the voices and visions of mothers. With them, we are powerful. Without them, we lose.

My mother was beautiful, brilliant, powerful. And whether you are a teacher, a doctor, unemployed, a sex worker, or a prisoner, so are you. I see you. I support you. And I lift your voice, and sing.

On My Childhood, El Centro del Raza, and Remembering

Esteli Juarez

I was raised by revolutionaries. My elders gave me a distinct advantage in life, and as a parent I intend on passing that advantage on to my children. Are you wondering what that advantage was? Consciousness. The ability to fight back against "the norm" both in direct action and psychologically. I was able to see the system and constructs around me as causing many more problems than they were fixing. I was also able at a very early age to see how some things in my life were not anyone's "fault." Many of the problems I faced and the people around me faced were due to systematic oppression, not the fault of any one individual. I knew very early on that the American Dream was a lie and rooted in colonization. Bootstraps with which to raise one's caste in this country are few and far between, and many times still rely on the good graces of the oppressive structure.

I was raised Chicana, in every sense of the word. Raised to have a deep understanding of my familial history, my social history, and the history of my people in this country. Raised to see injustice and fight against it. In law school, they teach you "issue spotting" or "how to think like a lawyer"; they didn't know I'd been doing that since birth. I remember being no older then five and being on my father's shoulders at a rally screaming "Hell no, we won't go." I wore a T-shirt to school in the second grade, on Columbus Day, with a picture of Indigenous peoples on a shore looking toward three ships, and it said, "Who discovered who in 1492?" One of my earliest memories is being in the house of my Ninos (godparents), Juan and Tina Bocanegra, and looking up at a black-and-white poster of Emiliano Zapata, my favorite revolutionary (that should tell you something about my childhood; I had a favorite revolutionary!) and the one my youngest son is named after. I did a report about Diego Rivera in the third grade, read *Bless Me, Ultima* at age seven, and my favorite movie as a child was *Zoot Suit*. I was raised . . . revolutionarily.

I had never spent a lot of time thinking about how this affected my life until the passing of Roberto Maestas, the longtime executive director of El Centro de la Raza in Seattle, in the fall of 2010. I did not know the man well, but he was a regular presence in my life due to his relationship with the city of Seattle, where I spent much of my youth, and with my family. El Centro is a piece of our history and a piece of power we have in that rainy city. For those of us idealists in this generation, for those who struggle for something better for our children, that place has become a beacon, a gentle reminder that change is possible. That sometimes our demands get met, but like everything else it is our job to keep them good. It is our job to keep working toward something better. Many of my friends have given their time at El Centro and it has created and forged relationships for those who passed through those doors, whether we were all there at the same time or not. I've met people long after their service at El Centro but their time there continues to bond us together.

El Centro is first and foremost a building, a physical space. It was an abandoned school in the Beacon Hill area of Seattle and in the fall of 1972, a group of Chicanos occupied the building. The creation of the organization and the occupation of the building happened out of community necessity. Chicanos, Mexicanos, Latinos had no public space in the city of Seattle, nowhere for people to gather, build community, access resources, or organize. El Centro has taken many shapes over the past forty years but the building still stands. It is still a place for people to gather, to build community, to progress. It is still a place where Chicanos and Latinos and other people of color go for touchstone, for support, for history, and remembering.

I was the first child born to my father during his involvement in El Centro. My mother was not around during my early childhood and I was raised by my father, the friends he made at El Centro, my godparents, and close family friends. I grew up in homes with pictures of Zapata and Che, where Spanglish was the only language spoken, where the subjects of colonization, imperialism, equality, and all things political and historical were discussed freely. I was the only seventh grader who was sent to the principal's office for defending Fidel Castro. The way I was raised also allows me to parent from that place. I may not have had the same experiences as my father, but I am able to bring those experiences, discussions, and viewpoints to my children. I am also able to parent without feeling guilt or pressure from a broken education system, as I am able to see where flaws in the system are and not place that burden on my children or myself. I am raising men, four of them, and this structure, this system, is not an inviting place for them. The way I was parented allows me and taught me to parent them from a place of liberation, progressive in nature, so that they will experience this system and their place in it differently.

When Roberto Maestas passed away, I called my father, one of the other founders of El Centro. My father recounted the story of the takeover for me. He walked me through the loss of the ESL program at what is now South Seattle CC. My brother's mother, Nancy Gonzales, as well as my other Nino (godfather), Roberto Gallegos, taught there. He told me about how they spent time trying to find a right location, how they organized the take over and how they spent months in that building with no power, until they won. He told me there are pictures of him studying for the bar exam by candle light, told me about how my Abuela (grandmother), La Santa Ramona Juarez de Padilla, would come and bring food, and how they would play hearts in the basement for hours. I try and imagine my grandmother much younger, and my father and Tios (uncles), too. And then he told me how it changed and how people's ideas of what El Centro should have been changed. Then, how people stepped away. When I spoke to Juan Bocanegra, one of my Ninos, he reminded me that "asi es la vida" and while I have fear for the mortality of my elders, this is the way it goes. We also spoke of re-membering. Re-membering. Piecing together stories to find truth, a change of perspective.

Sometimes tragedy forces us to reflect. The passing of a man I barely knew changed my perspective and made me realize that I was raised in a special place at a special time. To me ideas of justice, of change, of fighting for something better, those were not things I learned, they were instilled in me. As they will be in my children. Last week, my son Eli wanted a toy and reminded his younger brother that since he, as the oldest, is the leader he should get the toy and Tony handed it over. I pulled Eli aside and reminded him that yes he is the leader, but good leaders share with those who don't have that power. And he gave the toy back to his hermanito. Someday, my children will also realize their privilege.

II.

From the Shorelines to the Front Lines

Introduction
Mai'a Williams

All mothers have the potential to be revolutionary. Some mothers stand on the shoreline, are born and reborn here, inside the flux of time and space, overcoming the traumatic repetition of oppression. Our very existence is disobedience to the powers that be. At times, we as mothers choose to stand in a zone of claimed risk and fierce transformation, on the front lines. In infinite ways, both practiced and yet to be imagined, we put our bodies between the violent repetition of the norm and the future we already deserve, exactly because our children deserve it too. We make this choice for many reasons and in different contexts, but at the core we have this in common: we refuse to obey. We refuse to give into fear. We insist on joy no matter what and by every means necessary and possible. Mothers, especially radical women of color, working-class, marginalized, low-income, and no-income radical mothers, have sought for decades, if not centuries, to create relationships to each other, transformative relationships to feminism and a transnational anti-imperialist literary, cultural, and everyday practice. Sometimes for radical mamas, our mothering in radical community makes visible the huge gulfs between communities, between parents and non-parents, in class and other privileges AND most importantly the wide gulf between what we say in activist communities and what we actually do. Radical mothering is the imperative to build bridges that allow us to relate across these very real barriers.

a conversation with my six-year-old about revolution
Cynthia Dewi Oka

when 3 feet of sunshine missing two front teeth
asked me why do we need revolution
all i had was a grenade in my mouth.

i held him for a while and watched him draw
clouds and trees and ladybugs and a house
filled with everybody he loves

when was the last time we put to image
what we thought the world should be
when did it become enough to know
        how to promptly explode

i said to him he was much better equipped
to figure out the revolution than his mama
that if i don't he's got to disarm this bomb
        and throw it out the window

cause the revolution is not about self-defense
it's about self-creation, it's about seeing farther
than the walls directly in front of us

and my six-year-old has got a head start.

A Los Angeles Quartet:
Daily Survival, Body Memory, First-world Single Mama, Identity and Mothering
Fabiola Sandoval

---

i. Daily Survival

I have a nice desk job. Eight-hour days, flexible enough to take time to engage in my child's school activities. There are stories in my job. All those families that I help maintain their housing. I push paper for their housing. Many times I've said I'm a poet in an asset manager's chair.

Their stories balance it. Eye contact with colleagues, the tenants and promotoras, it is their stories that give dignity to it all.

With half custody of my daughter, the schedule flip-flops every week and once upon a time I believed since I actively mother half time, I self-described as a half time mama. Now though, I know I am a mama all the time, even when she's not with me. My ancestors and heart know more than what many eyes can see.

When I don't have her it's the plants I nurtured, the altar in the living room, the candles lit, the food cooked, the sidewalks walked on, other loves and their company balances her being away every two days.

Los Angeles-born-child-of-migrants, like the plants brought from afar, but now with roots deep they break concrete . . . wander in books, the Lincoln Heights library, friends near and in far away places, in memories, in the lives of my ancestors, in worldly hearts of those family and friends that stay.

I thank the Tongva people who were here before, the true natives to the Los Angeles basin; pray against this knowledge and amnesia and apathy overall. We know the ice cream man and his melancholic ways, sharing memories of his home state in Chihuahua, Mexico. The library workers talking with me, knowing a once long-haired stay at home mama with my scrumptious baby in a Snuggli and now a short-haired, on-the-go worker with my now six-year-old that loves books as much as she loves long dresses, dancing, and singing.

Often times the heavy parts of my job weigh me down, those unfiled papers that cover the desk and the floor in that full of healing posters/words office. I remember to listen to the every hour rings of the St. Vincent church bells and I'm grounded. It's a daily task to stay on that mindset.

Half custody does that to me too.

All the kids that aren't mine once tugged my umbilical cord when the little one was away, then I remember she's of the earth as much as my daughter, let go.

Now I'm looking for other work and going to take the custody issue to court. Yes, court. It's fighting for something different, so I know I'm changing and in my world, that's radical too. I've believe too much into a too small to fit in a box definition of radical even when that meant keeping me and my daughter and her father away from something that might help us along the way.

Some things get old, so I'm doing and writing the stories also for them to fly and let me fly in other directions.

Take comfort in gardening, biking, and meals with friends, writing poems, and listening to stories everywhere in Los Angeles even the birds chasing crows away from their nests, the hummingbirds getting nectar from our garden . . .

That's the balance of mama land, worker nice desk job, rooted like the native plants of Los Angeles balance daily survival . . . there's beauty in every blink.

ii. Body Memory

Yesterday I couldn't grasp all the stories; the young woman raped by her grandfather since she was two to twelve and his asking of forgiveness while he lay in his deathbed.

Remember the sister of one of my best friends growing up repeatedly raped by her father for years. All the other stories contained, details faded.

Then there's my own body.

It wasn't so bad. First the memories of my grandfather and his curious hands. They were the grandparents who lived in a nice house by a park, with dozens of trees and calla lilies in the yard and an outside dog, Tafi; the four-bedroom suburban home away from the one-bedroom inner-city home we lived in daily. My grandfather would get inappropriately happy when his granddaughters would visit, especially if they stayed the night, which I did a lot.

"Here's your favorite candy." Walking the dog every evening. After dinner, he would sit by me and force his hands on me, and then grab my hands to fondle him, watching MTV music videos for hours.

The days, he would want to get in the bathroom while I was there and I would push him out and lock the door.

It was a silent battle until it stopped, a decade of push, pull.

Then there was the family friend who the family helped after he migrated from Mexico, while he "played" with four-year-old me for months before I entered kindergarten.

Two other men on top of that, details too complicated to share, and I younger than fourteen they older than forty maybe.

As many families do, my family kept busy providing, trying to not lose their dignity in the fast city Los Angeles hustle, their immigrant labor too cheap they compensated with overtime. I am left to think that they must have had to abundantly believe in other people's good intentions, covering the amnesia of familial secrets of vulnerability and abuse, to make the sacrifices easier.

Over fourteen years have passed and I feel clean, unashamed most days.

Every day is a day to remember even when I do not wish to; my six-year-old reminds me of the vulnerability and magic of being young and full of wonder and the capacity for body memory to transform. I try not to get overwhelmed by being a mother to a daughter; in magic healing the body trusts our resiliency. She knows she's strong, powerful and her body is hers and to trust her tummy feelings, and then I let go. Let go, and hold myself tight letting go of my body memories turned outward to the world.

iii. First-world Single Mama

First-world single mama to one child in a non-profit world . . .
All of these labels
for others' comfort, than my own

let's play
for a minute

sure
I live in the first world
Not domestically partnered with child's father
Or anyone
work in a non-profit.

Let me add
for my sake
I don't identify as a single mama on most days
or as a first-world inhabitant
non-profit employee
I'm humana
writer poet mama
dancer . . .
story listener . . .
writing about story nuances and
Resiliency

Panel discussions on peace
building partners
tidy chairs and well seated attendees
looking up at the stage
experts talking
Amaya by my side
"we need to build trust"
"we need to ask families questions"
we do, we do
with the only child present in that room
we walk outside
play with the fountain water
pretending there were fish
in it
we chose
breaking free
of tidy sitting staring at the panel stage

speaking of family trusts and inclusion
building trust with make believe
stories with the little
one we are poetry
together

been on
kpfk and npr
paid to sit on at least three panels
four times flown to a conference
Partook in a fellowship for Latinas in non-profits
I wear one inch black pointy shoes almost every day
hoops or dangly earring that match my blouse
a paper pushing community based j – o – b
9 – 5 Monday through Friday
Hey, our ancestors did work hard to make sure we had a 40 hour a
week job
and people in the neighborhood & outside near and far wished they
have a job
to pay their gas bill
I can hear it, but I wonder
To be free . . . you do a b and c . . .
Free knowing the rent and food has a price tag
Dependents are counting on it
Free in an expensive first world

iv. Identity and Mothering

"I'm Mexican, Look I'm Brown!"

The little one and her cousin were playing in the living room early
that morning while I stole ten more minutes of sleep. My niece
speaks fluent Spanish and my little one knows twenty words in
Spanish.

"Mami, mami, she's saying I'm not Mexican because I don't speak
Spanish. I am, right? I am, I am!"

She runs in the room crying from feeling pushed out of the affinity group by her older cousin, who hasn't read any race books or engaged in identity politics at eight years old. She knows Spanish fluently and has visited Mexico a handful of times though.

These little ones both with curly hair, similar height and skin tone, slightly different facial features were challenged by language capacity.

I wake up half asleep and quickly remember what I grappled with at that age. With a light skinned grandma on my father's side, red headed bronze skin grandma on my mother's side. Stoic stern women, with a silent lion strength that is revered in this day and age, they carried the cross without complaining too much, some family member's would argue.

A common story, I swallowed the venom of self-hate early on.

From a family of visibly praying women, praying to Jesus almost every night was the next step. I prayed for my "darker" skin and brown eyes and mama's skin too and her thick accent.

Then I prayed for the big chi chis. The heart shaped hips.

Back to the room where I'm the adult in race authenticity and social rejection between the six-year-old and eight-year-old, I facilitate their disagreement the best I could.

"Use your words and they will change. Your grandparents are Mexican and so are you. You don't speak fluent Spanish, but that's okay."

She smiled.

We are Mexican, and we are Angelenas too.

Fluidity anchored in grounded-ness.

We have a globe to remember other parts of the world, and that our world is larger than our blocks and labels pushing the message "we know where we come from are and we're learning more of ourselves along the way, and on that note, let's learn about others."

It's all a process. Witnessing and guiding compassionately the little ones, being a mama that tries to live and not impose values (w/ my close family and friends' support), writing to process and reconcile the gaps. Gain power continuing to try when there's room for making it all clearer, like writing, to keep writing even when the voice says stop you don't know what you're doing.

We keep going, writing, witnessing, and trying.

Mothering as Revolutionary Praxis
Cynthia Dewi Oka

"For those who dominate and oppress us benefit most when we have nothing to give our own, when they have so taken from us our dignity, our humanness that we have nothing left, no "homeplace" where we can recover ourselves."
—bell hooks, 1990

"Motherhood is an act of defiance in the midst of colonization."
—Dana Erekat, 2006

The revolutionary struggle against a colonial, racist, hetero-patriarchal capitalism which has for centuries separated us; arranged us in structured oppositions to each other; reduced our bodies to raw resources for abuse, exploitation and manipulation; and, in the words of Frantz Fanon, occupied our breathing, is today the struggle for a world—no, many worlds—where we might exist and thrive as each other's beloved.

It is the struggle not only for a social universe that is meaningful and just, but lives that are inherently precious. It is the struggle against our elimination, our disappearance from each other.

Mothering is a primary front in this struggle, not as a biological function, but as a *social practice*.

As a system of organization premised on the private accumulation of profit, rather than the assurance of collective survival and well-being, capitalism requires that human needs be met while simultaneously being rendered irrelevant. This is why mothering, as a social practice, exists in a state of paradox—culturally idealized (i.e. in a white supremacist way) yet lacking in any social or economic value. It is literally *priceless*.

The ethos of mothering involves valuing *in and of itself* a commitment to the survival and thriving of other bodies. It presents a fundamental contradiction to the logic of capitalism, which unmoors us from each other.

Women of color have been violently punished and stigmatized for mothering. Black women were not legally allowed to marry as slaves; had to give up their children to their masters; were forced to care for white women's homes and children instead of their own; or lost their young to mass criminalization, incarceration, and poverty-driven violence. Meanwhile, indigenous women have endured the genocide of their communities and forcible sterilization by the state, been expelled from their communities by marriage laws regulating Indian status, or had their children taken from them and placed in residential schools and white foster homes. Today, hundreds of thousands of women in the Third World have to leave children behind as they go abroad in search of work.

Neither have women of color produced equally valued members of the labor force under the global capitalist regime: where white children are celebrated as increased human capital, Black, indigenous, and Third World children are lamented as drains on state resources, prospective criminals and more recently with the (racist) overpopulation discourse, as perpetrators of environmental degradation.

There is a vast store of experience, knowledge, and resilience in the lives of oppressed women who have made *continuing* possible for their communities even as white supremacist, hetero-patriarchal capitalism has intensified its efforts to deprive us to from the means of mothering ourselves and our communities.

Under neoliberalism, poor women's individual responsibilities to earn formal and informal wages (as part-time, contingent, flexible labor) while caregiving for family and community members cut off from state support, continue to multiply and deepen.

As one of these women, I can testify to the exhaustion, desperation, and isolation pervading such a life, as well as to the resourcefulness, strength, and revolutionary urgency with which it rewards me.

I maintain that this is a life worth keeping.

Perhaps the kind of home we need today is mobile, multiple, and underground.

Perhaps we need to become *unavailable* for state scrutiny so that we can experiment with reorganizing our social relations in revolutionary ways.

Against the rallying cry of freedom, I propose to embed revolutionary struggle in a politics of necessity and responsibility, a politics that enhances our *encumbrance* upon each other while rejecting the extension of our dependence on state and capital.

Many historical and contemporary social movements which have improved the lives of poor, working-class people and people of color have also reinforced our attachments to capitalism and nationalism; for instance, through welfare, pay equity, and citizenship. Working to sever our dependence on capitalist and nationalist institutions should be a priority in revolutionary struggle.

Mothering as revolutionary praxis involves exploring how we might reorganize ourselves to meet common needs in this historical moment, including the capacity to raise and nurture whole, resilient individuals as well as autonomous communities of resistance.

To revolt, we must measure the depth not of our victimization but of our capacity and resilience.

A Manifesto for Revolutionary Homemaking

The home is not a private resource that we draw from to do the real revolutionary work "out there." It is *the front of human sustenance* that is constitutive of hetero-patriarchal, white supremacist capitalism *and* its limits.

1. **Fight for the reproductive integrity and self-determination of all indigenous women, women of color, queer, trans, disabled, and poor women.** "We ought to be able to decide when and how we will conceive and with whom, who and what practices will be part of our pregnancy, what we allow into our body, where we give birth and with whom, how we feed our children" (Outlaw Midwives). No woman should go through pregnancy and childbirth in isolation and deprivation. Every community of resistance should have its own collective of capable and trusted midwives.

2. **Work toward sexual justice for genders that are labeled "deviant" by hetero-patriarchal ideology.** This means moving from a framework of consent to active co-creation of sexual desire and experience; extending bodily practices that bend gender identities and disrupt prescribed sexualities; ensuring that spaces of resistance invite and amplify the voices of gender-variant people; and equalizing material conditions of access to sexual fulfillment that is safe, dignified, and self-determined. This also means challenging the criminalization of sex work everywhere.

3. **Reclaim communal responsibility for caregiving, including childrearing and homemaking.** Stop expecting women to break themselves for other people's benefit in order to prove their worth. Recognize that time and energy are political resources we must redistribute. We can create childcare, co-parenting, and caregiver collectives to support the daily survival strategies of poor mothers and caregivers. We must enable their central participation and invite their leadership in revolutionary struggle. Further, we must challenge the exploitation of Third World women as domestic workers with precarious status from the understanding that collectivizing caregiving in our communities is linked to dismantling a capitalist empire that abuses Third World women's bodies as part of its infrastructure.

4. **Politicize familial love.** We need to be attentive to how power shapes our desires to be familiar and intimate with particular bodies. Might we go against class comfort in choosing the people

we share our lives with? Can we commit to intensely stigmatized bodies? We must practice partnership as mutual commitment, dependency, and alliance, where we invest not only in each other's specific struggles for justice but also in building and expanding shared just communities. Familial love can be a hub of resource sharing and a starting place to *open out* toward community.[1]

5. **Create structures of community accountability around intimate violence.** Survivors of intimate violence should have meaningful options outside the colonial-capitalist system of law enforcement and the prison-industrial complex which profit off of the criminalization of indigenous, poor, non-documented peoples and peoples of color. Intimate abuse can sever people's access to housing, family, community, economic support, and physical, affective and mental integrity. Every community of resistance needs to develop structures to create safety for survivors and hold perpetrators accountable. Further, we must reclaim the power and physical capacities to defend ourselves.

6. **Advance a justice-centered concept of health and develop autonomous spaces for healing work.** Oppression consists of violent and traumatic experiences that have become normalized and endemic. Without healing many of us are liable to reproduce the very dehumanization we claim to be fighting against. This is especially problematic in the context of communities of resistance, which are already combating heightened assaults by the state; and in the lives of people who cannot easily or safely access state provided health care (poor people of color, transpeople, non-documented people). We must resist the institutional pathologization of our responses to oppression. Every community of resistance needs a collective of healers.

7. **Develop radical, mobile, autonomous free schools that centralize the participation of children, youth and people excluded from hegemonic educational institutions.** For Paulo Freire, pedagogy is a means of "critical intervention in reality," a way of undermining the reproduction of conditions under which "to be is *to be like*, and *to be like* is *to be like the*

---

1   A powerful example of this is the Mobile Homecoming Project, where queer black feminist partners Alexis Pauline Gumbs and Julia Wallace journey in an RV through the American South to *make family with* black LGBTQ elders. Project details and updates: http://mobilehomecoming.org.

oppressor."[2] The public education system systematically dispossesses children and young people of languages, ideas, and subjectivities that are oppositional to those of state and capital interests. We must decolonize education by redefining the rules and forms of knowledge production.

8. **Create structures for the collective distribution of necessary goods**. Establish clothing exchanges, community gardens, and food/meal-sharing networks where people's contributions are proportional to their respective abilities.[3] Sharing homes can increase access to safe and dignified spaces of living while de-nuclearizing the norms of family. Importantly, we must extend home-sharing networks to folks in perilous conditions. For instance, poor single mothers and their children continue to be considered "unfit" to share homes with because their lives are perceived as burdensome and unstable. Create homes that can function as revolutionary hubs!

9. **Reclaim the process of art for facilitating collective critical reflection, connectedness and inspiration**. "Poetry is the way we help give name to the nameless so it can be thought. The farthest horizons of our hopes and fears are cobbled by our poems, carved from the rock experiences of our daily lives," writes Audre Lorde.[4] To the extent that art is a social process of perceiving, communicating and reconstructing our realities, it is necessary for growing our capacity to birth revolutionary vision. Develop multigenerational artist collectives responsible for engaging people in aesthetic processes to project the experiences and yearnings of our communities.[5]

---

2   Paulo Freire, *Pedagogy of the Oppressed*, 30th anniversary edition (London: Bloomsbury Academic, 2000), 37, 33.

3   The Rhizome Free Store models how this can be done. Rhizome Cafè is an activist café and venue in Vancouver dedicated supporting social justice struggles and movement building. Every month or so, Rhizome organizers choose a theme (e.g. clothes, school supplies, kitchenware, etc.) and invite people to bring in what they want to give away and take home what they need. For details, see www.rhizomecafe.ca.

4   Audre Lorde, "Poetry Is Not a Luxury," in *Sister Outsider: Essays and Speeches* (Berkeley: The Crossing Press, 1984), 36–39.

5   The Vancouver-based Press Release collective of movement poets is one such example. During the 2010 Olympic Winter Games, the group solicited poems from local community members and produced an anonymous chapbook entitled *Surveillance* documenting the destructive impacts of and grassroots mobilizations against the Games.

10. **Decolonize our relationship to the earth and other living beings.** Indigenous and peasant communities have been at the forefront of militant struggles to protect bio-regions all over the globe and to fight against their privatization, extraction, and destruction. We must retrain ourselves to see precious life where we have been conditioned to see only "natural resources," and participate in the recovery and defense of local knowledges and modes of social organization that were able for millennia to sustain relationships of reciprocity with the earth and all of its living beings.

Mothers and caregivers—particularly those who are poor—tend to be absent from the hubs of revolutionary struggle. They are busy making and defending homespaces; strategizing for the next check, the next hour, the next meal. They are out there demonstrating that it is possible and beautiful to continue under the most hostile and precarious conditions, even when they have to do it alone.

It is telling that communal mothering, childcare, and caregiving continue to be one of the most neglected interventions in revolutionary struggle by virtue of their being considered mundane and cumbersome, unlike "real" political work. When this happens, the message poor mothers and their children receive is essentially that their presence and participation in revolutionary struggle do not matter, that they have nothing to contribute.

"The quality that we call beauty . . . must always grow from the realities of life, and our ancestors, forced to live in dark rooms, presently came to discover beauty in shadows, ultimately to guide shadows towards beauty's end."
—Jun'ichiro Tanizaki

At this historical moment, we need to become skilled at mothering.

There will be no liberation without us knowing how to depend on each other, how to be encumbered with and responsible for each other. We will dream and never descend.

Super Babies
Sumayyah Talibah

mommy
i'm going to save the world one day
my oldest son told me
with pride
save the world
the baby
emphatically agreed
wearing capes
fashioned
from my head scarves
holding weapons
of green lego blocks
and paper towel rolls
they were ready
to conquer all evil

and my heart skipped a beat
as i wondered
if
at this age
they should be learning
to seek and destroy
because they're too young
to know about
grudges and guerrillas
and people who do wrong
to set things right
is this child's play
really
a game?

i wanna be a hero
they said
and go
to the rescue
save all the people
from harm
but everything they do
even tying their shoes
makes them
heroes
in my eyes

Doing It All . . . and Then Again with Child
Victoria Law

I first got involved in organizing and political work as a teenager.
I didn't have any resources, skills, or experience to offer, just an
inarticulate urge to change the way things were. I plunged into
everything I found with teenage enthusiasm: The summer I was
eighteen was the summer that Mumia Abu-Jamal, a political prisoner on Death Row in Pennsylvania, had been sentenced for execution. I spent every night working with an ad hoc committee
of squatters, artists, and anarchists to draw attention and support to his case. We leafleted and tabled, rode the subway till all
hours putting up posters about his case, contacted media, and
organized direct action demonstrations (precursors to the Black
Bloc that would later emerge and capture anarchist imagination
in Seattle).

Other nights were spent attending endless strategizing meetings to fight impending evictions of neighboring squats and community centers and, when an eviction or direct action did occur,
spending afternoons on the phone wrangling free legal support for
arrestees, nights at the courthouse waiting to post bail and days
attending trials. When some of the prisoner rights activists with
whom I did Mumia work talked about forming a group to send
free books to prisoners, I jumped in, remembering how eagerly my
friends, held first at Rikers Island and then in upstate prisons for
gang-related activities, had devoured the books and newspapers I
brought them.

Every Sunday morning, regardless of what I had done or how
late I had stayed out the night before, I rolled out of bed and went
to ABC No Rio, a local community arts center, to open up Food Not
Bombs. Every Sunday, regardless of the temperature or the weather
or how many other people showed up to help, I'd cook enough soup
or stir-fry to fill at least one five-gallon bucket and schlep it eleven
blocks to Tompkins Square Park to feed whoever was hungry.

My passion for social justice work literally engulfed my life—I learned black-and-white photography not as a fine art form but to be able to document instances of police brutality. I socialized almost exclusively with people who shared not only my political views but also my passion for putting them into practice. On the morning that a neighboring squat was to be evicted and two hundred dollars was needed for court filing fees to stay the wrecking ball, I emptied my bank account and lived off one cheap meal a day until my next paycheck.

This was the way my life was for four years. Then, at twenty-two, I got pregnant and decided to become a mother.

Just as I had made the decision to immerse my life in my political work, when I chose motherhood, I realized that my focus needed to shift. I could no longer put politics first and everything else, including my own needs, second. At first, I assumed that I would have to give up my activism. I would certainly have to give up going to protests against globalization or police brutality and avoid any other situation that might trigger the ever-so-eager NYPD to launch pepper spray, swing batons, and crack heads. I would have to devote all my time to caring for this helpless little thing that just wanted to eat, sleep, and be held. I assumed that I wouldn't have the time, energy, or inclination to continue my old life. And, because I had no role models to tell me otherwise, I assumed I had no other choice.

Before motherhood, I had gone to demonstrations, camera in each hand and a backpack full of film, waiting to capture the inevitable police misconduct, hoping to grab that picture that would mean the difference between a settlement and a dismissal.

As a new mother, usually with an infant in tow, I could no longer weave through angry or scared demonstrators or crawl through the legs of cops to get that perfect shot. I could no longer risk the threat of tear gas or batons. And I felt it was irresponsible to risk arrest with Siuloong still so dependent on me.

Still, I could not let go of what had become, for me, an essential part of my life.

Luckily, my childless activist friends would not let go of me either. They invited themselves over to see the new baby and incessantly asked when I would be returning to this project or that—with baby in tow. They enthusiastically offered to hold my newborn daughter not just so that I could move about more freely, but because they were genuinely excited about the new baby in their midst.

Thus, instead of dissolving into memories of pre-motherhood nostalgia, I shifted my social justice work. I turned my attention to more long-term projects, ones in which results are not instantaneous or even visible: I dove back into some projects, participating in every Books Through Bars packing session, handing the newborn Siuloong off to other willing arms so that I could fill a request or two. I wrote a grant for children's filmmaking and photo classes and found volunteer teachers.

I also began new projects, ones that I could fit in between the demands of a nursing newborn: six weeks after my daughter was born, I started writing to incarcerated women who were actively organizing and resisting their conditions of confinement. I wrote letters while waiting for the subway. At my minimum-wage office job, I alternated between data entry and research on issues affecting women in prison and organizations that might help them. While Siuloong napped, I incorporated those articles and the women's letters into a paper on women prisoners' resistance for a political science class.

Being a mother linked me to many of the women that I wrote to. As Siuloong became older and began to mimic my actions, usually onto the paper I was attempting to compose a letter on, the women became used to the scribbles and lines added to my letters. They shared their own stories about being separated from, or even losing, their children and constantly asked about mine.

My interest in their issues didn't end with the semester. Even after I had turned in my paper, I continued to write to the various women and to try to link them to advocacy and social service organizations that could help them.

The women's stories were both painful and inspiring. I realized that they needed to be heard by more people, not just by me. Still, the demands of that first year of motherhood—combined with the need to finish college and to work—prevented me from acting on that realization. The next year, however, one of those women pushed me to take further action: *I want to do a zine*, she wrote. *I want people to read about the injustices here and our struggles. Will you help me put it out?*

How could I say no?

With three other (childless) women who also believed in the idea that women prisoners' voices needed to be heard, I collected submissions from women incarcerated across the country. We edited and typed these handwritten stories, then laid them out and spent hours copying and collating the finished product into *Tenacious: Art and Writings by Women in Prison*.

That was just the beginning. With the formation of *Tenacious*, I began to see words—and printed matter—as valuable educational tools and ones that I could wield while still pushing a stroller to the playground. I started to see that I could use words to expose realities that wouldn't be heard otherwise and maybe even change people's perceptions on how the world actually was—and how it might be transformed.

When bombs threatened to fall on cities I had never seen and people whom I had never met, I felt compelled to turn my thoughts and actions toward the war. I bundled my daughter up and brought her to huge peace marches and smaller protests, taking pictures and chronicling our experience together.

But that was not enough. I wanted to do something more than just be another face in the crowd, another underreported number on the nightly news. I wanted to create something that showed the power of us, of mothers like myself who were outraged and who were taking action: I envisioned a zine collecting the voices and experiences demonstrating that mothers are not only angry but proactive in the anti-war movement. Mothers weren't visible in the early anti-war movement, but I knew that, despite hostility from both more conservative neighbors and childless (and thoughtless) anti-war activists, they were doing their part in saying NO to the war.

Both during and after pregnancy, I had heard comments from activists that women became depoliticized once they became mothers. I knew that this wasn't true, but it seemed to be a stereotype among the predominantly childless activists I came across. I wanted to create something that not only built bridges between mothers who were against the impending war, but also to rebut the notion that motherhood equals political indifference. My vision became *Mama Sez No War*, a sixty-eight-page zine that came out three weeks after the U.S. war on Iraq began. Zine-making became a political act. Since being the mother of a small child decreased the amount of risk I could responsibly take, I had to find other ways to protest. I put out not only my own experiences but those of women usually shunted to the margins—be they political mothers or prisoners—to challenge the way others perceived issues that don't impede upon their everyday lives.

With both *Tenacious* and *Mama Sez No War*, my daughter became my co-conspirator. We went to the office together and, in the evening, after most of the staff had gone either to the bar or home, I sat her on top of the Xerox machine.

She helped me make the master copy of each zine: after I placed each cut-and-pasted page onto the glass, she slammed the top down hard enough to make me wince. But, despite my fear that she would break the machine, I also saw the beauty of including my daughter in the process.

I incorporated Siuloong into other aspects of my postpartum activism, including virtually all of the weekly Books Through Bars packing sessions, nursing her as I attempted to address packages and then handing her off to one of the other volunteers so I could fill a request or two. As she grew older and began to toddle around, she pulled all of the George Bernard Shaw books from the bottom shelf and gleefully hurled them, one by one, into the recycling can. Now a veteran at the age of five, she helps me stamp the endless number of packages waiting to be mailed, then uses the emptied cardboard boxes as hiding spots.

When I began confronting my fear of public speaking and holding workshops on prisoner issues, Siuloong became a second lesson for those who attended: Shortly after she turned one, I was invited to talk about prison labor issues at a conference on prisoner activism. There was no childcare. I sat her on my lap and listened to the other two speakers. Siuloong decided that she wanted to nurse and so I pulled up my shirt and let her latch on.

She was still nursing when they had finished. I began my speech.

After the workshop, several people approached me—not only to comment on what I had said, but also on the fact that I had given a half-hour presentation on the history of prison labor and prisoner labor unions with a baby on my breast the entire time. "I think it's great that you had your daughter with you while you were talking," one woman said.

"Yeah," another agreed. "It made me wish I had brought mine."

A third person, a man recently released from prison, simply shook my hand and thanked me for the inspiration.

Since then, I've presented a number of workshops on prison issues. At one, I did so standing with a two-and-a-half-year-old Siuloong alternately in my arms or on my breast for most of my one-and-a-half-hour presentation on resistance among women in prison. Later that day, the conference organizers told me that they'd gotten feedback from a number of attendees not only about my workshop but also about how I had incorporated Siuloong into my presentation.

As Siuloong grew older and more able to comprehend concepts, my social justice work created new complexities in the way I parented. I can still take her to protests and demonstrations but now I have to explain the reason behind the march or rally and answer the succession of why's that pour from the mouth of any small child. Sometimes she thinks back to past events and makes connections: her one memory of the huge (unpermitted) February 15 march against the impending war on Iraq was of holding a giant cardboard crayon labeled "Crayons Not War." A year later, hearing a cover version of Bob Marley's "War," she asked, between bites of her dinner, "Mama, what's war?"

How to explain war to a three-year-old? The pregnancy and parenting books didn't prepare me for this.

I took a deep breath. "Well, war is when one country sends people to kill the people in another country."

She silently chewed her food and I wondered if my explanation had been too blunt.

"The next time there's a war, we should go out on the streets and march and say, 'No war,'" she continued.

"I don't know how you do it," my neighbor's girlfriend commented last summer. She was sitting on the front stoop smoking a midnight cigarette. I was just arriving home, having spent my Friday night developing rolls of film I'd shot at some protest or another.

At the time, I simply shrugged and mumbled, "I dunno. I just do."

But that's not entirely true. To simply say that leaves out the resources and community I've gained from years of being engaged in social justice work.

Staying involved in organizing can be draining at times. Even though Siuloong's father takes her for half the week, I often need that time to work and make money. Some days and evenings, I can fit in parts of my different projects without the demands of a small child distracting me. But there are still some nights when we stay out way too late because a meeting or work session goes overtime. There are still warm days when Siuloong would rather be at the playground but instead had to sit through a meeting or event indoors. There are still some projects and endeavors I've been forced to walk away from because my fellow volunteers refused to acknowledge, let alone accommodate, my concerns and needs as a mother of a small child. I walked away from an infoshop I had helped start when the other collective members repeatedly refused to address my concerns about not only the space's unsafe physical conditions but also the vicious dog that roamed freely and bit people without warning. When I brought these issues up, I was told, "Well, that's not really our concern. You chose to have a child." The most supportive response I ever got from that group was a noncommittal, "Maybe one day we'll have a childcare working group. But we can't make that a priority right now."

But I've also found that some of my projects—and the people involved in them—are willing to change to make sure that Siuloong and I feel welcome. Being involved—and making connections with the ever-widening circle of people in the various social justice networks—has increased the resources available to me both as a mother and as a person passionate about struggling for change. In talking with other parents, I realize that most don't have these same resources. Continuing to stay involved has helped me form a support network for both me and Siuloong—not only so that I can continue to do political work but also so that I'm not parenting in isolation.

Being around Siuloong during countless meetings, work sessions, and events acclimated many to the presence and needs of children and also allowed them to develop their own relationships with her. Some of these people have agreed to watch her so that I would have time to myself without the distraction or constant interruption of a small child. They not only occupy her attention in the same room while I finished laying out a zine or scrawled revisions into an essay I'm working on but also take her to visit friends in Queens or to walk along the beach in Coney Island. Sometimes, people I've worked with have gone out of their way to make sure that Siuloong and I have the support we need: two childless friends drove a few hours from their family's rural farm to Eugene, Oregon, specifically to help occupy Siuloong so that I could present my workshop on incarcerated women's resistance. They appeared at my workshop and, when Siuloong became too restless and demanded more of my attention, took her outside to run around so that I could concentrate on what I was saying. They stayed and ate lunch with us and then drove back. When she was two, one of my friends began taking her on the monthly Critical Mass bike rides, which she loved and never would have experienced with two parents who don't bike. When we needed a place to stay, a volunteer from ABC No Rio offered us his bedroom in a communal house and slept in the living room for several months. While we were there, Siuloong developed friendships with the other house members, who showed her how to play their guitars, read her stories, and took care of her when I had to go to the emergency room. After we moved out, they hosted a combined birthday party for her and two of the adult house members.

Our presence has also changed the culture of the places and projects with which we're involved. New volunteers now accept our presence without question. No one challenges our right to participate. Most see Siuloong's presence as a given, paving the way for other mothers and children.

Recently, Siuloong decided that she wanted to start volunteering at Food Not Bombs. The new group of volunteers, all in their late teens and early twenties, enthusiastically welcomed her. My only responsibility was to bring her to ABC No Rio and pick her up at the end of the day. They agreed to be responsible for her the rest of the time.

This past December, I traveled to Chiapas, Mexico, to attend the first Zapatista Women's Encuentro. For eight hours each day, Zapatista women shared their stories. Over and over, they stated that integrating mothers and children had been crucial to the struggle. Two little girls, ages nine and eleven, spoke about what the revolution has meant to them. They were articulate and obviously proud to be part of the movement. Young women who had been children when the Zapatistas rose up in 1994 also spoke, demonstrating a profound understanding and consciousness. Throughout the plenary sessions, children ran in and out of the auditorium to see and sit with their mothers or to be hugged before dashing off to play outside. Babies sometimes cried, but no one took much notice and, unlike meetings and events held on this side of the border, no one glared or asked the mother to leave.

I returned to New York reinvigorated and ready to continue fighting for and building a better world. Witnessing how mothers and children have been integrated—rather than excluded—from the Zapatista struggle renewed my commitment to continue including my own daughter in my organizing and activism but also to push others to create a movement where we all are welcome.

population studies
Cynthia Dewi Oka

"The proletariat in ancient society were those who were too poor to serve the state by holding property, and who served it instead by producing children (*proles*, offspring) as labour power. They are those who have nothing to give but their bodies."
　　—Terry Eagleton

1.
a few years ago, it coulda been me
loud lipstick wild carnival eyes
hair dyed orange & too-tight jeans
check the chipped manicure
check the oversize hoops
check the tattoos
fly dollar store spectacle
　　　　　　　bout to shipwreck on stage

if cancer hadn't killed daddy, i'm sure this would.
mama was stronger:
said nothin bout cigarettes in the stroller.

misunderstandings were understandable
i was the babysitter, of course
cause i was missing all the right implements:
　　　　　　baby daddy
　　　　　　diploma
　　　　　　dead end job
　　　　　　a valid ID

maybe i was more linear than rebel
maybe it was all the revivals mama dragged me to

eventually i made enough sense for grown-up feminism
& [most] people quit referring to my kid as The Mistake

eventually i got a green card to the State of Exception.

but a few years ago, it coulda been me
dollar store moral disaster
your Shameless little orgasm.

2.
i want to assassinate
every man
who's ever fucked
a mama
just to see

if her pussy's still tight

how much her dignity costs

whether the pain of labour softens
her face

        breaking under his fist

3.
remember when the city felt possible
like it could happen
musta been 13, 14
when i finished building
absolute infrastructure for survival in English
i stopped dreaming
forward felt unnecessary
when the city could wake up any moment
in my yellow brown palm

        we mortgaged a house on one minimum wage:
                my mom's.
            wore whatever came to us

from other people's garages
& never ever paid for haircuts.
one day i accidentally taught daddy
the English for 'slut'
while he was lopping off my braids
& saw a nascent breast.

when it woke up, the city stretched
& stared at me with omen eyes
nice haircut, it said. but you know what's nicer,
those tits.
and you have a great ass, for an Asian chick.
remember cement spin
joints hiss
backseat Notorious B.I.G.
misogyny is glass dew that ached
in my lungs rope and red
ribbons all the waist down

my friends had MTV & dances & Ziploc bags of weed
we went to church on Sundays
& Wednesdays
& Thursdays
& Saturdays
i have to say it wasn't about God.
daddy cooked giant pots of Balinese sambal
for all the homesick Indonesians
our insides burned and we wept while we ate
but there was never enough

Love
or stolen watches in our pockets.
remember lines we cut through the city
for a sense of trajectory
alcohol stained laugh on asphalt
& magic in our fists
remember the granite eyes of boys
bored with poverty
the city found it amusing

and passed a law [musta been 14, 15]:
you got to be hard
or terminal
or nothing at all

4.
we do algebra
in parking lots

how much to trade
each body part

how many hinges to loosen
and screw back in

how low the high
how easy we bleed

how long to hold
this breath before

finding ourselves
loved.

5. [a found poem]
there's nothin' more selfish than havin' a baby you can't pay for

that kid's gonna end up *gay* or *in jail*. just watch.

how many dicks you gotta suck to pay for school now?
lucky welfare got your back, huh.

these baby mamas. chasin dude after dude, like they want
damaged goods . . .
girl, one morning you gonna wake up 40, poor, fat and alone.
better make sure your shit's still tight!

how you gonna parent when you can't even put food on your own
table, huh?

thank god for those support groups

and those life skills workshops

just look at the statistics!

such a goddamn waste.
she was in accelerated
english,
don't you know? she had
potential!

you think *this* is what we migrated for?
damn babies havin babies

they done fucked up everything

6.
dream backwards

find the umbilical

at least try

She Is a Radical
Tara Villalba and Lola Mondragón

I.

At first I knew her only as "my mother"—*Nanay ko.* We know her as her daughters, we find her faults most easily: she nags too much, she understood nothing about me or who I was, she had given me nothing. I hated her food—it was always potatoes, I hated having to do "her" housework, I denied my mother in front of my friends, I was embarrassed by her, I was embarrassed that I had a *Nanay* and not a Mommy. She was everything, but she was also invisible.

And then I realized I wanted my mother by my birth bed. I needed my mother to make everything better, I wanted her to hold my hand as I struggled to walk, I wanted those fucking potatoes, she was the only person who came to mind, I called out for her — yelled for her, she became fully visible, suddenly she knew everything, she was the only one who could answer my questions, the only one who could calm us as we tried to calm our own children.

I realized she did give me everything. I chose to take on "her" work, and it turned out it wasn't just "her" work after all—it was every mother's work, it was work that only mothers understood was necessary for survival. The first time I looked fear in the eye because I didn't know where the next rent check would come from or how I was going to find bus fare to spend my last twenty dollars of food stamps and it was only the middle of the month, I wondered how many times my mother had been in this place, in this place of fear, in this place for me. I wondered how I didn't see her inhabiting this space, how she protected me from this space until she no longer could now that I was a mother myself.

I realized I learned to survive because I saw her survive. All of a sudden I felt so proud of my mother because she made me the mother that I am, and my daughter would survive because of my mother too, I could not take my mother off my lips, she's the first person I called with when I got pregnant, she's the first person I called the first time my daughter got sick.

Instead of faults, we see she is beautiful in her virtues and in her struggles, my mom is human, she is a mother just like me. I forgave her for her crappy potatoes because I realized how expensive meat was. I forgave her for nagging because now that I find myself nagging my own children, I realize how frustrating it is that housework never ends and that we never have enough help. I forgave her, I forgave myself for everything I put my mother through. Never again will I deny my mother, I think about her every day that I struggle, knowing she struggled the same way with me.

In that forgiveness, her humanity was restored. I loved my mother again. She is a radical, and I was the seed of her radical work.

II.

Memories of mothering my *manghud* came racing back—mixing his milk bottles, ironing his cloth diapers so they would dry faster, carrying him on my hip, burping him, picking him up after school at the bus stop—all before I turned fifteen. I never thought of myself becoming a mother of my own children.

Why was nobody pregnant until I became pregnant? Why were there no baby aisles until I had a baby? How did this other world escape me for so long? This world makes mothers and their babies invisible except on Mother's Day.

All of a sudden I discovered expectant mothers and their parking spots, there were pregnant women everywhere. All of a sudden I realized that the little seat in the shopping cart was not meant for my purse after all. I discovered the miniature carousels outside the grocery stores where babies squealed in pleasure for fifty cents a go. I discovered ABC and twinkle twinkle little star had the same melody.

All of a sudden I discovered children everywhere and all the rules, regulations, expectation, and *saway* that came with having those children: always be cheerful in front of your children, never use four letter words, never never ever hit your children . . . in public, always use the car seat, immunizations are required by law, homework DOES matter in kindergarten, you can't take your own children out of school just to have fun with them on your day off, police are our friends.

Despite the optimism, we discovered our children experience racism, sexism, oppression because they are children of color. When we let our children roam around the park at what we perceived to be a safe distance, we discovered that the police would approach and protect certain children from predators, and treat other children as predators. That's when I realized I had to protect my children from the "guardians" of our society. I discovered I was becoming a radical.

III.

Before children, we could always give away and take back our bodies from our lovers, friends, and family. Now there is a life growing inside of me that I cannot take away so easily. The longer it goes, the harder it is to take myself away from this being. We become two beings in one body, two spirits fused with the same blood but separated by the membranes of the placenta. From one heart we hear two heartbeats after ten weeks. And then radically it becomes surreal to accept a stranger's hands in my most privately kept possession—my womb, my vagina, my breasts, my clitoris is exposed and visible to a world of strangers. Laying on the birthing table, my daughter was literally being ripped out of me, stranger clamps, stranger vacuum, stranger hands. She got pulled out and so did the pain. And my heart got ripped out of me. And forever more she would be my heart outside my body. I had transferred ownership of my heart into hers. This body is no longer my own, it is for her use, for her survival, for her to take and do as she pleased. Because I had given myself completely to my child in a radical sharing of the one body I have.

IV.

The birth of my child was the birth of a radical. I no longer had the luxury of dying young. My lifetime grew long enough to want to see my children's children. My dream of a young radical martyred for *la causa* was OVER!!! I was now in it for the unglamorous long haul. But what surprised me was that I became the most effective radical after the birth of my children. They were my reasons to be radical.

To be their mother I learned to be a warrior. I had to fight for my way. Why couldn't I give birth in a tub? Why is that backward?

I had to fight to give birth at home. I took back my body from the hospital strangers and promised to share it only with my daughters and sons to come. I had to fight for my daughter's name. I had to give up my name for my son's name. I had to fight to breastfeed in public, to disregard the discomfort of other people at the sight of my nipples. I had to fight to get time to pump at work. I had to fight to get back into my pre-pregnancy jeans. I had to fight for weekends with my children because their father didn't think I deserved it. I had to fight the urge to always fight those who looked down on my "poor brown children."

I have to fight their teachers who want to put them in English only or English learner classes, who tell them that the University of California is too high to aim for, who compliment our daughters endlessly for being beautiful, exotic, obedient, and good caring generous citizens who are always ready to help their teachers and by extension, the public good. We have to fight pediatricians for our children's right to natural, herbal, or traditional remedies, so *curanderas* aren't out the window anymore. We fight police to stop criminalizing our children and their classmates. We fight Regents, School Boards, Superintendents, Legislators, Governors, and policies that erode our children's chances for public education. We fight for our children who are the faces targeted as the designated laborers in our society—the waiters, the custodians, the maids, the nannies, and if they are lucky and work hard, the underpaid teachers, nurses, daycare workers and soldiers. If they are unlucky and are "lazy" they are the laborers behind the bars at San Quentin making Victoria's Secret *chones* and Texas Instruments. We fight for small pieces of city space so we can teach our children what tomatoes look like attached to their parents. We fight to clean up messes including ones we didn't make. We fight for the rest of our natural lives and this is the most radical fight I have ever fought.

VI.

For us, mothering is the root of my connection with my own mother. From her roots, I became the seed of her radical work. From that seed I set my own roots, and my own children have become the seeds of my radical work. So as my children get older and they begin to look at me as "just their mother," I can have patience for the time when they too can forgive me and wait for the seeds of their own radical work. And I hope for the radical that they are destined to become, because I am in their blood. We were once two spirits in one body, and two bodies in one being. And she is the radical seed that is the root of my radical work.

My Son Runs in Riots

for Oscar Grant & other warriors
7/8/10
Christy NaMee Eriksen

I don't use playpens,
my son runs in riots.

He took his first steps towards burning buildings
and he carried a molotov cocktail in his right,
draggin his blankie in the left gripped tight,

half brushed cotton, half tear-stained satin,
he lets the tail gather the dirt and screams of the street,
he can't sleep without it.

When I sing lullabies
we are often running
and he keeps up cause
he loves the sound of twinkle twinkle
little star
to fire alarms.
He think ashes are diamonds in the sky.

I breast-fed for a year,
as recommended,
and weaned him to household chemicals.
We are only as strong as the bomb we mix
and my son's lungs glisten.

Listen:
A brown mother's love is her biggest protest.

I take my son to the picket line.

I tell him he is worth the peaceful world,
the clear sky,
the songs free people sing.

My son full of beauty
and dangerous
thoughts
stands up,
sucks on a switchblade and takes off.

He met men with gray hearts and silver badges
and he has
bullets in his back,
he has
bullets in his front,
he has 56 baton blows, six kicks in his ribs and

when you watch the video
it's tough to tell whose son it is.

They wanna wipe away our tear gas

But they won't let us cry.

III.
The Bottom Line

Introduction
China Martens

I'm waiting two months to see a doctor (at the sliding scale clinic) 'cuz I've been coughing for five months. Poverty is my reality. I don't have post-poverty trauma. I feel so alienated by all the post-poverty talk that's going on around me. I mean people should be able to talk about what's going on with them—their feelings. And that's why, in a way, the internet is so weird—you can compare a vast amount of personal world-views and see what is really going on and also you can compare yourself. When you don't see yourself, you become, or feel, kind of odd and unarticulated. To articulate yourself would seem perhaps, that you are to be questioned or blamed, misunderstood, or just silence. The odd, in its lack of familiarity, has a different relationship, to the whole.

Poverty, in the present, doesn't seem to articulate itself very much in the mediums I frequent. It feels hard just to say: *I am here.*

For some reason this week I feel there is this batch of post-poverty talk. The trauma of post poverty. Running out of money and not having money for a certain amount of days (five?) with knowledge that money is coming—but that sets you to panic like the old days were and you hate that feeling. One person on Facebook went as far as to say that she felt, for her, having money was even more stressful than not having money. My opinion is that money changes you on the point of contact. That's why she can say something like that. I've seen it happen in myself. That it's a whole new game as soon as that money hits—on the point of contact—wham. LIFE *is stressful.* But like they say, mo' money mo' problems—give me your problems! You know the money is going to run out. Well I don't even have the money so I'm already run out. Is it more stressful to contemplate being where I am, then to be where I am? I know everyone stresses about money. But post-poverty trauma seems a kind of nice place to be.

I don't begrudge people getting stuff, or even their getting nice stuff posts. I really don't! I do feel resentful a bit that when everyone is talking, no one is like: I'm poor now. Or dealing with this issue now. That it's something almost illegal to express. Almost without a language to express.

I do hate the kind of posts that throw out a superficial awareness of privilege—like about going to the dentist, how it's a drag but they know they are privileged. And I wish I could go to the dentist!

How would I want them to say it? Hmm. I guess its not about the way things are said: its about the ways things are. I just want to be able to go to the dentist too. But really, who are you saying that kind of thing for? I think you are saying it for other privileged folks. To show you know something. But you don't really feel it or you wouldn't say it like that. To get to be: I know I'm lucky—I have what you don't—and then complain about it. But I also know this: everyone complains about everything: that is how the world is. There's always someone with more, someone with less—so you can't get ALL caught up in it. To say or do anything is to cause a problem.

Still. Poverty is Violence. Poverty is crushing violence. Poverty is current. Poverty is NOW. Now is resisting Poverty. Poverty is not the only pain. Pain is despair. Despair is hopelessness. Children are Hope. Hope is the current, changing, moment, living, rising, being born, and resisting, existing, in poverty. There are different kinds of poverty. The kind that crushes, that Kills. And the kind that is ordinary, everyday, enough, still, Home, growing from little: we have a lot.

Single Mama Moments
Christy NaMee Eriksen

Single Mama Moment # 15

your son is angry
his arm wild
he scratches you.

you say NO
and you give him the stink eye
two
seconds,
you're the bad guy.

he stares back
second by second softening
and he grins like
it's over now, lets be friends, and you

mush into a million kisses
the good guy.

Single Mama Moment #24

two xylophones
and you are
writing a symphony with your child.

his arm in rhythm
in love
in focus

and as you tink tink tink
your eyes meet
and your jaws open wide in
rock star smiles.

oh,

someone should take a picture.

Single Mama Moment #41

the baby has a fever
and you need to leave to get Tylenol.
he wants to be held
tight
with both arms but

you need to put on your jacket.

do you:

juggle baby
one arm at a time
balanced in the crook
as you unsuccessfully snag your arms in
(might take a while)

or put baby down

and throw the jacket on in seconds

as he howls?

Why Don't You Love Her?
Norma Angelica Marrun

March 10, 1994. On my twelfth birthday I had to make one of the biggest decisions in my life. I was given two choices. My first choice was to return to Mexico with my mother. My second choice was to get adopted and remain in the United States At the young age of twelve I made the decision to remain in the United States I did not know when I would ever see my mother, father, or siblings again. If I returned to Mexico, I knew my family was not financially stable to provide me with an education. On the other hand, if I stayed I knew I would have better opportunities to pursue a college education.

Before coming to the United States, I was aware that my mother and I were undocumented, but I did not exactly understand what it meant. November 1994, my mother gave me a small yellow button with the number 187 crossed out in red to pin on my backpack. California's Proposition 187, known as "Save Our State" initiative, the people of California declared that "they have suffered . . . economic hardship caused by the presence of illegal aliens in this state . . . and are suffering personal injury and damaged caused by the criminal conduct of illegal aliens." (Proposition 187, 1994: Section 1). According to William V. Flores (1997), "Politicians from both major parties clamored to 'close the border' and to deny public assistance, public education, and health care benefits to the undocumented."[1] Like many other undocumented immigrants, we were seen as an economic problem; however the primary population that was being targeted was dependent wives and children of undocumented workers.

I remember my friends at school asking me "why do you have that yellow button on your backpack"? I remember telling them

---

1   William V. Flores, "Citizens vs. Citizenry: Undocumented Immigrants and Latino Cultural Citizenship," in *Latino Cultural Citizenship: Claiming Identity, Space, and Rights*, edited by William V. Flores, and Rita Benmayor (Boston: Beacon Press, 1997), 255–77.

that it was a bad thing because they had something against us Mexicans. Those *gringos* don't want us here! When Proposition 187 was passed, I began to understand and feel what it meant to be undocumented.

My mother was tired of working seven days a week, of earning 100 dollars per week, but most of all she was tired of being exploited by her own people. On my twelfth birthday she returned to Mexico. Seven years went by with very few memories of my mother. Why can't I remember if she called me or wrote? Did she think about me? Did she worry about me? Did she ever wonder about my future? I do not remember if I sent her pictures of my eight-grade graduation, my first school dance, prom pictures, or my letters of acceptance to college.

A year after my mother left, the adoption process began. I remember the day when my adopted mother and I went to the Mexican embassy in San Francisco, California to file the paperwork for my adoption. My adopted mother was carrying a folder where she placed all the legal documents. She handed them to the friendly and handsome Mexican officer. He looks through them; he stops and looks at my mother, "Oh I am so sorry, *señora*, but you are missing one document and unfortunately without it we cannot begin to process your application." My mother had taken the day off work and I had to miss school. The not so friendly officer admires my mother's ring. A relative had given my mother the ring, but she took it off and handed it over to the officer. That day the application was processed. It was not until my eighteenth birthday that I was granted legal status in the United States and a year later, I went to visit my family in Durango, Mexico.

In the last two years, I have tried to confront my biological mother about how she felt about my adoption, but she always finds ways to not talk about it. If she was here in the same room with me I would say the following to her:

Ama, I am not mad at you, if anything I admire your strength and courage for choosing to leave Mexico. You came into this country in hopes of finding a way out of the poverty and marginalization we experienced in Mexico, but you realized that things were just as difficult in the United States You have been working all your life and I know your body is exhausted. You lost your mother when you were only eleven years old. As a child you were forced to work in the bean and chile fields. At home you were physically and emotionally abused by your father and uncles. You had the courage to leave your home and find work as a domestic worker. Why do you always say that I don't love you? It hurts me when you tell me that I don't love you. You say that I love my adopted parents more than you. Please do not make me choose, it is not fair!!! It is not that I don't love you, but I really do not know who you are. You will always be my mother and I have so much respect for you. Why is that every time I try to talk to you about these things you accuse me of being bitter and cold-hearted? You always make yourself the victim and make me feel like the ungrateful and angry child. I am tired of you telling lies about me. Why do you tell my sister, my brother, your family, and your friends that I don't love you? It is painful when people ask me, why does your mother think that YOU DON'T LOVE HER?

Mothering
Vivian Chin

I'm sitting in a courtroom, behind a wooden fence-like barrier, an audience of one. My son is on the other side, sitting next to the lawyer, a woman who is biracial (white mother, Black father), who was recommended to me by someone who is biracial (Black and Chicano, adopted into a white family as the tenth, final child, the sole adoptee). But I'm not thinking about all of these racial measurements, and I've stopped saying that I'm half-Japanese and half-Chinese, since such percentages and fractions seem absurd. I'm not thinking about my own racial anything right now. There's a man up on the witness stand, testifying, looking ahead, looking at the prosecutor, looking at my son, looking at the lawyer, looking at me.

—He looked too dark to be just *Caucasian*, the man says.

Would I call him a man? He's more like a sad, greasy white guy. But, what? What?

Look. Look more closely. My son is as white-skinned as you. He's lighter-skinned than me.

—He looks like a white version of you! a friend joked when he was about twelve.

So where is this darkness coming from? From me? From my son's clothing? But wait—I bought him fancy clothes for this court date. He's not sagging in big jeans and a white T. His hair is lined up, trimmed close to his scalp. But really, couldn't anyone tell from looking at him that he's Asian and white? Or have we become darker in this courtroom? Guilty = dark. The greasy white guy sees darkness because he thinks my son is guilty.

I gave my son a good birth. Having read *Birth Without Violence* as a teenager in the bookstore, or maybe just listened to Frédérick Leboyer on the radio (that's what we did in the '70s, before YouTube), I knew I wanted a home birth. When I was pregnant, I was living in a shack, a rustic cottage at best, next to a frat house, behind a house divided into rented rooms. I was squatting there. I didn't have to pay rent because the rent board had ruled in my friend's favor, before she moved and let me live there. I didn't answer the door for about five years. I'd go hide in the bathroom. But I found a way to have a midwife instead of a doctor, to give birth on the floor of a shack instead of in a hospital with my legs up in stirrups. As long as I had a female enough body, I wanted to see what it would be like. I wanted to have a baby, to have a child, to see how I would raise a child differently, as a revolutionary act beyond the reach of mainstream anything.

I think I have failed my son. I think I did my best.

When he was about eleven, I remember getting more than one call from the mothers of kids whose house he was visiting.

—I just wanted to call to tell you what a pleasure it is to have your son here! He's so polite and well-behaved!

I was depleting my savings to send him to a "love everyone" private school, where the kids wrote about how when they grew up they wanted to adopt brown babies. Brown babies unlike them and like them.

A social worker came to ask me questions after my son was born.

—How will you feed him? Are you working? Because you know there are women who trade their babies' formula for drugs.

She said she was there because the baby was born at home and I was unmarried. As if I accidentally gave birth at home, and this would make sense because I wasn't married. I told her I was nursing my baby. That's what breasts are for, right? Twenty years later and I still remember her name—Becky.

A beginning Japanese language textbook will teach you how to say: My child is stupid and ugly, but at least he's healthy.

This explains a lot. My mother's first language was Japanese, although she was born in California. We don't brag about our children. We teach them to have different personalities: one for inside the house, another for outside. This isn't about "use your inside voice" or a parent's euphemistic request to a child to be more quiet. This is about being modest to a point verging on abuse. At the same time, I did try to do damage control. I told my son I loved him. (Why would anyone do that? What—you think your kid is stupid and doesn't know you love him?) I tried to use language to describe feelings. On a good day he *can* do this.

—TAKE ME OFF YOUR TAXES! Everyone else got money back from taxes. They just made up a job and got money back. Why do you walk around scared of everything? ALL I WANT IS A CAR.

I'm not sure how I ended up with a six-foot-long leech in my house. Does this have to do with the economy? He's so angry his anger is consuming him. When he was about two, my shins were covered in bruises. He kicked me. I let him kick me. I must have told him to stop, but he didn't see a need.

My phone buzzes with a text:

> u cant move out on minimum wage
> ur so full of shit u havnt offered
> anything reasonable il always
> remember that

I delete it. Get that poison out of my phone immediately.

He always had good aim. When he was still in diapers, he'd play catch with his friend. Toss the fuzzy ball to the Velcro mitt. His friend would throw the ball behind himself, and my son would throw the ball and hit his friend in the head. When he tossed his toys at me and they beaned my, I'd blurt out, —Goddamn it.

Pretty soon he'd say goddamn it every time he threw something.

My sister changed it to: Cat got it.

It was easier then.

The first time he was in court, I just paid a public defender. She was a poorly dressed—ugly shoes, corduroy pants, bad sweater and blazer—white woman who said she usually defended murder cases. She didn't defend anything.

My son was made a ward of the court. I don't even know what that means, and I write that sentence in the passive voice because, at this point, I don't know who is doing what to whom. I could just say that the juvenile justice system is consistently doing injustice to juveniles and leave it at that. On another hand, there's also so much more going on, or is there?

If you Google "ward of the court," none of the results will be very helpful. The term has a special meaning in California, but exactly what that special meaning is, is not clear.

The intake person ran after me and came up to me to ask me:

—Did you ever live with your son's father?

—I think I've answered enough questions today, I had the presence of mind to respond. I can say that knowing that the law has intervened and stuck its nose into my private life makes me more angry than I could bear. But I did bear it. And I do see that it's completely not just about me, not at all. The criminal justice system casts a wide net, very finely woven, and it can catch whoever it pleases, and, of course, release whoever it pleases.

There's a judge who works in Juvenile Court in Alameda County. They call him by the first letter of his last name, which sounds Greek, maybe. People say that his son was beat up by dreadheads, so, before your court date, it's best to cut off your locks. But who wants to do that. The judge is a man who sits in his robe, high above everybody else, and emanates hate like no one I've ever witnessed. Hate blows out of his pores like the AC vent on an airplane until it fills the whole courtroom. The kids say he drives an Aston and plays basketball at Mosswood Park. Someone should jump him, they say.

The intake probation officer pushed a piece of paper in front of me and told me to sign it. It said something about how I understood I could be imprisoned or fined if I was found to be unfit or negligent as a parent.

The next time a probation officer told us to sign a paper my son asked,

—Do we have to sign this?

I'm telling you, my son knows how to handle those people better than me.

The PO said, —No, you don't.

I was torn between feeling so much pride for my son and wanting to choke the PO.

In part what happens is this: People feel like they got nothing to lose. In this world you're either predator or prey.

How can I, a person who tests 51 percent white on stuffwhitepeoplelike.com, respond? Is there a support group for parents of color of biracial teens who identify as hard and of color even though they look racially ambiguous and live in the cuts, in the upper-class hills? Now when my son steps out the door and waits at the bus stop across the street, the undercover cops will pull up on him and demand a search. Some cop in a special unit van told one of my kid's friends that they think he's involved in something up here in the hills. Some big time something.

If you get home supervision, then you have to go out to the right place to pick up the monitor. You'll get a sheet of paper with confusing directions that's been Xeroxed so many times it's hardly legible. You drive out to the suburbs, where the houses are all defaulted. You go into some building and get directed to a phone on the wall. You call the right number of someone who's inside, in an office. They'll tell you to make an appointment and come back later, or drive to another office, but they can't tell you exactly where it is.

To install an EM, you have to have a landline. You hook up a box to the phone line and it can tell where you are. If you try to talk on the home phone, it'll start making awful sounds and you have to hang up. Electronic monitor, ankle bracelet, house arrest. If you step out of the house at the wrong time, you've violated. I push my son back into the house when he starts to step over the threshold to pay the pizza delivery guy. Now they have a GPS monitor so you have to wear this other thing on your belt along with the strap around your leg. To get it off, once you've completed your time, you have to call in and arrange an appointment. If you try to go to the closest place to do this, they might tell you that they don't have the proper set up to remove it there. Just say you can't get to the other place. Go to the closer place. They'll hand you a pair of scissors. That's the set-up needed to remove the monitor.

Now that he's no longer a minor, I am grateful that he hasn't been arrested again.

My phone buzzes.

> better let me know
> something now if i leave
> this house now im going
> to get money or die tryin

He's seen one too many action movies.

His good friend doesn't have a place to stay now. His mother got put in a rest home because she had another stroke or her kidneys are failing or diabetes is overtaking her. The older sister is staying with her baby with friends. The younger sister is staying with her boyfriend. The grandfather is staying with his woman. He could stay with his aunt but her house is dirty. In his mother's apartment, he had to sleep on the lazyboy.

I rent a house. If my son's friend comes over and they have to run to catch the bus down the street, the cops might drive up to them, handcuff them, and say that there've been a lot of home burglaries lately.

My phone buzzes, this time with a call.

—When other people start affecting me negatively that's when I get mad. I want to be fucked up. I want to be in jail. You been bullshitting me all my life. You haven't helped me one bit. You think you have but you're not really doing anything. You don't help me with shit.

It just makes me want to die. I *am* calm. I don't care. I'm calm.

I can't go on. I go on. I don't know what to do. I sit here writing. Putting this into the computer. Write more. Sit on the floor. Meditate.

The well-dressed expensive lawyer did her job.

—It's clear something happened that night, but it's not clear exactly what.

The judge, a calm Black woman recites a list of possibilities, going on slowly and methodically, until she finally explains that the case is dismissed. Now I must slowly pay the bill that I put on a credit card.

Those with money pay with money. Those without pay in other ways.

I don't remember dropping my son when he was a baby. What causes extended larval stage, neotony, in a young man? I know with polliwogs it's about not getting enough nutrients. Their tails won't drop off, legs won't grow.

I feed my son with my own anger. With my despair. All I can know is that things don't usually stay the same forever. Or is it that pain can lessen, become stronger, or stay the same? If I can get under it, what does it feel like? What can I do to alleviate suffering? All suffering. Breathe in, breathe out. Breathe in pain and suffering. Breathe out, smoke dissipating in the wind.

Brave Hearts
Rachel Broadwater

I have been trying to find the eye of this story. Was it the moment that I first laid eyes on Kayla? Was it when my sister called, scared, having locked herself in the bathroom with her baby trying to her best to both protect them and calm her own fears? There are too many events that have transpired in all of our lives for me to just point out one and say with absolute certainty "aha" and x marks the spot. All I can do is put down the words and hope they make sense.

I am a mother with two children. One is my daughter and the other is my niece. They are eight and nine, only a year and two weeks apart. When we are together people always ask me if they are twins. The girls find this amusing. My daughter giggles behind her hands and my niece just shakes her head. People tend to assume that my daughter is the older since she is taller. It took a while for my niece to be okay with the fact that her younger cousin was taller than she. When people would bring up the height, Kayla would proudly say "I'm still the boss of her."

My husband and I have been taking care of my niece off and on since she was a toddler. She has been with us steadily for three years. My sister left her abusive, mentally ill husband on Mother's Day three years ago. We had talked about the possibility of Kayla staying with us while she got herself together. My sister, like many women in her position, thought that somehow she could change her husband just by the sheer force of her love. He had an abusive upbringing that was complicated by a late diagnosis of schizophrenia and manic depressive disorder. She had tried her best like so many do. But that day she could no longer do it. Could not take another time calling the crisis mobile unit to have him taken away. Couldn't call the cops again because he was out of control. Most of all, she could not stand to have all of this going on while her daughter was watching, always watching. Seeing her parents fight since she was a baby, she would pantomime her parents. She had a dark half-moon-shaped scar under her bottom lip where she would bite to ease the anxiety of watching the two people who were supposed to love each other and her rip each other apart.

I knew that the day would come eventually but still when it did it was still somehow a surprise to me. My husband, daughter and I were at my mother's house to celebrate the holiday. My mother and I have had a strained relationship that seemed to loosen up with the birth of my daughter. We set aside our disappointments in each other to focus on this amazing and enchanting person that had come to be. My mother beamed at the interactions between myself and Madison. She was so proud she would tell me.

I'm not sure if my mother ever held the same sentiment with regards to my sister having Kayla. My mother and stepfather had been concerned about her husband upon meeting him. He was in a down cycle and met them with a dull affect and monotone answers to questions. He was nothing like the engaging personality that was my husband. When my sister became pregnant and was subsequently engaged to be married, their concern turned to worry. On our weekend dates after she spoiled the girls, made small talk, our conversations would eventually gravitate toward my sister. My mother would ask if I thought Jessica was being abused. From the outside it seemed like she was simply expressing maternal concern. But while her words spoke of concern her eyes held me in high esteem and approval. I was the daughter who did it right, found a nice man, got married, bought a house, and had a baby. I was the frugal one, the responsible one. I was the good mother who read to the girls, exposed them to culture and new experiences. My diligence transferred to my mother in pride and thus self-approval that she had done it—raising me in any event—the right way. She took pride in the people who took note of Madison and Kayla's well-groomed appearance, their manners and precociousness when they were with me. I seemed to be everything my sister was not. My position of being the responsible one meant that I was the one who was be my sister's keeper. I was the one who offered her a place when she attempted over the years to leave her marriage. It was me who delayed going back to work so that I could watch Kayla while my sister went back to school because she could not afford daycare. I became her refuge, the open arms and heart that were always available.

I always knew that it was going to be me. It was the way in which both my sister and I were brought up. When my sister and I would fight, my mother would pull us aside and tell us solemnly that we were all we had. We had to take care of each other. We knew that her mother had taken ill when she was young (her father having died years earlier) and had died when she was a teenager. We also knew that my mother had bounced from her older siblings homes. She never spoke of that time but we knew from the simple fact that she never mentioned them; there were never any excited call us to let us know that Uncle so and so or Aunt so and so were on the phone for us, that it must have been very bad indeed. So when we looked at our other's face, we would grudgingly mumble sorry to each other. That was never good enough for her. She would make us look at each other eye to eye and say sorry. It never failed to make us laugh. I could tell it made my mother glad knowing that her girls would always take care of each other.

I never noticed the noose slowly tightening around my neck, restricting both air flow and creative energy. I also never realized that by instinctively swooping in to help Jessica, I was absolving my mother of her own responsibility toward my sister and her situation.

I find myself thinking back to that day from time to time. I usually do that when I think of how far Kayla has come. It was such a difficult transition for her. Despite the fact that she had stayed with me before, she knew it was not like the other times. For some children in her circumstance, they will vacillate between clinging and pushing away. For Kayla, the only option she seemed to exercise was clinging. She hugged and kissed and wanted to be reciprocated. She snuggled, nuzzled, and every other in between. She wanted to call me Mommy.

It was decided that Kayla would stay with us until Jessica was able to establish herself. She had to start from scratch in a way. She had not worked in over three years. She needed to get a job, an apartment, hopefully a car. Kayla was told these things by me and her mother. We got her into therapy so that she would have a safe place in which to explore her feelings.

Through patience, diligence, love, and a good sense of humor from all of us, our family really started to take shape. We had our routines and quirks. The girls in particular interact much more like sisters than they do cousins. Now that Kayla had settled down a bit, I could give them each the kind of attention that they needed and deserved. There was peace in our little valley. And I thought that it would stay that way for a while.

"Titi, Mommy wants to talk to you. And guess what? I'm going to live with Mommy this summer!"

The news stunned me, so I did not reprimand her for jumping on the couch. I recall talking to my sister and hearing her joy. She had been approved for a two-bedroom apartment so now Kayla could come and live with her. I knew this was really big news for her and did not want to dampen her spirits.

I always knew this arrangement was temporary so then why were my fantasies crushed? Why did I feel sucker-punched, rushing my sister off the phone so that I could get some air? The rational side of me reminds me of the fact that Jessica and I agreed in advanced to discuss any major changes before disclosing them to Kayla. The idea was to present a unified front with whatever the situation was. Over the next few days with Kayla's erratic behavior and Madison's anxiety at the prospect of her losing the person that she loved the most seemed to solidify my position. My indignation was really a thin veneer for the complex emotions that were quickly consuming me.

Why am I so reluctant to let her go? Do I really believe her life will be all fire and brimstone if she were to leave too soon? I think in Kayla's perfect world her mother, her new baby brother, and our family would all be able to live in a big house all together. She could skip from my room to her mother's, happy as a lark.

She had no car in a town with very little public transportation; no school busing and she had just gotten this job. Not only would she have Kayla and herself to take care but also her toddler son who came unexpectedly nearly a year and a half before.

For those in our family who were privy to the new information, there was concern that Kayla would want to stay for a little while and then come back to us. There was concern that Jessica would not be as constant with Kayla's studies, her emotional progress. I shared those sentiments myself in addition to a disturbing trend I noticed happened on several occasions when Jessica would come to visit. Despite Kayla gushing to her mother on how much she missed her and wanted to see her, when the moment actually came

Kayla did not seem comfortable to be with her. The visits rarely played out the way I imagined it did in either of their minds.

My sister wants her in the summer so that she can get used to the area but I am more worried about Kayla getting used to her mother again. I suggest for Kayla to stay with her for the summer and on school breaks. That sounds good. But a nagging thought comes to my head. Am I coming from a space of pure benevolence? Do I have right to lay down any conditions? Is this simply love for my sister and her child the desire for them to have the best relationship possible or is it my own rigid parameters of what I think a mother-daughter relationship look like? My writing reflects my own personal philosophy that poor mothers do not equate poor mothering. With all of my concerns, am I betraying those principles?

In the days following my sister's announcement, I think back to when Kayla first came. For months I held, rocked, read, snuggled, set boundaries, wiped tears and snot, talked through tantrums. I would sit cross-legged on the floor while a sweet, confused little girl was under a bed finding the dark and dust bunnies easier to tolerate than her own harsh realities. She was not the only one who suffered.

When I was comforting and consoling Kayla, it meant that I was not with Madison. She either stayed with Daddy or tried to occupy herself as best as she could. We would always talk afterward. I would explain and assure her that I loved her and she was important but right now Kayla needed a little extra loving. That is a lot for a five-year-old to take in. I gave her extra hugs and kisses, went on nature walks, and had a weekly breakfast date just me and her. She would look at me with those sweet eyes and say, "That's okay, Mommy. Go with Kayla." I wished some days that she would just have a meltdown. I wished that she had fallen on the floor, kicking and screaming, tearing down curtains yelling, "No fair!!! That's my Mommy!" Her understanding only made me feel that much worse.

Despite the difficult months in the beginning, we were a family. Many a night my husband and I watch the antics of the girls with a twinkle in our eyes and a smile that said "Just look at those two hot messes." We watch them interact and share not just clothes and toys but something else; the exchange of ideals, strengths, and vulnerabilities. The joy and privilege of witnessing the both of them grow before my eyes, to see the progress and to be amazed at both of their individual moments of emotional bravery and clarity is something that I treasure. I guess part of my fear is that when Kayla leaves, our life together will become nothing more than a hazy dream that becomes more and more indistinguishable with time.

While I cannot ignore Kayla's progress and her joy, I am becoming increasingly uncomfortable with the rose petals that seemed to be thrown my way when people learn of our family structure. Their eyes grow wide and warm at the same time. I am told I am a good mother, a good person. They see the children benefiting from something that is deemed endangered; an intact Black family structure. I have had friends, family, and strangers alike come up to me and comment what a lovely family we are. From the outside we seem to be a throwback. I stay home while my husband works. He is the spiritual head of our home while I tend to the hearts of the children. People see clear enunciations, vivid lines where our paths cross. Very few don't realize there is no rigidity or power struggles. They don't see a couple determined in their own ways to reject those things that bind us, prohibit growth and joy.

I cannot continue with a selfish trajectory. I know that my sister having her daughter will allow her to regain her sense of pride as a mother. Despite the fact that in allowing Kayla to stay with us was the most loving and selfless thing she could have done, for many she is just another Black mother whose child is with someone else. The fact that her daughter was not with her was confirmation to many in her predominantly white community that Black women were predisposed to a destructive, irresponsible, pathological maternal narrative. I cannot imagine how that must feel for her.

In contrast, it seems self-evident that Kayla benefits from a traditional, heterosexual, Christian family structure. That is problematic for me in light of the countless single Black women who are taking care of someone else's child and they are deemed an extension of what they identify as my sister's particular pathology. When those women pass by with their families, they are not getting the adulation that my husband and I get. What they do is no different than what I do and, quite frankly, our positions are not equal and if anyone deserves rose-petals and cream pie, it's them.

So then why, I ask myself, am I holding onto this for dear life? Fear.

The fear that somehow in giving up Kayla too soon, I would repeat the cycle of my mother's inability to be emotionally available to us. My mother, with a traumatic childhood, unexpected pregnancy with me at nineteen and subsequent shame from being young and unmarried with a child, was so eager to get rid of that mark that she thought marriage was the only way to absolve her from something from which she did not need absolution. She was desperate to reclaim her self worth in the form of someone who was not interested and did not feel that she was worthy of that prize. She was not elegant enough, educated enough. She was just an unmarried woman with two kids. My sister and I were constantly appraised by this person and consistently found as deficient as my mother. It was excruciating for mother. She thought that if only we were neater, took better care of our things, then it would be all right. We could live in a real house, with a yard and go on vacation twice a year . . . if only.

After years of contorting her self worth, she finally won the prize: marriage. It was no accident that it happened after my sister and I were out of the house. Jessica and I tried to make amends with the situation. We would go out together, spend holidays together and my mother was happy. She had the family and home that she always wanted but it was not open to us. When my sister went through the hell that was her marriage, my mother never opened that home to her. She never said, "Baby, whenever you need me just call me and Mommy will come." I have often asked my sister if she offered to help her get out of her abusive marriage. She always shakes her head. There is always an uncomfortable silence between us for a while.

But is my memory of my mother that stark? I can still see her with Madison as a baby singing Sade's "By Your Side." I can still see her swaying Madison to sleep and singing the lyrics.

"You think I'd leave your side/baby you know me better than that/you think I'd leave you down/down on your knees/you know I wouldn't do that."

That was one of my favorite songs for nursing Madison. I would marvel at her perfectly crossed legs, so ladylike, and her hand on my breast. Watching my mother, I believed that was not only true in relation to my mother and my daughter but for me and my mother. But I know better than that. She does not have the capacity to be there for my sister and me in our time of need.

Writing those words is akin to watching the coffin of a loved one drop in the ground. It is real, then. You can no longer intellectualize it. This has informed my mothering from the beginning. I never want either one of the girls to come to me with tears in their eyes, lumps in their throats, and resentment in their hearts and say "why didn't you . . ."

I cannot allow that fear, however justified, to take over my judgment. I am focusing on loss when there is so much to be gained. Not just Kayla being reunited with her mother, but also discovering and putting into action a greater concept of what love can be and is.

What does my situation say about love and how we love? For one thing, it is not always immediately illuminating. As we get older, we achieve understanding and grace when we see how the fire of love and sacrifice begins to thaw the freeze of our misunderstanding/hurt/our sense of abandonment. Kayla won't fully understand until she is older, I am certain, of her mother's deep abiding love and how it manifested itself in her mother letting her stay with my husband and me.

My daughter will know that love is not an either/or proposition, but should be viewed as an and/with. The reason that I took Kayla in is that I love her. So by that same logic, I have to let her go when it is time. I have to be fearless in my love and have the confidence that all that we have collectively imparted to Kayla will not slip out of her head and heart like eggs onto a plate.

Every day I cry a little. Sometimes from joy, sometimes from sadness. But every time I let go, I get something back. I believe in my heart of hearts that every time I have taken the time to be patient with the children, somehow someway it is a balm to my mother's spirit. For me to hold Kayla back would strip it all away. Love makes you vulnerable, but it also makes you brave.

Scarcity and Abundance
Autumn Brown

Driving home the other night, my husband Sam and I were flipping through radio stations and we landed on the Laura Ingraham's conservative talk radio show, where she was interviewing Governor Nikki Haley of South Carolina about the Republican perspective on improving the economy. As is typical of these conversations, the issue of business regulation came up. Ingraham referenced a new government requirement that businesses with over fifty employees have a designated room for breastfeeding expression. Ingraham scoffed, and both she and Haley called the measure ridiculous, saying that the last thing businesses need right now is to be saddled with further regulations.

I was floored. How strange it was to hear two professed conservatives—who in the same conversation extolled the virtues of a bygone America where people put families first, and criticized the Obama Administration for not getting Americans back to work as fast as possible—unable to see the logic in a regulation that enables working mothers to provide the best nutrition possible to their children AND show up for work with the knowledge that they can use their breast pumps in relative comfort and privacy. Their perspective—that we should not saddle businesses with further progressive regulation in a time of economic downturn—represents what I have come to call Scarcity thinking. I will explain more about that in a minute.

An extreme counter to this is an extraordinary story coming out of the Powderhorn neighborhood of Minneapolis. A forty-five-year-old woman was raped in a public park by a group of teenage boys while cross-country skiing with her two children. In the wake of the attack, the woman posted in an online community forum about her gratitude for her friends and neighbors who supported her and her family after the incident, and said that she is now trying to hold her attackers in compassion. The community held a vigil in Powderhorn

Park a week after the attack. The response in this community is an example of what I have come to call abundance thinking.

Scarcity thinking says that there will never be enough of anything—love, food, energy, or power—so we must horde, or conditionally offer and withdraw, what we have. Scarcity thinking says that we cannot expect others to provide what we need, and that creating systems to ensure that basic needs are met are pointless exercises in altruism. Abundance thinking says that together, we have enough of what we need, that there is enough for all of us if we recognize our essential interdependence. Abundance thinking requires that we share our struggles and our rewards. Abundance thinking trusts that if we develop relationships based on sharing our struggles AND our resources, we do in fact have enough of everything—love, food, energy, and power.

As a parent, I often see the difference in Scarcity thinking and Abundance thinking as they play out in my family and in the other parenting relationships I witness. The Scarcity perspective in parenting is that because there will never be enough of the things we need, we must teach our children early on to rely on themselves for everything. For example, this perspective leads parents to not appropriately comfort their children—the theory being that children must learn to "self-soothe" and comfort themselves. Scarcity thinking leads parents to ignore essential information that their children offer to them.

I know my children, and I know that they cry when something is wrong; they want to be held when they need to be touched. They seek new physical and emotional and kinetic perspectives that come from being touched and held by different people, and being *brought with* on my journeys through the world, instead of left behind. This teaches me about Abundance thinking in parenting. It teaches me that if I give my children an abundance of love and attention and comfort and time, then they will seek out and replicate relationships of abundance in their lives. By doing this, they co-create a world where abundance relationships and abundance thinking is normal.

I was raised by parents who loved me abundantly. They were not and are not perfect people, but they parented from a place of unconditional love and support. When I was in high school, my mother caught me looking at pornography on our home computer.

I was embarrassed and ashamed, but the way she handled it was transformative. She told me that she was concerned about my looking at porn not because she thought it was dirty or shameful, but because she wanted me to understand that what was represented there was not what actual sex looked like and felt like. Since she knew my sexual experiences were relatively limited at that point, she did not want me to have an impression that in order to be beautiful, sexual, and desirable, I would need to fall in line with the picture of sexuality represented in the porn I was looking at. This was a formative moment for me as a sexual creature, and it made me seek out romances where it was my innate, creative sexuality that was affirmed, not my ability to perform specific sexual acts or my approximation of the figure, hygiene, and experience of a woman deemed culturally desirable.

Not too many years later, I met and fell in love with my partner, Sam. I recognized him as being my life partner within weeks of meeting him, because I felt in him the ability to love me abundantly, and when I met his family I saw that they also had abundant love. In finding each other, and in choosing to commit to being with one another, we were co-creating the world we had been taught by our parents does, in fact, exist.

Abundant love is deep and difficult. It is love through choices. I am someone with anger management problems, and yet I choose to not use violence as a way of interacting with my children. I recognize that it is a choice and that I must actively engage in making the choice EACH time the opportunity to use violence presents itself. I am someone with a wicked memory and ability to hold a grudge, and yet I choose to see my children with new eyes each day as they teach me who they are becoming. They learn, they change. I learn who they are and I change my perspective of them. I am someone with fairly rigid morals and ideas of equity and justice, and yet I flex my mind and spirit around my children and my sisters and my parents and my parents-in-law and my husband and my brothers-in-law and all of my extended family, so that I can understand their choices. It is tough—really, really tough. It means a lot of tears, and it means hard conversations about race and politics, economies and families, trauma and forgiveness.

Abundant love means that each time I think my heart cannot contain any more joy or any more sorrow, I have to stretch it even wider. Abundance thinking recognizes that I can do this. Abundance thinking is not naive, nor is it idealistic or utopic. It can be awful because it means I often feel so vulnerable. But I also experience levels of elation that are beyond anything I have encountered through the use of external substances. I experience it making love to my husband, who still excites me more than any other person could after eight years together. I experience it falling asleep next to my son, whose face is my face, and my mother's face, and my grandfather's face. I experience it breastfeeding my daughter. I experienced it giving birth to both of my children. I experience it when I look at my husband holding both of our children. I experience abundance because I expect abundance, and because humans are social creatures, we live up to cultural expectations, whether they come from outside of us, or from within.

I also experience abundance through our social, financial, and cultural struggles. Sam and I are a mixed-race couple and we have had two children in the last three years, during a time of extreme economic upheaval. Both of our children were born in Brooklyn. We never had enough money to pay for childcare, but we realized early on that if we were going to make it work to have a family, we were going to have to depend on our community. It tested us, tested our politics, and tested how deeply we trusted others. But we set up a network of friends and family who we could call upon when we needed childcare, who were willing to do it for free or for trade, or at a very low cost when we could pay, and because of the strength of that network, we were able to maintain, and even deepen, our involvement in political and organizing work. And when it became too expensive and overwhelming to stay in New York City, we moved back to Minnesota where we lived for a time with Sam's parents in a multi-generational family home. We now live in our own home on a piece of land that borders the land of Sam's parents: we grow food on our land, and we forage in our woods, and we teach our children to love and respect life. We still struggle financially, as each new year brings new seeds and changes to our already abundant lives. We bear the burden of our socialization and sometimes we feel like we are not everything we are supposed to be—as parents, as college graduates, as working people. Sometimes we succumb to that Scarcity thinking. But sometimes, when we can release that burden, we see how truly fantastic our life is, and how we are living in alignment with our values here and now more than ever before. We come alive in that abundance thinking, and then we are more in love with each other, and with ourselves, and with our children, than we ever have been.

When I see or hear or read scarcity thinking, it makes me want to reach out to those who propagate it and tell them about my home and how I came to be here. Because there is enough of everything we need here, in spite of how we struggle. It makes me want to tell them about the mother in Powderhorn Park. Because there is enough love in that community to heal the mother who was raped, to heal her children who witnessed the assault, and to heal the boys who attacked her. I do believe this. It makes me also want to tell them about the legislation on accommodating breastfeeding mothers. Because there is also enough space and resources for an agency that employs fifty people or more to have a room for a breastfeeding mother to express milk in private, so that she can still give her child the best start in life, in spite of having to or choosing to work outside of the home. That is not a belief—that is physical reality. And I have learned that if I am going to change someone's mind with a story, it must be a story of abundance. Scarcity reinforces fear. Abundance ignites the imagination.

The Clothesline
Layne Russell

My clothing is dancing without me.
Outside, clean, brilliant in the sun,
it dips and bobs merrily while I worry over pots and pans.
Drunk with power, it knows
I am a woman
and as long as I look right, I may *be* anything at all.
my underwear twists and shimmies
between sheets held up by clothespins,
like a modest mother with towels
while her children change after a day at the beach.
Try to explain the liquor on your breath in bad shoes,
or bad shoes, with liquor on your breath.
Henry, I cannot be a new wearer of clothes.
God knows I've tried
but you've never had to face down a pediatrician
with an underweight child and frayed hems.
You never explained your domestic economy
to a social worker
in a conservative skirt or otherwise.
You never had to assert your transcendence
to anyone who stared at your breasts, sweat-stained from honest
work or armored in starched cotton.
Emma, the revolution was a bust,
but my clothing is still dancing.
It dances without me,
while I worry about taxes and forms and court dates and principals
and whether we look well enough to get away with what we are.

This Is What Radical Mamihood Looks Like

Noemi Martinez

Noemi Martinez y familia live on the Frontera of Texas/Mexico.

By definition, we shouldn't be here. Yet we diverge on this Border, creating new language, discovering hybrid ways of communication where we tell our story with historical reconstructions that dislocate others inaccuracies. We have become primary sources, witnesses to each other's histories.

Shadows of the Martinez familia, photo by Jonathan River Martinez-Hernandez Estero Llano Grande State Park, Weslaco, Texas

Jonathan River and Noemi

Noemi and Jonathan River

Jonathan River with Marley, at Sal Del Rey, Edinburg, Texas

Noemi, Winter Brooke, and Jonathan River with Marley

IV.
Out (of) Line

Introduction
Alexis Pauline Gumbs

In my academic work I have often been asked how I can possibly talk about queerness and mothering together. Some queer theorists treat it as an oxymoron, believing that a person could be a mother despite their queerness, or queer despite being a mother, but they are hard pressed to believe that mothering could be the queerest thing that humans do. In this section, we look at queer mothering in a broad sense. Our definition of queer is that which fundamentally transforms our state of being and the possibilities for life. That which is queer is that which does not reproduce the status quo.

It is important to us to feature the voices of people who identify as queer and to highlight their mothering practices, and it is equally important to us to highlight the queerness of mothering as a practice itself. We are looking at mothering as an investment in the future that requires a person to change the status quo of their own lives, of their community and of the society as a whole again and again and again in the practice of affirming growing, unpredictable people who deserve a world that is better than what we can even imagine.

In this section we remember that many people do the labor of mothering without the luxury of the status of "motherhood." In the United States Black mothers have not been seen as entitled to "motherhood" no matter how many people they have worked to nurture in their own families and as domestic workers for centuries in this country. Immigrant mothers are often excluded from "motherhood" as motherhood is a category of citizenship and as we can see from the many parents and children who are being deported away from each other right now, rights to "motherhood" are not respected for non-citizens. LGBTQ people in the United States face barriers to parenting and legal hoops that deny them access to the people that they mother. Just yesterday a friend who came out to her mother reached out to me horrified because *her* mother threatened to take away her son, unable to imagine that a lesbian could be a good mother. And many people do the labor of mothering who would never even dream of identifying as mothers, even though they do the daily intergenerational care work of making a hostile world an affirming space for another person who is growing mentally, spiritually, physically, and emotionally. And some queer mothers, like the mothers of houses in gay ball culture, boldly honor the fact that they mother queer youth whose families have often rejected them. The queer thing is that we affirm each other beyond the limits of our bodies, our limits, and our imaginations. Mothering is a queer practice of transforming the world through our desire for each other and another way to be.

Forget Hallmark:
Why Mother's Day Is a Queer Black Left Feminist Thing
Alexis Pauline Gumbs

After reading:
The Anti-Social Family by Michele Barrett and Mary McIntosh (1982)
Fear of a Queer Planet, edited by Michael Warner (1999)
Aberrations in Black: Toward a Queer of Color Critique by Roderick Ferguson (2004)
"Of Our Normative Strivings: African American Studies and the Histories of Sexuality" by Roderick Ferguson (2005)
"Queerness as Horizon: Utopian Hermeneutics in the Face of Gay Pragmatism" by José E. Muñoz (2007)
"A 'New Freedom Movement of Negro Women': Sojourning for Truth, Justice, and Human Rights during the Early Cold War" by Erik S. McDuffie (2008)
Blood Dazzler by Patricia Smith (2008)
Something Like Beautiful: One Single Mother's Story by asha bandele (2009)[1]

My mother is Black. So the means through which I was produced is a matter of national instability. My mother is Black. So the trace of slavery waits every moment to ink my body with meaninglessness. My mother is Black. So my living is a question of whether or not racism will be reproduced today. My mother is Black. This same piece of information threatens my survival. But my mother is Black, which is at the same time the only thing that makes my survival possible.

It's early morning. I am a little bit drunk on the sound of rain, but it occurs to me that I should get (you) ready for Mother's Day. It is very easy to notice that I am obsessed with mothering and mothers. "Mother" is the single most interesting and confusing word that I know. Next to Black.

---

1   Outside of the above timeline, see Audre Lorde's "Litany for Survival," Cathy Cohen's "Punks, Bulldaggers, and Welfare Queens," and Hortense Spillers's "Mama's Baby, Papa's Maybe," which I did not reread this week . . . but have completely internalized such that I should be understood to be citing them no matter what I am saying about anything.

And here comes Mother's Day. For me, this year Mother's Day means a million things. Expectancy, fear, obligation, inspiration, joy, admiration, deep reflection. A few weeks ago my mother told me that she thinks I will be "such a great mother." It struck me that while I have always dreamed of becoming a mother, and intended to become a mother, it still comes as a surprise when anyone affirms that it is something that I can do, SHOULD do even. Because I live in a culture that criminalizes Black mothers for creating and loving Black children, a culture that criminalizes Black kids for being born. And Latino kids too. I have been taught that mothering is something that happens to you, and you deal with it, and fight for it, swallowing down shame and living with the threat that the state wants nothing more than to take your kids away from you in every way imaginable.

But it is not my mother who taught me that. My mother repeats again and again that mothering us is her greatest accomplishment, like asha, mothering is her enduring joy and triumph despite everything. And trust, she has other great accomplishments. My mother, not through perfection, not through ease, but through sincere struggle, intense and sometimes even overwhelming love taught us something in her very being. My sister (now an ambitious account exec in New York) once confessed to me that though it might seem unfeminist, the only thing she really cared about, the one thing that she knew she wanted to do for sure in life was to be a good mother. And I told her what I more recently wrote in a poem to one of my feminist theory students, who blessed us by bringing her daughter to class, "mothering is the most feminist act of all." My mother, like every Black mother, has been slandered. But we know a lie when we see it. My brother wanted to punch every producer of CNN's disgusting "Black in America" series for daring to suggest that being raised by a Black mother was the key liability destroying the life chances of Black people. How dare they? How dare they? When our Black mother is the only reason we know how to breathe and survive despite the toxic racism filling this world. How dare they?

It is no mystery why it is a cultural truth that talking about a Black person's mother is a great way to unleash a universe of anger. Our mothers are slandered every single second of every single day. The media does it like it's its job. And indeed it is.

And here is the risk. All this talk of mothering, all this affirmation and privileging of mothering puts me at risk, not only in a mainstream

narrative working to reproduce a nation built on racial hate and genocide, but also on the academic queer left. It is not very queer of me to
keep talking about my mother this way. In fact (as Michael Warner suggests) the only queer way for a Black person to talk about a mother is the
"irony" of the house mother in Black gay ball culture. CNN is dead to me.
The deeper betrayal is that queer studies participates in the slander of
the Black mother, agreeing with the story that says she should not exist.

Has Warner not considered (as Cathy Cohen makes very clear
in "Punks, Bulldaggers, and Welfare Queens") that Black mothering
is already a queer thing? Because we were never meant to survive.
So the Queen Mother in the house movement is not just throwing
shade, the queen is doing the necessary work of mothering. Of saying
these bodies Black and queer almost to redundancy, these spirits that
every facet of our society would seek to destroy, MUST survive and
WILL transform the meaning of life whether you like it or not. That
is what a Black mother does. Sincerely. No irony. It is no joke.

So this week I have been picking a bone with a queer theory
narrative that sees mothering as the least radical thing one can do,
in so much that it becomes irrelevant to the majority of the discourse on queerness. Clearly, like Moynihan, they don't know my
mother. Asserting that the labor of mothering is always in collaboration with a reproductive narrative, always reproducing heteronor-
mativity, ignores the fact that there has been a national consensus
for centuries that Black people should not be able to mother. Every
force, from coercive sterilization, to the dismantling of welfare has
been mobilized to try to keep us from doing it. Where has dominant
(read white) queer theory been while politicians have been rant-
ing and raving about how welfare queens, (which despite the actual
statistics becomes a code name for poor and racialized mothers)
are going to destroy civilization as we know it not only by creating
Black surplus children, but by influencing these children with their
deviant and risky and scary behavior? And isn't this the organizing
desire of queer theory . . . to destroy civilization as we know it?

I just wish everyone would listen to Cathy Cohen (who by the way
is a Black co-mother to a beautiful fierce Black girl child) so I wouldn't
have to stand here screaming (or more accurately sit here taking, decon-
structing, and rebuilding the premises of queer theory all week long).
But here is the quick and dirty of it: mainstream queer theory was inau-
gurated by Warner's edited volume and influenced by a Marxist femi-

nist tradition of critiquing the heteropatriarchal family as a complicit force in the reproduction of capitalist oppression. And they throw the Black babies out with the bathwater of their universalism. The "tyranny of motherhood" as described by Barrett and McIntosh does not leave room for those other deployments of "mother" and "hood" (excuse me "inner-city") in the American vernacular of culture of poverty discourse.

This is why Hortense Spillers should be required and repeated reading for queer theorists. Four words. "Mama's Baby, Papa's Maybe." Which means there is no reason that the act of mothering would reproduce patriarchy, or even take place within the confines of patriarchy along normative lines because the practice of American slavery has so fundamentally ripped the work of mothering from the bodies of Black mothers, forcing them to do the labor of mothering for white and Black children while fully denying them any of the authority of motherhood by killing and selling away and raping and mutilating their biological children and their chosen kin. (I have written before about my discovery, while reading slave code, that even a free Black mother had no legal right to defend an enslaved daughter from abuse by a slave master.)

The complexity of the term "mother" (next to "Black") requires a queer theory that deuniversalizes race and highlights the function of racism in reproducing the heteropatriarchal status quo. Cathy Cohen, Roderick Ferguson, and José Muñoz do this work of reminding us that Third World Feminism and the Third World Gay Liberation movement are an alternative starting point (contemporary with the Marxist feminist arguments that Warner's version of queer theory inherits). Their work is crucial because it says something very obvious. We are people of color. The whole system wakes up every day trying to exterminate our bodies and our spirits. Our very survival is queer.

We were never meant to survive, and if mothers are part of why we are here (and they are), then they are the queerest of us all. But this is not even news. If we remember what Black women have been up to in the United States, we can just go ahead and let go of the assumption that mothering is conservative or that conserving and nurturing the lives of Black children has ever had any validated place in the official American political spectrum.

Eslanda Robeson   Shirley Graham Du Bois   Maude White Katz
Charlotta Bass   Mary Church Terell

Take the fierce Black women writers, mothers, publishers, actresses, activists who would become the Sojourners for Truth and Justice and their work starting in the 1940s to protest the imprisonment of Rosa Lee Ingram, a Black mother who was sentenced to death for standing up for herself, and defending herself against a white man who tried to rape her. It was Black women activists who changed her sentence to life in prison and then eventually (after twelve years of incarceration) got her released from prison. And always, always the key word in their organizing strategy was "mother." Their understanding of Ingram, who was willing to fight to keep this violent man away from her body and away from her children, epitomized the term "mother" for this set of Black women revolutionaries. They framed the state's violence against Ingram as a violence against Black mothering itself. How dare this Black woman take a stance against rape? Standing against rape is a mothering act. How dare she threaten the perceived truth about what happens to Black people, that Black bodies are infinitely rapeable? How dare she stand ferocious, daring and teaching? This is what will happen to you if you come at me.

This is the act of mothering that mobilized a national movement, Black women gathered twenty-five thousand signatures for a petition in 1949 . . . way before the era of the text message e-blast petition. They made it an international human rights issue, contacting every single member nation of the UN. And I need you to know this, remember this if you remember nothing else: On Mother's Day, exactly sixty years ago the Black left internationalist feminists of the Ingram Committee sent TEN THOUSAND MOTHER'S DAY CARDS to the White House and scared Harry S. Truman so bad that he made up an excuse to miss their scheduled meeting the next day.

Ten thousand Mother's Day cards from Black women to the white house. Stolen holiday. No justice, no peace in the form of ten thousand paper-cuts. A floral dare saying: celebrate this. This is what mothering means: organized support for radical self-defense. **A complete refusal of rape by any means necessary. Ten thousand Mother's Day cards. A threat saying we are Black mothers. We are survivors. Try us.**

Forget Hallmark.

Have a revolutionary Mother's Day, people.

Three Thousand Words
Katie Kaput

I can't write anything that will tell you what you need to know; my story at twenty-eight years of age is a tangled embroidery ready for the scissors and knife. I can list fragments of identity: transsexual single homeschooling queer radical Italian/Irish-American mama, but I can't weave a story anymore. My tongue is stilled by such powerful forces it's a wonder sometimes that I can eat, that I can breathe:

A) My story is not only my own,

    1) and my children will one day read the things I have written about them and cluck their tongues and roll their eyes or flush with embarrassment,

    2) and my ex will read my story and be hurt and angered by any mention of her actions or words and their effects in my life,

    3) and yet there is no story to my life, no wisdom to impart, or brutal lessons to learn, without including this:

        a) Rio, my nine-year-old first born, who wore his filthy train engineer's cap seemingly every day of the first five years of his life like a good baby crusty punk, had this to say today, "If all your potential was visible on your body, like a hologram of your future, you'd know what things to just give up on without even trying . . . but then you'd never know that you can change your hologram potential if you try."

           i. I agreed with him, but later I realized that our society is already like this. What else is all the testing and tracking at school? What else are our assumptions about other people and ourselves based on race, gender, class, sexuality, temporary able-bodiedness, and so on?

           ii. I'm really glad we homeschool, and he was home eating lunch when this thought occurred to him so we could talk about it.

b) Robin, who is almost five but capable of more wistful nostalgia than an entire high school reunion of former football stars and cheerleaders, misses living in the country, as we did for the last year his other mother and I were together.

  i. It has now been two years since we lived in the country.

  ii. Robin would like a pony.

    ✘ The wages of a writer, jam-maker, odd-job-doer, occasional nude model, and homeschooling single mother do not provide for ponies.

      ⚞ Being a nude model is not the worst job I have had.

    ✘ I would also like a pony.

  iii. "The country" is probably really "when my parents loved each other enough to live together," of course.

c) My ex didn't even like me to write about things that happened between us when we were together and the things were overwhelmingly positive.

  i. I have always tried really hard to paint everyone close to me in only glowing terms in print.

    ✘ I don't want anyone to sue me.

    ✘ I don't want anyone to be really, really mad at me.

B) My story is unintelligible to you if I tell it truthfully:

  1) because I am not a thousand words of explanation of what it means to be a transsexual mother, to be a young mother, to be a girl who people have only known as a girl since she was thirteen.

  2) I am not three thousand words devoted to explaining the violence that cis women (women whose gender identity matches the gender they were assigned at birth; women who are not trans) and trans men commit against my sort of woman. It is not usually the murder, dismemberment, and beatings cis men give us along with their sexual desire, their objectifying glances and pockets full of money. More often it is exclusion, verbal violence, and

assumptions about what growing up a trans girl means in this society. I have been excluded from enough resources, gatherings, and social situations to fill my day planner a thousand times and to meet my needs for medical care and counseling, but I am not three thousand words of complaint and explanation, of trying to get you to see me as what I am: a girl like you, a mama like you, a person like you.

3) There is no standard girlhood or motherhood; that I am too weird to be understood is an accident of statistics. There are not enough of me to comprise a community, a voting bloc, or an anthology.

Among many things, I am this attempt at speech, with all its omissions and overly long explanations I give only grudgingly: I dropped out of high school two years before my then-partner and I decided to become teen parents (and by decided I don't mean decided to keep the baby, I mean decided to make the baby).

Years before I was a high school dropout, in seventh grade, I daydream in class, read anything-that-isn't-assigned, write things for which I can't "earn credit," and measure my friends carefully, knowing that soon will be the time to tell them I'm a girl, despite whatever assertions some guy with a medical degree made after a cursory examination of my vulnerable, little baby body when I was born.

Being a transsexual girl in junior high in the Midwest, every day is a chance to cultivate my budding case of post-traumatic stress disorder, whether being voted "most likely to be gay" at the end of sixth grade, having my arm held to the flame of a lighter by a boy who seems to be second guessing his decision to make out with me in the school bathroom, or listening to a constant stream of the wrong damn pronouns.

After school, I take care of my little sisters, watch *Sailor Moon* episodes with them and play Bikini Kill and Huggy Bear seven-inch records for them, lay the groundwork for my own dream of having a family, and feel sick in my belly thinking of my inability to get pregnant: at twelve, I want a uterus so much I would gladly shave three or four decades from my life for one.

I am thirteen years old, and my mom is crying; my dad has told her I'm a girl.

I am sixteen years old, and my mom is crying, my dad is furious: I've stopped going to school a month before, and the school has finally gotten around to calling. I don't answer when they ask what my plans are. I know I'm not going back to school, or anywhere that feels like it, ever again.

I am eighteen years old, and my girlfriend of a few months asks me to move across the country and have a baby with her. We read Ariel Gore's *The Mother Trip* and somehow come away from its depiction of total gut-wrenching, vertigo-inducing chaos thinking, "Oh my Goddess, we have to do this! Now!"

And we do, and my first child is born when I'm nineteen. I'm old enough that other parents tell me I'm not really a teen parent and yet young enough to receive head-shaking, tongue-clucking "babies having babies" comments on the bus, to be assumed older sister or babysitter at the park.

I cradle him every night, talk to him and sing to him all day as we shop for groceries and play at the park and cook dinner for when his other mom gets home from college. She is studying to be a nurse. I talk about becoming a librarian, but my attempt at getting a library assistant certificate, undertaken during the pregnancy, ended in disaster when the head of my program couldn't find an elementary school in Portland, Oregon, willing to have me as an unpaid intern. I was the only one in the program who couldn't be placed: it didn't escape my notice that I was also the only trans woman in the program.

More even than because of my tendency towards curling up inside my snail-shell in response to transphobia (young teen years of spitting and hitting back at my tormentors having been replaced by apathy, lethargy, and fear), I don't want to go back to school because I have already begun planning to homeschool my son.

John Holt wrote, in his book *Teach Your Own*, "What makes people smart, curious, alert, observant, competent, confident, resourceful, persistent—in the broadest and best sense, intelligent—is not having access to more and more learning places, resources, and specialists, but being able in their lives to do a wide variety of interesting things that matter, things that challenge their ingenuity, skill, and judgment, and that make an obvious difference in their lives and the lives of people around them."

As soon as I read those words, I know that the interesting things I've done, the things that have mattered, the challenges that have improved me as a person, are all things I have had to grasp for myself against institutional resistance, from school or from boring, poorly paid jobs. I have been raised in a culture of specialists and babysitters who have decided what things my peers (of age, of class, and ultimately of the vast majority of humanity however different our circumstances may be) and I should do, learn, and be.

I know that I don't want this for my son, and I know that the things I plan to do with my life and the people who are in my life will provide him with lots of opportunities to apprentice at challenging things. I work at the library as a page (the bottom rung of the ladder: we can't even share a union with the clerks, let alone the librarians) when my partner is available to be with our son. We live with her family for a while, then get our own apartment through the city-owned low-income housing program in Palo Alto.

Our apartment is beautiful to me: we have a garden on the balcony and my son, two and a half years old, has his hands in the dirt as often as he can. I paint his nails sparkly gold while he sits in his special blue plastic chair among the strawberry blossoms and pots of edible flowers. Inside, we decorate with art our friends make, old postcards, and paintings my partner painted, of burning houses, cars on fire, and people lost in mirrors.

"I liked going to school," my partner says. "I think it's good for kids. And he needs friends."

"You never said you liked school before." This argument is old, yet we are repeating our lines like the other has never heard them before. "He'll have friends. It's hard to get through life without making a few friends."

She I insists that he will go to preschool when he turns three; I insist that I'll help him find friends, and I do. One day a week, at a park less than two miles from our house, a big group of home-schoolers gets together to play. We go every week, walking at whatever pace suits us, throwing sticks into the creeks we pass and talking to the ducks, squirrels, and trees.

He doesn't go to preschool.

My partner becomes sick and is hospitalized; I call in sick to work for two weeks. She is hospitalized again a month later and I lose my job. Our rent is sliding scale and our families help us, so we still have somewhere to live.

She gets better and manages to carry on with nursing school. We have a second child. Since losing my job at the library, I have worked only odd jobs, gotten money from writing a few times, and stayed at home with the kids. She and I fight a lot about whether what I do is work, both raising the kids and writing, and about whether I should have to work toward a career with as much earning potential as hers.

I feel like she is a stranger; she seems to feel like I'm a child, naïve, stunted as much by my ideals as my traumas.

We leave the city and our amazing friends for the rural coast of northern California, to be near her family and live on the land on which she grew up.

The kids and I learn to make a chicken coop (plenty of geometry and other math in that, as well as other practical skills!) and raise chickens, spend time flying kites at the beach, comb the woods for beauty and treasure. We sing, constantly, folk songs and songs we make up:

Foggy day, another one on the coast yeah
it's a foggy day, guess it's just like most
we're gonna ride our bikes,
we're gonna fly our kites,
we're gonna make the most of this
foggy day . . .

My partner and I are fighting more and more often, so I look hard for work and find no one at all interested in hiring a long-time stay-at-home mama with no high school degree who also happens to be transsexual.

The kids and I are very lonely: there are hardly any homeschooling families nearby, and I am a bright red-nailed sore thumb. At my now six-year-old son's baseball game, my partner is clearly embarrassed by all the staring going on. She asks me not to come to the pool with her and the kids on her day off.

We ask her parents to watch the kids and we go for a walk.

Very quickly we are crying, angry, sad, full of respect, hate, and love for each other, and . . . single.

I am crying so much that I go lie down in our cabin. "I can't face the kids right now."

But I do, at dinner that night. Of course we tell them nothing. There is no script for this, so I let it sink deeply into me, so it becomes simply the truth before saying anything. Part of feeling this, of learning what is true is starting to do a zine again, for the first time since my oldest was a baby. I let myself draw and make little comics of adventures the kids and I have and of my neurotic process of realizing I'm a person who might like to date someone or feel cute sometimes. I write about sex, money, chickens, street harassment, transmisogyny (that particularly virulent intersection of misogyny and transphobia that impacts trans women, especially the feminine among us, and is perpetrated by cis women and trans men as readily as cis men).

Putting what I can find of my voice out into the world feels intensely liberating, scary, and exciting. I start making up songs, sing:

i'm gonna start a little game
where you have to drink every time i say
i'll learn to love myself

i think you'll be
comatose by 7 o'clock
it's not like i'm not lovable
i'm so lovable
it's not like i'm not sweet
i'm so sweet my teeth are falling out

it's just there's me when i think and me when i look
me when i wish and me when i look
yeah i'll learn to love myself
learn to love myself
learn to love myself
drink up!

My ex and I try to live together for a few months, moving to Portland to end the isolation for the kids and me that my zine has started breaking for me.

It doesn't work, and she wants to move back to the small town she grew up in. She gets an attorney and files for sole custody of the kids and the right to move them back to rural northern California. I raise money from friends and family and hire my own attorney.

Things go okay, and we stay. We make deep connections with homeschooling friends. I fall in love with another mama and we have a complicated, beautiful sort of family. Her three daughters are at least cousins to my sons and sometimes are the sisters they never knew they had. It doesn't always feel like it's going to work, but the connection is real and resilient between our families, even during times we have broken up.

I struggle with money, work at a bakery the two days a week the kids are with my ex, make some money writing, do more nude modeling for a website whose name includes a slur for transsexual women but pays well, nanny with my kids in tow. We have housemates, live in basement apartments, sometimes throw ourselves on the mercy of friends and family.

I am so glad I can be home with my kids. I love sharing the learning process with them, love their curiosity and my own, love late-night math, old movies, and studying the history of film, teaching ourselves stop motion animation, gardening, talking about radical history, urban design, and space travel. I love having community that cares for each other in the form of my partner and her kids and in the broader homeschooling community and with the handful of radical queer folks we connect with, childless though they are.

Most of all, I love the time we spend playing and talking and enjoying each other's company. This is what makes me feel successful no matter how much I struggle with money, direction, self-doubt, utility shut-off notices, relationship growing pains, men saying rude shit to me on the bus, cis women saying rude shit to me at queer feminist dance parties: We are happy and as free as we can be. I would live in a van or a friend's spare room and do unsavory things two days a week to have this love and joy all the rest of the week long.

> "Whatever an education is, it should make you a unique individual, not a conformist; it should furnish you with an original spirit with which to tackle the big challenges; it should allow you to find values which will be your road map through life; it should make you spiritually rich, a person who loves whatever you are doing, wherever you are, whomever you are with; it should teach you what is important, how to live and how to die."
>
> —John Taylor Gatto

my first poem
as a radical mother
alba onofrio

---

written for Adelani in august, 2010
after an engagement
with June Jordan's poem "A Couple of Questions"

What is my job—
as your mother
as the lover
of your father
and your future

How many meetings can we make
How much anger can I take
How much pain can I hold
How many people can I hold down
while being held down
while lifting you up
to dream, to be
seen and heard and whole
and wanting to wildly create
the world I don't know,
haven't seen, but I'm wanting to dream
with you, my sweet
my sweet
my innocent, my pure,
miraculous, breathtaking child

Do I show you the truth
this mess of a place you've landed here with me
how to anticipate what they think

and what you're "worth" and what I'm worth

Worthless and priceless
can they be the same
Do I teach you to survive
to protect your body and your soul
to lay low
to get by
do I teach you the codes
or do I just
let
you
go—

Do I steel your body and mind
or do I steal you away:
cocooning, embracing, and just letting you play
and sing
and enjoy the day
and the sun
and the stars
and the rain
letting you be wildly your own

Do I harness that potential
do I dare clip those angel wings
do I keep you safe and home with me

Does any hurt help you
Does any help hurt you
Do those headlines and being on the front lines
of every march and plea for sanity to the powers that be
cut down on the probability
of you creating
that world that we've never known
never seen
never tasted
'cause honey, we're reaching hard to even dream
much less embody and be

'the way,' the light . . . of a new day

Do I let those pretty wings free
to 'be all you can be'
while the hunters' sights are set on you
on me
on we
this community of radicals and queers

Tell me, what *is* my job
as your queer, brown mother
as the female-bodied lover
of your father
who art in heaven, hallowed be thy name . . .

Rise my Phoenix, Rise my little Sun
Show us the way to Heaven
Make this world your own.

Beacon, Bridge, and Boulevards
Gabriela Sandoval

October 7, 2010, in Santa Cruz, CA
I am sitting in my therapist's office, staring off into the little glass ball on the windowsill that houses several tiny shrimp who have already exceeded their life expectancy by years. There are tears running down my face. I am unsure if the tears are because I continue to be stuck in this psychic place or if it is because I am so angry to continue to be stuck in this psychic place. It occurs to me that I have found something to write about.

August 2010 in Chihuahua, Chihuahua
It's late. I've stayed up with my twenty-year-old niece wasting time on the internet while she studies. A friend sent me the call for papers for an anthology entitled *This Bridge Called My Baby*.[1] I can't think of a single compelling thing to write. I assume the days will melt away and in the whirling routine of summoning patience, returning to daycare, sleeping, commuting, eating, teaching, contemplating the good exercise will do me, sitting in administrative meetings, cleaning, and savoring quiet, playful moments with my daughter I will not likely find an idea worth translating into words, let alone find the time to print it on paper.

The only thing that comes to mind as a viable topic as I drift into sleep is fear. Fear. I dismiss it as an unworthy topic for exploration and laugh at myself for even considering that I would admit my fear to anyone, let alone a community of readers whom I do not know and who may never know me.

October 14, 2010, in Santa Cruz, CA
I am sitting here, again, beneath the large grey painting of a blue bird and its egg. They seem lost from each other. I stare down at the intricately patterned rug. My leg bounces. I usually run out of time.

---

1   The original title of this anthology when the call for submissions went out.

I can't stop the tears from trickling down my cheeks. I wish the time would speed up. If it is so clear that I am unhappy in my job as a tenure-track university professor, and indeed, that I have generally disliked it for nearly seven years, why can't I do something about it?

My therapist is insightful. She's smart and sensitive. I've known quite a few therapists in both professional and social capacities. I even considered becoming a therapist once when I stood at a fateful fork in the road. I trust her. If I had a relationship to save, I would bring it to her. She notices the miniscule shift in me. "What are you thinking?"

I have an idea for this anthology. It's about how my daughter is a bridge. At the tender age of two years, she has already served as a bridge away from toxicity, away from falseness, dishonesty, dearth of integrity. My life is massively more functional for her presence in it. Decisions I should have taken years and decades ago, paths I should have walked, joyfully, willingly, happily so many times, paths obfuscated by indecision, by feelings of unworthiness, or deserving, they burn bright and clear in my mind's eye, simply because she is present in this world.

My therapist laughs. She suggests I should write a piece about choosing to risk homelessness because I am currently on a bridge to nowhere, a path that will surely hollow me out, leaving me empty, my light further dimmed if not rendered a smoldering mass of ash. She is not trying to be funny. She is serious, and, I realize, so am I. If you are reading this account of my daughter's gift to cross even the most turbulent waters with her magical eyes and her brilliant smile then know that I have opted to take the only truly viable path away from the ivory tower and its golden handcuffs. I may not ever be able to take those off, but I will rip them out of the ivy-covered walls and walk away with my head up. I'll turn and say, quietly, with the deadliness of an asp, "FUCK YOU" to an institution that proved mind-numbing, kept none of its promises, sought to erode my self-esteem, made me a less prolific writer and stunted my creativity and imagination, pimped me out, tokenized and silenced me, showed no loyalty let alone professionalism. I may end up without a job, I may have to move back in with my elderly parents, I may lose every last bit of that little bit of hard-won financial stability, but if you are reading this, I've found my way and I have to thank my daughter for that.

February 2007, San Francisco
Everyone told me I had to go see the "gay astrologer" when I moved to San Francisco. I finally managed to get in for an appointment. She looks at my chart and tells me that there are foundational aspects of our lives that are based on occurrences in the first few years before and after we are born. She tells me that for me these are scarcity and impossibility. Your parents were experiencing acute scarcity when you were conceived.

They were. My parents and their three adolescent daughters moved from Chihuahua in 1972, two years before I was born. My father worked in a dog food cannery while my mother—who had stayed at home with her three daughters before immigrating to southern California—packed chiles seasonally the rest of the year sewing bows and other accents for pennies each onto lingerie she couldn't afford to buy. I am sure they wondered what they would do with a fourth child to feed and clothe.

You do things because you think they are impossible. You went to the university because you didn't think you could. You got a PhD because you thought it was impossible. You landed a plum job with the University of California because you thought you couldn't. You will likely get tenure because you think you can't. And you will stay there, because of the feeling of scarcity. The thing about you is that you shine when you are on the right path and I can tell just by looking at you right now, that you are not on the right path.

When will I have a baby? I am preoccupied with this because I inseminated myself a few days prior. She tells me that she does see a communally cared for child in my future, but not in this year.

A week later in San Francisco
I am pregnant. She was wrong. And what else might she have been wrong about? I will have a Scorpio child to contend with. I am ecstatic. In a few weeks I will be out dancing. I'll feel cramps, then blood. I'll run to the bar next door and feel as though I am drowning in my own fear in that tiny bathroom stall. I'll wait until the following morning to go to the emergency room where the doctors will tell me that my hormone levels are not high enough for me to be pregnant but not low enough for me not to be. The most likely explanation: that I was pregnant.

April 2011

By the time you read this I will be long gone. Please don't look for me. I won't be holding office hours in my office in College 8. I won't be standing in front of 240 students required to take research methods before they graduate. I won't be in attendance when the faculty sit at that long table for an hour and a half each week. It's possible you might find my book in print some day. There are a few articles. You may be able to locate some students who can attest to the fact that I cared about their education. Don't bother looking for me down those hallways. They are empty. My daughter practiced her first steps and then running up and down those halls. She attended a few meetings and played in my office. Then one day, she showed me how to open the door and taught me how to walk out. Don't bother looking for me at the university. You won't find me there (unless she decides she wants to study there one day).

If you are reading this, it is because I have risked everything— gambled it all—in order to ensure my daughter never sees me unhappy with the choices I've made, in order that she never come to believe that she must stay in a path that makes her anything less than ridiculously happy, in order that she know that her life, her work, is up to her. She taught me that, it's the least I can do.

Epilogue: February 2012, San Miguel de Allende, Guanajuato

We are living in San Miguel de Allende, a small central Mexican city designated a World Heritage Site by the United Nations and home to one of the oldest arts schools in the Americas and to the only government accredited professional midwifery school in Mexico. I am the Academic Coordinator of this small school with huge ambitions, primarily to place one professionally trained midwife in every rural community in Mexico and Guatemala (that's over a hundred thousand midwives!).

I moved here with my partner and my daughter three months ago. We brought only what fit in our suitcases. Without a car, I pick my way carefully through cobblestone streets, loath as I've been to give up heels completely.

I remember another therapist I knew once, in another life. It was the end of the year, 2004, and the foggy days in Santa Cruz had driven me to find a therapist. How could I feel so unhappy if I was back in sunny California after so many years of self-imposed exile braving graduate school in overcast upstate New York? I'd applied to over fifty jobs, interviewed at three schools, received two offers. How? How could I be unhappy in the only Latino/a sociology faculty position in the state of California. Every time I met a Latino/a sociologist, I was greeted with phrases like, "*You* got the job I wanted so badly!" and "I wanted that job *so* much!" I blamed it on the fog rolling off the bay into Santa Cruz and sought help.

One day, this therapist sparked my ire. He said, "This is not the job for you. Finding the right job is like trying on a pair of shoes, when it fits, you will know." I seethed. I stewed in anger for days, weeks. Didn't he know I had struggled for so long to obtain that PhD? Didn't he understand this was the ideal tenure-track faculty position? I hadn't attended school for over a decade to be told this wasn't the right "fit" for me! Moreover, I hadn't attended institutions full of people eager to tell me the only reason I was present was because I was a woman of color and a queer one at that, that the only reason I was allowed entry was because of all the quotas I filled. No! He had to be wrong.

I think about that metaphor every time I walk these uneven stone-lined streets, every time I escape a near-spill on the dusty, narrow lanes. That tenure-track position was like a pair of gorgeous, soft, black, leather, pointy, stiletto-heeled boots I once owned. It didn't matter that the path was smooth. It didn't matter how much I loved them, the way they looked. They hurt me.

My daughter taught me this. Sometimes—probably most times, the difficult path—in this case, the one that pays less, offers less security, provides less status—is right. Sometimes even the most comfortable shoes hurt when you are walking the right path. The intangible rewards of struggling slowly up and down these narrow streets holding the small hand of the feistiest child I know, well, it's not like walking on clouds, but it does make me slow down and smile. And I don't need a therapist anymore.

In this Pure Light
Zuihitsu for a son
Cheryl Boyce Taylor

1.

October 2008

I'm in the waiting room at UCSF
my son is about to have a kidney transplant
my daughter-in-law is the donor

a dear friend gifts my daughter-in-law a silver necklace
from it hang three pearl shaped hearts, for love, strength and hope
I ask to wear the necklace during surgery

2.

November 1970

Dear son
On this joyous morning sheets still smell of birthing
our newborn inheritance between us
still an unburned bride my body blooms
become   river boat cave grave village
your small mouth sewn to my blue flesh glows

your twin brother
gone to meet the breath of God waiting in that field of light

son
you are my pillar tree wealth straw-broom looking glass wings
currents scream temple fire
break the night light the city love

does the organ of the heart shiver in this pure light
or does the light shiver in the presence of the heart

3.

I so want love
can this dyke-mama body absorb all that light

bombastic red
I rouge my mouth
ease out the door
my tightest dress the green brocade
piano plays

a little sign
    fuck me and my poem
written on the bathroom wall

last night we were the blues   I was her obsidian spine   she my
unbeatable raft
a sharp stone fell into the great smile that was her body

4.

June 1985

The house on Merrick Boulevard

my son's dad tells him I am a lesbian

he screams and cries roars his rage
earth hums with ache
one snapped tree broken at it's center
he is 15   my son a delicate kiss slips from my palms

I fear this death more than I fear my own

pain has slimmed me

the next few years I grow a Judas body   a false tongue my eyes a watercraft for the Gods
my son grows into a thousand distant mornings
the questions of his body a crooked dirt road narrow in the damp of boyhood much later he becomes a spell maker
      I adore his sensitive words

5.

Last night on the phone my son hums me one of his new tunes
tells me *I always knew I'd be a rapper of positive thoughts*
he tells me *I love my grandmother but when she tried to pray my hip hop dreams away*
I would repeat in my head *I will have my music I will have my music someday I will I will*

his body became a temple for hip hop

When I found out my son was a diabetic
I wished to make his curse mine inside I burned with blue shame I had given him bad sugar
I had given him my diabetes

four needles   four shots of insulin
four shots of insulin   a handful of pills
that's what it takes to make my body work each day   four Peri exchanges
                    that's what it takes for my son's body to work
                    each day
             Mother's day 1999
             my son calls to say
             he needs a kidney

6.

That night I beg God to give me the burden forgive my sins is it because I love a woman
God
I make a pact

God
I swear I will—

7.

I paint my face holy
the color of white apple blossoms

8.

On the flight to Oakland I pray and pray
my son is getting sicker I don't know how to comfort him
                   My grandson David meets me at the airport
        he hops on one leg all the way to the baggage carousel
I'm gonna give him my kidney he says
I will I will   I'm not scared ah nothing—
he is eight

We go directly to the hospital my son is asleep
I sit at his bedside and wait
two A.M. the phone rings my girl is on the line
how did the test results go she asks
                         we are quiet for a long time

My son stirs
the phone drops I hug my child   I hold his hand in mine kiss him
squeeze him
until he says
ouch ouch ouch ma

Queering Family
Ariel Gore

The universe is made of stories, not atoms, the poet Muriel Rukeyser said.

I know some things about this universe.

I taught a memoir-writing workshop called *The Language of Your Life* in Portland, Oregon, for a decade. I've taught an online writing workshop for another decade. I've edited an alternative family magazine for the better part of twenty years. And in doing so I've read into the lives of more than five thousand writers—most of them U.S or other Western storytellers born in the 20th century.

Five thousand lives. Five thousand stories.

So many atoms bumping into one another.

I've learned a lot about family.

And what strikes me most profoundly, five thousand languaged-lives in, is the immense psychological damage that is the direct result of the marketing of an idealized American nuclear family.

Nucleus / what is central / the positively-charged mass within the atom / it's not surprising that we've used the same word / nuclear / to describe both the intimate lives we were all supposed to strive for and the greatest threat to humanity we ever created / this is war / this is the language of your death / stay alive / thrive / if you're going to be a target, make sure you're a moving target / the positively-charge heart within the story.

The idealized nuclear family is: Mother + father + kids. Parents are mid-twenties to late thirties when the first kids are born (idealized age increases over the course of the 20th century). All family members are straight, middle class, middle- to high-income, able-bodied, mental illness free, pretty, happy, successful, and white-identified.

Any short falling in any of the above categories is one's own or another immediate family member's fault and may be addressed via all known control and escape mechanisms—preferably administered behind closed doors—including but not limited to: Verbal shaming ("what will the neighbors think?"), neglect, nurturance-withholding, financial withholding, domestic abuse, sexual violence, nonverbal shaming including the invocation of "family secrets," alcoholism, drug addiction, and illicit sexual escapes.

We are stories of quiet incest under powder-blue sheets and capitalist failures drowned in cheap, imported vodka. We are the shame of my father's mental illness. (We are not the shame of my grandfather's military defense corporation or my great-grandfather's earth-mining operation.) We are muttered judgments "their daughter is a lesbo," and "leave the meat for your brother." We are immobilizing anxiety the source of which we can't quite put our finger on.

All this to say that, No, I'm not interested in any of your "gay rights" or "women's rights" or "funny-looking people's rights" that will get me access to or membership in this cultural disaster. I don't want to join the country club and my desire to ride on by has nothing to do with sour grapes. If the universe is made of stories, not atoms, like Rukeyser said, then I'm an expert in the universe by now and I know a black hole behind a country-club façade when I see one.

In truth, I want only a few of things vis-à-vis this idealized nuclear family:

To be a threat to it.

To thrive outside its boundaries.

To live to see the end of it.

To use my limited talents and energy to be of whatever help I can as those damaged by its legacy begin to heal, make art, and build lives free from its intrinsic violence.

The notion of a threat is, of course, subjective.

I find it amusing that to be a threat to the nuclear family, all one has to do is live happily (or in honest depression) outside of it.

Teen mom. Welfare mom. Single mom. Smiling in the newspaper. Happy in her little urban apartment. First book deal just signed. I think I was twenty-six years old when *The San Jose Mercury News* called me "conservative America's worst nightmare."

And I thought, *Seriously?* Because *my* worst nightmares were all violent and terrible—the tragedies that people and communities cannot recover from.

They must live sheltered lives, I thought, these conservative Americans, if *I* was their worst nightmare.

I hadn't even publicly come out of the closet yet.

"The queer is to destabilize the norm," my scholar friend Christa Orth told me when I asked her what that word meant, anyway. "To queer is to make identity, gender, sexuality, family, and community moving targets."

To have grown up in a 20th-century family is to become a target.

To have a child is to become a target.

They want you not to reflect the idealized nuclear family but rather to strive for it and live in perpetual emotional shame and commercial want.

I set out to write an essay about queer parenting, but only came up with 5/7/5. Haiku:

I had a baby.

But I didn't register.

Spring. We'll travel light.

V.
Two Pink Lines

Introduction
Mai'a Williams

When I was pregnant with Theresa, I told my mother that I wanted to give birth with a midwife. She kept mocking me about how I needed to go to a doctor, not just get some dirty woman who barely knew what she was doing. My mother was born in 1952 in rural South Carolina Black middle class. The first generation in those Jim Crow days who was birthed by a doctor. It was an achievement for the community.

And those women, those midwives, who had for generations saved the community, were now stigmatized and castigated as 'dirty' and 'unlearned,' 'unkempt' and 'backwards.' Even as midwives, day after day, brought our poor rural communities who lived on the brink of starvation, malnutrition, physical exhaustion, psychologically traumatized, through the dark days. They not only midwifed our survival but our triumph.

They are proof that birth is not so much about the equipment we bring to a birth as a midwife, doula, assistant, sister, mother, it is about the quality of attention that we bring to it. They not only knew a mama's name and her health history, often times they knew her family, her friends, what she grew in her yard, her daily habits, her favorite foods. They let birth be intimate, by being intimate with mamas. They let birth be spiritual, by calling on the spirit. And they succeeded against all odds, especially compared to today's home birth midwives and OBGyns.

Often in Black communities we hear about a crisis of leadership, a crisis of community, a lack of accountability to each other within Black communities. I don't think it's a coincidence that this crisis of leadership (which is normally envisioned in the social imagination as a lack of Black male leadership) started about the same time that our Black midwives of miracles began to be outlawed. The mama/midwives who with every force of their beings kept our mamas and babies and alive and thriving. In the foreground and the background, midwives stood on the shorelines and front lines of our peoples survival and had an infinite number of lessons to teach us about community building, radical love, miracle making, how to give birth to leaders and revolutionaries.

They taught us to break apart and be a revolutionary for our children's survival.

And that breaking apart that mamas do has the potential to turn mamas into revolutionaries, because you see the world differently. You know differently. You read the news differently. Your poems are different.

Black midwives, granny midwives, unlicensed midwives saved us as a people and helped our communities give birth to revolutionaries, agitators, militants, freedom fighters.

*

Birth is smelly bloody dirty messy bestial, whether it is vaginal or surgical there is no easy way out. The epidural can ease the pain but not the existential fear.

You will be turned inside out. If not during the birth, then during the pregnancy, if not the pregnancy, by the nursing, by the sleeplessness night, the mind-bending loneliness, sooner or later you will break down. You will think, believe you cannot go on. You will realize that if you ever thought that facing yourself, the bloody, ugly, sublime truth of yourself was the ultimate responsibility, you were wrong. It is to face yourself and realize you cannot run away because another life, your child's, depends on this ultimate self-encounter.

Welcome to mamahood.

I am trying to articulate the blood and muscle, the tears, the shaking, how it is no longer really a choice, of whether or not you will have the courage to not run away from your own fear, panic, lack of self-control. It is something beyond and before courage. It is a visceral sense that vulnerable, quivering life is breaking you and you have to let it. It is not self-sacrifice. It may not even qualify as love. It isn't sweet. It isn't romantic. It may traumatize you, keep you up at night, the memory of that moment when you had to face your worst and best and really you aren't sure if you came out the winner or the loser.

The only word I have is revolution.

But time and time again, when the mothering gets tough and you wonder how how how you are supposed to stay patient when you kid is driving you up the wall, when you feel like you are falling behind on everything, work, school housework, field trip permission forms, doctor visits, visa appointments, the bureaucracy of every day life. When the bills pile up and you are counting coins, you will come back to that moment. You will think quietly to yourself, *'remember when life itself broke you apart, shattered you and made you the earth that made your kid possible?'*

Well if you did that, then you can get through this as well. And for better or worse, you will.

Step on a Crack:
Parenting with Chronic Pain
Claire Barrera

If not for the danger of electrocution, I would be writing this from my bathtub. That little ceramic container of warmth has become a refuge for me that I retreat to one to two times daily. Since my daughter, Paloma, was born twenty-one months ago it's been one of the few places I can be totally alone. It's a safe, quiet place I can sink into myself and reflect. It's also one of my most effective painkillers since being pregnant and then breastfeeding and caring for a child have significantly reduced my options in that category. I like the encompassing pressure of the water against my skin. Its simultaneous softness and weight calm the buzzing of my over-stimulated nerves and relax the defensive grip of my muscles. At the end of each day, when my pain and exhaustion tend to peak, I can't wait to get in the bath.

In fact, Paloma was born in warm water. I had planned a water birth in our home, and when the time came, I was eager for the midwives to give me the go ahead to jump in the tub. By then my contractions were going strong and there was a powerful ache in my lower back and pelvis as my baby's little body continued to move down. The water supported me and it also provided a sweet transition for Paloma as she left the womb and entered the world.

In every way, the pain of labor was the opposite of my chronic pain experience. Amazing hormones of joy obviously had an influence. But to begin with, the very foundation of the pain was opposite. While my chronic pain was evidence of trauma and malfunction, the pain of labor was caused by the incredible transformation of my body as it produced life. There was and would be no injury. While with my chronic pain I normally felt fear and disconnection from my physical self, during labor I felt a complete trust of and love for my body and its innate abilities. I was grounded inside myself, present, feeling the power of the pain of my contractions as they did their work.

After Paloma was born I was sure I would be able to hold onto those feelings of fearlessness and connection to my body. Unfortunately, it wasn't so easy. During my pregnancy I had for the most part experienced a lessening of my pain. Post baby, my pain has returned, though somewhat altered. I don't actually feel all the time how I felt during labor, but my memory of it is an awesome reference that I feel lucky to access when I'm really struggling with my pain.

I knew before getting pregnant that parenting with chronic pain would pose challenges. So far I have only had time to experience what challenges exist for the mother of a very young person. Struggling with those challenges, I began to wonder how my mother had coped with having major depression while she raised my sister and myself, and decided to ask her about it.

"I found being around you guys to be helpful when I was feeling depressed," my mom told me on the phone. "In the beginning I didn't suffer from post-partum depression, I suffered from post-partum ecstasy." We both laughed. I asked her how she found ways to not take out her depression on us when we were older.

"When you were old enough I explained my depression to you in age-appropriate terms," she said. "Mostly I didn't struggle with depression around you guys. I did get into psychotherapy and also that was around when Prozac first came out." My mom did tell me about a time when my sister lived with her and I did not, when she became very depressed after she split with her partner of five years. They went on a road trip together to lift her spirits, but it didn't work.

"On the ride home I just felt so dead and flat, and I said to your sister, 'I just feel like I'm looking out at a desert and there is no oasis in sight,' and your sister said to me 'I'll be your oasis, mom' and it was so touching, but I knew she shouldn't have to be my oasis. But that's how it was, I was depressed." My mom cried a little telling me this story. It made me think of times when I've been short tempered with my baby because of my pain and the guilt I feel after. And it reminded me that we have to know we are doing the best we can and our children will still thrive.

I certainly haven't experienced the post-partum ecstasy my mother did, although there have been many moments of joy in these first two years of life. One of the biggest challenges I have faced is the lack of sleep and how it affects my body. When I don't sleep well, it seems my body never relaxes enough to get a break and heal. I have been blessed with a child who wakes frequently, even more than most babies I know. That means the next day is worse than the day before. And unfortunately, carrying a heavy object all day long (something I never did before I had a baby) has increased my old pain and created some new spots of trouble in my back and neck. That has a lot to do with nursing as well. More pain means less energy and patience for my daughter and my partner, which I feel is the biggest issue I struggle with as a parent with chronic pain. I just have a shorter fuse. I imagined I would be the most patient parent in the world, and I'm not.

One day when Paloma was around three months old, I found myself literally yelling at her because she wouldn't nap. My back was hurting very badly and I was exhausted from waking with her five or six times a night. Afterward, or course, I felt terrible. It was a wakeup call to take more breaks and get more help.

It's not just the deficiency in maternal patience that I have been surprised by. I'm sure nobody's expectations for parenting completely match up with the real deal, but it does seem that parents with chronic illness specifically struggle more with having to give up on a lot of the parenting techniques they wanted to use. At least, that's the impression I got surfing the parenting forum on Mothering.com, where there were a few threads for parents with chronic pain and chronic illness. Most of us on this discussion board are believers in attachment style parenting, yet there were so many posts from mamas who had to stop breastfeeding or cosleeping early because of the pain they experienced, or who couldn't wear their babies in slings for the same reason. Other changes might include less financial stability than anticipated due to doctor's bills or inability to work, less energy and patience for parenting, and decreased mobility that limits things like trips to the park.

There is grief when one has to let go of these desirable gifts one wants to give one's child. I sometimes feel resentful that I spent so many years as a nanny wearing other people's babies and now I can't wear my own for more than ten minutes. I also plan to stop cosleeping at a much earlier age than I anticipated, because getting my body comfortable enough to sleep is enough of a challenge without adding a squirmy baby into the mix. In addition to grief I feel guilt about denying my child these good things, and find my-self at times feeling shame in the presence of other mamas who are parenting a different way.

It is widely acknowledged that in Western culture we expect parents, especially mothers, to always act like they adore children and parenting, and that they can "do it all" with grace and ease. I have found that the radical/natural parenting community is no different. Many mom acquaintances of mine do not deign to share much of the difficult moments they experience as caregivers. The need to present as though one is successful at mainstream parent-ing techniques has simply been substituted with an alternative. One is expected to breastfeed, babywear, make all your babyfood from scratch, unschool AND work, etc. etc. with a smile on one's face. I find this discouraging and not radical at all, and I don't see myself, as a mama with a disability, reflected in that reality.

Like so many other aspects of life with chronic pain, as a parent I've had to redefine what I think of as a successful and fulfilling life. It takes a lot of work to let go of my idealized image of family life. But the more I'm able to do that, the more present I am for my baby, and the more creative I am at replacing the things I wanted with new concepts of parent-child interaction. We can use the stroller instead of the sling and still enjoy our walk. We can play in the pool instead of the park, especially since we both love the water.

In a sense, having chronic pain helped me develop the skills I would need to be happy as a parent, and for that I am grate-ful. Many parents I have met have shared with me that they lost many friends once they started having children. In young, punk, queer community, being a parent can mean social death. For my part, I can't miss something I didn't have in the first place. By the time my daughter was born, the friends that might have dropped away had already done so long ago, when I first developed chronic pain and could no longer participate in the same activities. Those friends that stayed were tried and true, loyal folks who have since become aunts and uncles to my daughter and allies to me as a parent.

Invisibility is another identifying characteristic of those of us who have kids as well as those of us with chronic pain. When events and activism are not made accessible, let alone centered, around us we are not only left out but it even appears we do not exist. Chronic pain helped me find ways to participate in my community that were accessible to me, and I have used that as a parent.

Lack of time and lots of stress have been characteristics present since I developed my pain and definitely since my daughter was born. While doctor's appointments have been replaced by endless diaper changes and nursing sessions, lack of sleep has remained a constant and grating feature of these past few years. I certainly use similar coping skills for both issues in this case, such as making time to care for myself and asking friends to help me get things done.

So, having pain has been both a barrier and a teacher for me as a parent. More than anything, I don't want my struggles with pain to color my daughter's childhood in an unhealthy way. I want to care for myself and work with my feelings so that Paloma doesn't have to carry them for me. I've had to expand and amplify the skill set I've developed as a person with chronic pain. Taking time away from her and talking to people about the hard times helps me with my short temper. Getting friends and family to babysit even for an hour or two gives my body a break from the grunt work of hauling around a child. Making space to be with my body in a positive way, either in the bath or in a dance class helps me pass on the concepts that our bodies are our wonderful allies, not our adversaries. On a day when I am struggling with a flare up, I sometimes just stop and remember, image by image, those amazing few days when Paloma was born. And I believe that if my body and I can bring forth life, we can find a way to be happy and healthy in this world.

Birthing a New Feminism
Lisa Factora-Borchers

On December 20, 2009, I gave birth to two things: a 9 lb. 7 oz. son and a new feminism. It was the third time I had undergone surgery; twice to remove ovarian tumors and cysts and once to remove a breathing boy.

By nightfall, I was vomiting from the drugs administered for the C-section. After an excruciating vomiting episode, my head hit the pillow in utter exhaustion and Isaiah, my new son, began to cry out of hunger.

I looked at my body. Like a meticulous and tedious film director wanting to capture every detail of a flowerbed with a camera, I surveyed every inch of my body. I started at my feet.

My legs were still buzzing numb from surgery. To keep from forming blood clots, my legs had been strapped to a pumping machine. Two pieces of plastic swathed my legs. They hissed when they squeezed my calves and lazily loosened after three seconds of tight holds. The noise prevented me from deep sleep and made my legs sweat. A catheter was inserted. I saw the bag full of my urine with taints of blood. It was a horrendous sight.

The dressing over my surgical incision covered the most tender and vulnerable part of my birthing body, the exit wound of my baby.

An ugly red rash had exploded onto the top of my chest. Its bumps were just as unsightly as they were itchy. A reaction, maybe, from the hospital gown? Or hormones?

My left hand was a splotchy mess from a messy IV insertion. Mounds of clear tape awkwardly held in a needle and dried blood itched under the surface. It was hooked to a machine, beeping and regulating my body. Bags of I-don't-know-what dripped into my arm.

My right arm tried to secure Isaiah in an awkward position so I could breastfeed him. His desperate attempts to latch on were beyond painful, but with the help of countless nurses and my husband, he drank.

Gulped, really.

My normally brown face was gray with remnants of drugs and fatigue. No food. No water. Only ice chips. My water was taken away when I greedily sipped too much at once and, consequently, vomited into the pan again.

Later, to help stir bowel movements, an enema was inserted.

As I surveyed my body, I saw every orifice of my body was either plugged, bandaged, bleeding, dry, or fatigued. And as Isaiah drank, my breasts ached with new agony, unfamiliar with this new demand for nourishment and, suddenly, as if my leg pumps, catheter, IV, and surgery scars weren't enough, I began having more contractions. My uterus throbbed with an intensity that made my eyes close.

"The hormones stimulated by breastfeeding will cause contractions. This will help your uterus descend and go back to its normal size," the nurse assured me.

And Isaiah's latch intensified.

Never, in all the days of my life, had I ever undergone anything so life-giving. Never had I myself been so life-giving. Every part of my body was simultaneously healing and giving.

Through the pain, the lactation consultants were so beautiful and caring, I wanted to weep into their laps.

They gently touched, massaged, and handled my breasts. The nipples, swollen and red, screamed with pain at the slightest touch of a hospital gown. Maya, a middle aged woman from Russia, was sharp, informative, and decisive. Her teaching was fast, her hands careful, but her eyes were business. She recognized the pain, she knew how difficult it was to remain even. Myra understood that I was this close to losing my sanity.

She understood that while the vagina or, in my case, the abdomen, was the door to life in the womb, it was the nipples that were the entry point of survival for my son. The body, my body became a poem, a poem of survival.

I stayed in the hospital room, save two hours to walk down the hall for a parenting class, for four days straight. Because of the drugs my dreams were in neon, and because of the milk coming in my breasts were engorged. What I remember most clearly about that period in my life was how unbelievably gentle and kind people were in my time of vulnerability. My body was an open wound and nearly everyone that saw it treated it with reverence and me with care.

One night, when Isaiah was fitfully sleeping and my mind had time to expand on something other than my own physical state like a loose leaf lightly touching a windshield before moving on, I thought about Feminism.

"I'm now a mother. Never again like before. Never just I." These thoughts raced in my exhausted mind. My life just took the most radical turn. The morning I went into labor, I had made myself chocolate chip pancakes and six hours later, I was responsible for the well-being of a human being. Everything had changed in the blink of an eye. And in that change, I came to a realization that there were two kinds of feminism. The Feminism of issues and the feminism of our lives.

I realized the Feminism that is perpetuated in mainstream and mainstream-like media is not the feminism of our lives. It is the Feminism of commerce. It is the Feminism that picks and chooses the winners and losers, the visible and invisible, and accessible and ignored. Its capitalism agenda selects and focuses upon what will sell and conflates material gain with spiritual progress; things that bring pleasure, not transformation.

The Feminism that has stepped on the backs of women of color and ignored the backs of trans and disabled women is the Feminism that camouflages itself with diverse panels and collectives but neglects to modernize its definition of social liberation in the era of digital media. It is the Feminist theories stuck in the academy and conferences in affluent hotels with no outreach to make it more accessible for marginalized folks to attend. This Feminism is the reordering of the so-called patriarchal hierarchy. It loves to hear itself talk and self-congratulate for working on issues relevant only to individuals like themselves.

This is the Feminism that has the time and luxury to ask leisure questions such as, "Why don't you identify as Feminist?" as it obsesses over semantic identity and invests front covers of magazines and features to the evangelization of the feminist identity, rather than the feminist agenda that addresses power inequality and human suffering. Mainstream Feminism boasts the art of uplifting the already privileged and ignoring the women whose heads are in toilets cleaning those same women's bathrooms. The conversation of the privileged is prioritized over the pleas of the oppressed.

The purpose of feminism is to end itself. Andrea Dworkin called it one day without rape. The purpose of feminism is to one day find ourselves where we don't need to fight for human rights through the lens of women's oppression. Note: I didn't write that the purpose is to bring down the man. The purpose is not to have a female president. The purpose is to transform the infrastructure that holds kyriarchy in its place. Replacing men with women—of any race, ethnicity, creed, or ability—who refuse to acknowledge the insidious and mutating face of gender oppression is not forward stepping. It's a perpetuation of history.

And so the question comes: how invested are you in the liberation of women?

Because if you agree that the liberation of all women carries more weight than the identification as a liberal feminist, the feuds over whether feminism is dead become irrelevant. The uproar should be about dying women, not a dying Feminism.

There was something so entirely miraculous about those four days in the hospital. I witnessed myself birth life. Bones from my bones. Blood from my blood. Life from my womb, I brought a person into the world. From two, I grew my family to three.

This awesome mystery/reality settled itself in bits and fragments.

My father told me that the birthing woman is different afterward. Her power is different. She herself is different.

My power is different.

For months, nearly everyone I encountered—friends and strangers alike—offered their opinion on what parenting should and would be for me. It was in that hospital room, where Nick slept uncomfortably on the couch without shaving that I, hooked to monitors and machines, understood a profound difference between us as parents.

Parenting is the responsibility that we both shared. Together. It would be the late nights of feeding, rocking, and soothing that we'd walk together, he and I. To me, motherhood is a state of helpless yearning. The world shows itself in full color the first night you become a parent. You begin to yearn for the impossible: guarantees of safety and justice. And recognizing that impossibility often made me tearful. But I didn't want to spend my life crying over impossibilities. I suddenly had this crazy urge to clean up the world for my son. I needed to organize.

The feminism of my life unfolded in a love story that resulted in the birth of my son. That gift of love expanded into larger insights about my feminist perspective for life, not issues. Gathered at my bed was my mother, the woman I've thought of and written so much about, the woman who I have processed more than any other human I've met. My father kept stroking my hair and muttering concerns over my bruised and broken body. Mainstream Feminism's interest in westernized notions of individualism glossed over my culture and ethnic identity.

The feminism I had begun to build was a house of love that no longer shunned my parents out of intergenerational and bicultural frustration, but embraced our difficulties and disagreements. Filipino culture was not something I needed to understand, it was something I needed to live out so race was no longer referred to as an agent of my parents' Filipino heritage, but of my uniquely formed Filipino identity.

Nick held the can for me while I vomited. He wore scrubs and, in the delivery room, wore a surgical mask. The shade of the scrubs made his hazel eyes deep green. I saw him between hurls. I saw my son. Our son. Epiphanies come in such strange moments. As Nick gently wiped my face after vomiting, I knew that wherever I went, he would need to be welcomed, too.

The language and polemics of inclusion is still a muddy trench for feminisms. What exactly does "women" mean, and who is excluded from that title? And where was I going without my son? What was I creating if not a world that had a space for him? I didn't want to go where my family would not belong. There was no separation between the world I wanted to build and my son's future. I wanted freedom for both of us. Mine and his.

The Feminism of issues serves its purpose well. It informs us of the problems. But we're more than issues, are we not? Isn't our life worth more than the issues?

The feminism of our lives is the story of love, survival, testament, death, and epitaph. It is what we dedicate ourselves to and what we will pass on as truth to our children. Whether or not we identify as "feminist" is a sandbar to the oceanic movements of feminisms.

There is so much work to do, so much silence to break, that for the brief minute of a life where I get to use my voice, I am not going to expend my breath on explaining whether or not I identify as feminist. Transformation does not have a name or a label, it has a sound.

Listen. Listen closely. Can you hear it?

The revolution will not be a movement. It will be Birthed.

Choice
Esteli Juarez

My father is one of seven children (that lived, there were others that passed at birth or early in life). He's the baby. My grandfather, from all accounts I've ever heard, was not around while my father was growing up. I acknowledge that this experience was different for my uncles and aunt and they had more positive relationships with Jesus Juarez, Sr. I have never heard anything good about him from anyone. He died the year before I was born and my father did not attend his funeral.

I did grow up hearing of another man, Marcelo Herrera, the man my brother is named after and my Tia Lita's husband. Marcelo who was practically my father's father, who loved Lita at a time when she was "sick" and no one really understood what was wrong with her. Marcelo who helped raise his wife's sister's children as his own when their father wasn't around. You see, there were times when my grandmother, La Santa Ramona Juarez de Padilla could not care for her children alone so her sister, Lita, and her husband Marcelo, took them in and they lived together in a one bedroom home, with an outhouse, in Roswell, New Mexico.

I heard lots of great stories about Lita growing up. She hated English and wouldn't allow it to be spoken in her house. She said it sounded like dogs barking. So, in a time in New Mexico history when children were PHYSICALLY PUNISHED for speaking Spanish in school, my Dad and Tios HAD to speak Spanish at home. She would cook for all nine-plus of them on a little wood burning stove and make the best tortillas and café. She thought indoor plumbing was gross and refused to put a toilet in the house.

She also couldn't have children. When I was a young woman I asked my father why Lita and Marcelo had no children, why had he named my younger brother Marcelino Herrera after Marcelo, and he told me it was because she couldn't have children. You see Lita had epilepsy, something that runs in my family, and at that time women who were "disabled," "retarded," or "insane" were FORCEFULLY

STERILIZED, and the epilepsy made her all three of those things. So when she was a young woman a doctor, a medical professional, TOOK HER CHOICE AWAY. Lita and Marcelo didn't have children not because they couldn't afford them, didn't want them, or couldn't care for them, to the contrary, they cared for many children. Lita never got the chance to decide whether or not she wanted to have children, she was, very literally, stripped of that right.

As a young woman I was horrified to learn this. That some-one with more education and power took advantage of my Tia and took her UTERUS. And even more horrified when I learned later in life about the campaigns against Puerto Rican women, both on the island and in the States, and Native women in the 1960s and '70s that essentially did the same things. Hundreds of thousands of Native and Puerto Rican women were sterilized, many of them without knowledge or consent or with the belief that the process was reversible.

The older I get the more passionate I become about retaining control over my body and allowing other women the same oppor-tunity to do so. This is why I attended the Women's March in DC in 2004. This is why I was in *The Vagina Monologues* in college and that experience inspired me to direct a production for three years while in law school. This is why I work with victims of domestic violence. To help them regain power and control over themselves.

I gave birth to my first son at twenty-one, then the second one at twenty-four, and the third one at twenty-five. Some older woman once told me that my feelings about abortion, about Choice, would change once I held my first child. When I got pregnant with my first child, I was in my last year of college, I had just applied to law schools, my boyfriend at the time had two children, was in the mid-dle of a messy divorce and lived across the country. We discussed it and having a child didn't make any sense, it wasn't logical. I sat in the lobby of Planned Parenthood waiting to be called back and decided at that moment that I was going to have that baby. I walked out and my son has been changing my life ever since that moment. Since the birth of my first son, I've only fought harder, believed stronger, and wanted better for them, for their future and for their future part-ners. I try and teach my children about the control they have over their own bodies. As they age I try and show them respect over their choices by asking them for kisses or hugs, not by taking them. The only way to show them how important Choice is to show them all the choices they always have by nature of being men.

Choice to me is not just about abortion. It's about all the choices. It's about the choice to be able to conceive children at all. The choice to keep my body intact and not have a government tell me when I should or should not be allowed to carry a child or not carry a child. For marginalized women in this country the issue of choice is not as simple as the right to abortion because this government practiced involuntary hysterectomies on so many of our mothers, grandmothers, sisters, elders, and Tias.

A woman's right to choose goes both ways. Is the right to choose to continue a pregnancy but it is also the right to choose to get pregnant in the first place. I will fight for a woman's right to choose until the day that I die. I will fight for every woman I've loved who's been abused by a man and had to make the hardest decision she's ever had to, choosing to continue with a pregnancy and the abusive relationship or not. I will fight for every girl who has been raped or molested and wound up pregnant and has to choose between keeping that baby or living that trauma over again every single day. I will fight for my Tias and the choices they never got.

Postscript

When I was a kid there was a rumor that my Tia Teresa (the only sister my father has) was able to have kids but didn't get a period. Ever. I used to pray that whatever that gene was, that I had it. It sounded awesome. Not until the year that I turned twenty-seven, until after writing the first draft of this piece, did my sister and then my cousin, my Tia's daughter, tell me that my Tia had been forcefully sterilized before the age of thirty. A woman who read at about a first-grade level until she was forty was robbed of her choice. My Tia Theresa, like my Tia Lita, has epilepsy. Unlike Lita, her reproductive right was stolen in the 1970s not the 1930s and not because she has epilepsy but because she was poor.

This March my Tia Teresa was one of the planners of the Mil Mujeres March (Thousand-Woman March) here in New Mexico. It was a smaller-scale version of the March for Women's Lives that happened in Washington, DC, in 2004. It was my sons' first march and rally, but I'm sure it won't be their last.

The Darkness
Fabielle Georges

I still remember it. We were sitting in a church that looked more like an auditorium. There were hundreds of plainly clad people sitting in the pews with us waiting for something to happen, someone to speak. He was there, in his seat, looking up at me. His face inspired the birth of a memory that was not my own, but my known. I thought on this memory, this chant hissed at little Black children by their mockers:

> Nigger, Nigger never die
> Shiny face and bulging eyes

And that was what he looked like with his shiny face and bulging eyes. He was as dark as I, maybe a dash or three darker, with eyes just as big as mine. His lips were too grand for his infant face and his nose flat. He was me, looked like me. I felt inclined to love him, so I did. I loved him and I felt close to him. But I was upset, disappointed because he looked like me, was me.

But this was just a dream fueled by my pregnancy, muddied with late-night eating. He, in reality, was still the eight-month tenant renting space in my womb.

This dream reached me often. Not too often, but often enough to goad a kind of fear. I was afraid that my son would come into this earth bearing the same shameful sin that veiled my existence: this dark skin. I was afraid that he would have to work, as I have worked, to ignore or excuse a color that refused overlook my lineage and skip to someone else's line of ancestry; this darkness that has followed me since before the birth of my father's mother's mother. These possibilities secretly scared me for I could not openly admit that I was still ashamed of my color.

I spent the years prior to his conception reminding myself to love my self. I read the clichéd inspirational pamphlets dressed in the sleeves of books on self-love. I listened to the stereotypical voices of tan-skinned speakers talking about this darkness and celebrating it and, for some time, I let the nominal power of this darkness stimulate my esteem. I walked in this skin and built up four walls of explanations and pardons around me. And around these four walls of explanations and pardons existed four thin, meager veils of love and acceptance. But his arrival was near. These flimsy veils disintegrated from the bottom up and I was simply left with my excuses.

There was a Black baby on top of the cake at my baby shower. My light-skinned, silky-haired aunty jokingly said that this is him. This would be my son. Through the cringe that my face, dark, was aching to present I smiled, laughed, "No, that isn't him." This plastic figurine had a dark, shiny face with these big, protruding eyes. I didn't want this to be my son. I didn't want to have to excuse his color along with mine. The work would be too difficult.

Heavy thoughts carried me through my pregnancy. I fretted over my midwife maybe failing to see that he may have Down syndrome, the ultrasound technician neglecting to tell me that my son may not have all ten fingers or all four limbs. I feared the possibility of autism, malnutrition at birth, and sticking to my birth plan. I worried over having the darkness swallow him and raising him sans the help of his father. I worried over hindering his ability to live without added judgment. I worried.

He was born healthy. I sighed. He was wonderfully cranky, beautifully agitated, and fresh. He existed with all the parts intended to support his physical survival. He is a nice light brown and thin-lipped like his father. His hair was fine and straight and nothing like the clutter of curls I wore when my birthing was complete. His eyes were large with wonderment and since they were married to the lighter, thinner looks of his face, they did not seem aggressive or oppressive. They seemed . . . awake. When I saw him I said aloud "I didn't think he would be this cute." The nurses laughed, his father smiled, I sighed.

I threw away the pending shame that loomed over my pregnancy, for he was here and the darkness has not devoured him. But as the days passed and he grew, his straight, fine hair began to curl at the root. This curl, as his father puts it, was evidence that his hair would be "nappy, tough, and rough" like mine. Days after the days passed I asked his father how long it would take for his real hair to grow through. How long would it take for it *nap* up? He didn't know. I waited. I waited to see how his hair would grow out and if his skin would stay the same pretty color it was.

I have seen other babies near me and far away. Some were light, brown, dark, white, tan, mixed. They were all lovely, but whenever I saw a dark baby I felt like I was obligated to take on the task of finding the beauty that should be there, but was hidden beneath their darkness.

The shame that swaddled these thoughts was locked in my silence. I loudly declared with my hair, my clothes, my literature, and speech that the darkness, Black like me, was the way to be. When I said it I believed it. Sometimes I still do. But then, I look down at his sweet, brown face and relish in and at the sight of him. And, inside of myself, I sigh a sigh of relief that drips thicker than the concealed contempt I have for the darkness that I can only love in public.

It would be commonly pleasant for me to end this on a beat of wellness and acceptance; to say that I have learned my lesson and resolved this outstanding issue. Alas, the truth prevails and the truth is that I haven't. I am still ashamed and afraid of this skin and appeased by the verity that my child, unlike me, will not have been left victim by the darkness. I sigh.

Birthing My Goddess
H. Bindy K. Kang

My father's migration to Canada was floated on a dream of a new beginning, fully equipped with possibilities and a transformation from poverty to the "immigrant dream" of financial stability and comfort. My mother's hand in marriage was "arranged" by her parents who also knitted and tilled dreams of escaping poverty. What they left behind was everything. A language they could easily dance with, family and friends they grew up with, a space in time they could live and dream in. After my mother's arrival, my parents had their Punjabi Sikh wedding, the *Anand Karaj* (the ceremony of bliss) at one of the oldest *Guruduaras* (Sikh places of worship) in Canada. The bliss was followed up with my prompt arrival nine months later, while my sister, three years my junior, was planned. Our births were marked with gratitude and joy. We never felt the chill of not being a boy until much later. And never did we feel it from our parents. Family members would comment that it was unfortunate that my parents didn't have a boy and only had girls. I would overhear these comments and see sadness behind a mask of indifference on my mother's face. My father never showed sorrow. Maybe it was there, hidden somewhere, behind that neutral mask. But maybe, just maybe, he didn't have any sorrow. The sadness I saw in my mother's eyes was deeper than sorrow, it was shame for not being able to produce a son.

I was a child that always needed answers, so after hearing one too many of these comments and seeing the look on my mother's face, I confronted them.

Why do people think you need to have a boy?

People just think so.

But why?

When girls get married, they leave their parents but boys don't, they stay with their parents and look after them.

Why can't girls look after their parents?

Because they get married and look after their husband's family.

I am not going to get married, I won't leave you, and then, you don't need a boy.

A smile crept on my mother's face and that was the end of that conversation. My parents tried to have a third child, but they weren't successful until years later. My mother thought she was experiencing the early stages of menopause (at age thirty-nine) but she was pregnant with my little brother. When my parents found out they were expecting, the doctor asked if they wanted to know the sex of the child but after a short discussion, my parents declined the offer because it wouldn't change anything—they would still have the baby, they would still love the baby and the baby was a gift from the Divine. As my mother relayed the news to my sister and I (both in our teen years), we thought she was joking until our family doctor called and without a hello, enthusiastically shared: "Congratulations, it's a boy."

While the home front was soft and calm, the extended family began a dizzying demonstration of weird questions—asking my mother what she had eaten, chanted anything special, did a special type of worship ritual, basically, what had she done to bring on this little boy miracle. This crazed excitement frightened me. What was it about this boy child that made him the miracle baby? What could he do that I couldn't? Carry the family name? At that point, I was still never going to get married and I was going to take care of my parents. But even if I did get married, I would take care of my parents (which is exactly what happens in most families). I love my brother, with all of my heart, and I am happy to have him just the way he is. I was involved in his care from day one, his baby smile lit up our family, his toddler laughter filled our house with a refreshing happiness—but if he were a girl, all of this would have been true too.

What was wrong with my family? Why wasn't the sex of the children as important to us as it was to our extended family?

I always go back to that eight-year-old explanation that in Indian society, a boy child represents old age security because he will take care of you, provide food, shelter, clothing and medical care. He will take you to the doctor, he will protect you from harm and 'he' will be there when you pass away.

Years later, my eighty-three-year-old grandfather was on his deathbed. He had four daughters living locally and four sons (ten children in total). The four daughters organized their lives around his hospital stay and saw their father every one of those last eighty-eight days. The four sons visited infrequently. Just before his passing, my grandfather shared his regrets, his last stories and his last words with his daughters. The most poignant was that if he could have a life re-do, he wished that he could have had ten daughters.

Our household, to all extents and purposes, was feminist. My parents shared all of the household and childcare responsibilities. Both parents worked outside the home. And when my brother was born, my father was on a pension and was his primary care provider. In some Punjabi households, the men were privileged with patriarchal benefits of being the rulers of the house. But that was far from our family culture.

My parents were Sikhs, and we, children, adopted Sikhi as our way of life and our spiritual space. Sikhi originated in Northern India in the 1400s with the first teacher or Guru, Guru Nanak Dev Ji, who challenged the status quo. He didn't believe that we needed spiritual conduits to reach the Divine, so no priests, no Brahmins, no Imams, we could connect with the Divine individually. There was no hierarchy of caste or class in his philosophy—everyone was equal. Devaluing women and girls was challenged—particularly with the ritual of sati (widow burning), which the Guru banned. I grew up in this progressive religion in which women were equal to men, where everyone was equal. The first scriptural Sikh mantra is Ek Onkar, which represents a philosophy of oneness. If everyone is one, there are no hierarchies, no one at the top or the bottom.

I often heard of the devalued position of women and girls in Indian society. But I always thought that the Northern state of Punjab, where the majority of Sikhs reside, was different. There would be more people like my parents. Sikhs have spiritual teachings that do not devalue women and girls. Despite an egalitarian religious philosophy, many Sikhs have continued to see girls and women as less than their fathers, brothers, husbands, and sons. Sikhs aren't supposed to put stock in the caste system but our last names give away our caste identity, and many Sikhs don't appreciate marrying out of one's caste. As progressive as our spiritual philosophy is, the cultural backdrop has yet to be confronted and abandoned.

Being born in Canada, many people would think that I have it "good" because I don't have to live with a particular brand of sexism, but Canadian society is not removed from sexist beliefs and values. There are gender barriers, there are double standards, there are binary roles—the packaging is just more sophisticated and subtle.

Being born outside of India, in a family that looked, talked, and walked like feminists, I have had the opportunity to be critical, to question these stagnant beliefs that position me, and my gender at the bottom, at the back, or even render us invisible. My voice is as loud and vital as any man's. My views are essential. I am valuable to my family, to society, to my ethnicity, to my religion, to my nation and to humanity. I matter.

Before I became a mother, gender discrimination always spiraled my attention into its destructiveness; now that I am a mother, all of this matters exponentially more. I bridge today's reality to a future that will honour my daughter for her gender. I bridge my dream of equality to a pragmatic reality. I bridge this mirage into something tangible, touchable and edible. The bridge, the bridge that I must be, requires a constant engagement with people who say things like "boys are better," or cage children into strictly policed gender-boxes. I long to see a place where my daughter never feels the shadow of invisibility, the second-classness of her gender, or that somehow she is less than the XY configuration.

During most of my pregnancy, I purposefully excluded gender markers when thinking of her, or talking about her. Whatever her gender was, she was wanted and loved. She was wanted and loved before she was even dreamt of. She or he or somewhere in between didn't matter. My partner and I were going to be guardians of this little soul and we would serve, protect and love whoever arrived. We would reach deep into our own souls and find a limitless love that would shelter our child from anything we remotely saw as dangerous, and we would wrap our child up in hope, light, and love.

As we moved through the pregnancy, we decided that we wanted to know the sex of the baby so we could prepare. We wanted to have her name picked out and the clothing organized. We wanted to be ready to welcome this little soul and be (somewhat) prepared for the monumental transformation from being a couple to being parents.

My partner and I are of South Asian ethnicity, specifically Indian lineage and our ancestral roots link us to the Northern Indian state of Punjab. We both grew up in Sikh households and I, more than my partner, identify Sikhi as my spiritual path. We were both born and raised in British Columbia, Canada. And we want to raise our children here.

My doctor has known me for the past fifteen years but her receptionists don't know me as well. I informed my doctor that I would like to know the sex of my baby. And she suggested that I have my ultrasound done at week twenty-one so that the technicians would be able to better identify the sex. In British Columbia, the sex of the baby is not investigated for non-medical reasons before week twenty. The federal government introduced the Assisted Human Reproduction Act in 2004 to legislate the use of reproductive technologies. Among what is not allowed under this act is the use of reproductive technologies to select the sex of the baby. Because the local health authorities will not do abortions after week twenty for non-medical reasons, informing parents of the sex of the unborn fetus after week twenty should not result in sex based abortions— so that is why we have to wait until week twenty to find out the sex of the baby. The local news media has reported that communities in British Columbia and Ontario with large South Asian populations or large Asian populations have disproportionate numbers of male births. While the Assisted Human Reproduction Act does exist, Canadians can easily access sex-determining ultrasounds prior to week twenty and also access abortions just across the border for a fee. Some American clinics are purposefully advertising in South Asian and Asian newspapers because these target markets are known to have a preference for boy babies.

When the receptionists were told to schedule an ultrasound appointment at week twenty-one for me, they all began asking why I wanted to know the sex of my baby. The newest addition to the reception staff made faces as she called the hospital's ultrasound lab. She purposely booked my appointment in week nineteen. I asked her why she did that and she said, "Well, that is what they had." I called the ultrasound lab the following day and re-booked my appointment for week twenty-one.

When I returned for my check up two weeks later, again, I was bombarded with questions: "Why do you want to know?" I joked about being a Virgo and needing to be as prepared as possible. But that answer did not suffice. If I was white, this answer would have been good enough. But I am not white. My name screams of difference. My skin announces ethnic stereotypes long before my non-accented Canadian English surprises onlookers. I am catalogued into a homogenized identity that South Asians are baby girl killers. Writing those three words: "baby girl killers" makes my stomach churn and suffocates my heart. I am not sure I can even leave it in this text. I am so broken and tattered with the notion of female infanticide. I am horrified that I, a feminist, a Sikh, a woman, a mother would be linked to something so revolting and criminal.

Week after week, my desire to know the sex of my baby was brought up. Week after week, I felt as if I had to defend myself. Week after week, I could see what floated through their eyes as they watched me, I could see their eyes looking at me like I was a part of this heinous violation against humanity.

When I did finally have my ultrasound, I poured out a river of defensive chatter, how I like to be prepared, how my partner and I really want a girl, how I am a feminist, etc. so the stereotype of the 'baby girl killer' would not follow me. I would sacrifice myself before I allowed any harm to come to my child, how could anyone think I would kill my baby? Me. How?

The results were inconclusive. They were 75 percent sure it was a baby girl so we had a 3D ultrasound done. She was a girl!!!! All of the most amazing yipees, yays, va-vay-vaas!!!! I released a sigh of gratitude. I could use the name I had secretly held in the furthest corners of my soul. My partner was elated, and felt overjoyed that he was right that she was a girl. I cried tears of joy. Years before, while completing my master's degree, I researched feminism and Sikhi. Out of dusty library stacks, I serendipitously found a book on Sikh women with my daughter's soon-to-be name nestled in one of the stories. To capture the beauty of her name, we spelled her name phonetically to maintain the Punjabi pronunciation. Her story echoed the fundamental Sikh principle of *Ek Onkar*, of one-ness, that "there is no enemy, everyone is one." My daughter's name is a constant reminder that we are one, living in a flow of oneness, even when we are repelled by each other's differences.

With the shopping done, the name in place, we eagerly awaited for Dayven to arrive. As Dayven grew, my womb expanded and my blossoming belly became a discussion site for strangers, acquaintances, friends and family members. When I went to drop off my partner's dry-cleaning, the owner politely asked how far along I was. Then she drifted into a conversation about how I was carrying and how she was certain I was going to give birth to a boy. Both of us share Punjabi ancestry, so I felt I needed to tell her that I was happy to be having a girl. When I announced that it was a girl and how happy we were, she looked at me puzzled and remarked that there was no way I was having a girl: "You are carrying like you have a boy." No matter what I said, or how loud I said it, she was adamant that I was having a boy. Along the way, I had numerous conversations with strangers and neighbours of South Asian or Asian ancestry who claimed that I was having a boy—never leaving room for the possibility it was a girl. I started to wonder: if by saying it was a boy, and denying the vagina I saw in the 3D scan, are they collectively willing a boy? Perhaps it was to uplift me from the sadness I must be feeling underneath my gleeful, radiating smile?

One person did say, "Well, maybe the next one will be a boy." Trying to come from kindness, I began my baby-girl-monologue about how happy I was to be the mother-of-a-daughter and what an honour it was to birth a Goddess. The polite stare I received in response left no more words between us.

When the voices of disappointment didn't reach me, they landed with my feminist siblings. One day, when my sister was visiting my uncle and his family, questions regarding the baby's sex began flying around over tea and samosas. My sister excitedly reported "it's a girl." My aunt responded, "Don't say that, how could you say such a thing, you had a boy first, how could you wish that on your sister." My sister, a fellow feminist, began her baby-girl-monologue about how we, in this generation don't believe in favouring boys over girls. After a number of back and forth exchanges, my aunt finally whispered that she couldn't help herself, this is the way they grew up.

While it was convenient to pigeon hole that generation as bowing to the silent, audible, and deafening institutionalized patriarchy that had seeped into our collective consciousness, the voices of younger cousins began echoing the supremacy of a boy over a girl. When my fourteen-year-old male cousin asked if we knew what the sex of the baby was, he refused to accept that it was a girl, and continued to reason with me that having a boy is better, and that I should be wanting a boy first. As his older brother stepped in and told him to shut up, I wondered if he was suggesting that I abort this child so that I could configure a boy first?

Throughout my pregnancy, I was humbled by the creative Goddess energy housed within my body. Upon her arrival, my little Goddess filled my heart with the deepest joy I have experienced. As her beautiful body lay in my arms, she was my heaven. I finally embraced my own Goddess nature, I stood alongside Durga, Saraswati, Laxshmi, Quan Yin, Sitara, Athena, Isis and Mother Nature. I am so honoured to have joined the mama warriors before me, with me and who will follow me.

I share this piece because I have such reverence for motherhood, for the power of a woman's body, for the feminine, I am so humbled by the shakti force within the female body. As a mother Goddess, who gave birth to the same energy, to another Goddess—I continue to wonder, how can the feminine be devalued?

Within the Punjabi culture, a new mother may return to her natal home to be cared for forty days by her natal family. I elected to spend a few weeks with my mother Goddess. At Mom's home, I received numerous visitors, mostly from our large extended family and everyone excitedly greeted Dayven with love and kindness, and of course the customary awwws and coohs that babies elicit. One of my aunts, has three sons, and has longed for a daughter of her own. During her baby Dayven visit, she reported that she was hoping to adopt a baby girl from India. Everything in my being has longed to adopt at least one child, so I was glued to her every word.

As my aunt sipped her tea, she began sharing the horrific details of an interview she had recently heard on a local Punjabi radio station. A female doctor was visiting Vancouver and participating in a host of interviews about current-day female infanticide in Punjab. While my aunt shared the doctor's story, I covered Dayven's newborn ears, I wanted none of this trauma to slip into her soul. I left the room with tears streaming down my face, wishing I could have done something. Even now, I shiver from the images that were seared into my heart and soul as my aunt imparted this act of institutionalized and culturally sanctioned violence against the feminine.

The doctor and her husband were on a rural medical outreach visit and after finishing up at a temporary clinic, they were walking along a dirt path and noticed dogs attacking something on top of a pile of dung patties. The doctors couldn't make out what was being attacked, but they felt a chill, something was not right about this picture. As they got closer to the dogs, they made a gruesome discovery; these wild dogs had ripped a baby girl's body to pieces. This baby girl's family left her on a pile of dung patties to be ripped apart like an abandoned animal carcass.

My daughter sleeps soundly a few centimeters from me, and every cell in my body would protect her from harm. That baby girl was no different than my daughter, the same alert baby eyes taking in the bright new world around her, the same laughter that can bring joy to the darkest moments and the same sweet skin to kiss a million times over. But my child lies on top of an organic soy-based mattress, safely sleeping while her mother lioness watches over her. That baby girl deserved to live, to be cherished, and loved. That baby girl deserved to be a baby, a child and a grown woman, instead, that little Goddess was ripped to pieces by wild dogs while her parents, grandparents, aunts, and uncles were safe and sound somewhere.

After weeks of reading of female infanticide, sex selection abortions and surplus male populations, as my daughter slept in my arms, I went to my mother with a web of questions. I could not understand how this was happening in the Sikh dominated state of Punjab. The same Sikhs, whose religion espouses gender equality?

Mom, I don't understand, why did they kill girl babies in Punjab?

I don't know.

But did you ever hear about this? Maybe in the village? Someone distant in the family who had done this? Supposedly it is still happening and Punjab has one of the highest problems in India?

Bibi (mom's mom) used to tell us that her Dadi (paternal grandmother) would kill off the girl babies born to Bibi's mom.

But why?

I don't know, if it was a girl, she would kill the baby, but your grandmother survived somehow, and one of her sisters, but the rest were killed by their own grandmother.

But if you keep killing off the girl babies, how do they expect their sons to get married, there will be no girls left to become women?

I know, and that is what used to happen, in a family, only one brother would get married and the others remained shurdhay (without a mate).

But was it because of the dowry, what was it?

Well, in the old days, the Muslims would carry off (abduct) the girls, and the families wouldn't want their izzat (name, reputation) ruined so they would just kill off the girls, so it wouldn't happen.

But what if their daughter never got abducted? Couldn't they protect their daughters? And how was it girl's fault if she was abducted? Why kill her?

That is what they did in those days.

After my painful journey into the literature and my family history, I return to contemplate how the preference for sons and subsequent murder of daughters can be written on me. Unilaterally, placing all South Asians into the category of daughter-murderers is problematic. Not all Muslims are suicide bombers, not all white men are serial killers, and not all South Asians have a preference for boy children. While Canada boasts a multicultural ethos, Canada was founded on the white colonizer identity where Aboriginal and visible minorities are under the watchful gaze of the declining European-ancestry-majority. While racism has moved from an explicit, colonial space into a softer, implicit form, racism still thrives in Canada. "Paki, go back to where you came from" sits side by side with "but why do you want to know the sex of your baby?"

My movements as a South Asian ancestry Canadian mother were and are under surveillance. While I agree with having regulations to prevent sex selection abortions and any and all types of violence against children, targeting specific communities as "baby girl killers" furthers the notions of us and them. It expands dominant racist ideologies that magnify the "backward" cultures of the undesirables.

I want to conclude with a letter to my daughter (and her future siblings) in the hopes that she will never feel the patriarchal chill of the "boys are better" camp. I also hope that it inspires more of us to question dominant ideologies that undermine children's freedom to run through their own fields of happiness.

Dear Dayven Kaur (and her siblings),

I dreamt of you long before you were conceived. I dreamt of you before I could even fathom becoming a mother. I knew I would hold you in my womb with the warmest embrace. I knew that each moment you grew inside of me, I would know that Divinity existed. A miracle such as you could not happen without the hand of something more powerful than us humans could imagine.

I want you to know that when you grew inside of me, I thanked every Goddess and God, from every tradition, for the miracle of you, my daughter. I found your name within the pages of a book on eminent Sikh women. Your name means the Divine and the Sikh woman who held your name in the 1600s believed in equality and the principle of *Ek Onkar* (oneness). When we knew you were arriving, as a daughter, your father and I cried tears of happiness—the kind that we have never felt before. My heart has expanded beyond my human body, beyond my everlasting soul and beyond all space and time. I love you without boundaries, without conditions and without contradictions.

I am here to serve and protect you. And I will carry out this sacred honour beyond my grave. My soul has given itself over to being your mother, a mother that will not rest. A mother who will support you to dream grand dreams with red, luscious curtains and your personal orchestra. I want you to do what moves your soul. I want all of the goodness inside of you to fearlessly exist in everything you do. I want you to dance to your internal, Divine rhythm and forget the boxes the world confines us to. I want you to have wings of freedom, to do what your heart desires. I hope that the wisdom of your foremothers and forefathers graces you at a tender age but, that you still can run through fields of wild flowers without worrying about dirtying up your shoes. Your body is a temple for your soul. Every cell, every neurotransmitter, every breath is your body worshiping your soul. I want you to always remember your sacredness.

A long ago time, our ancestors thought girls were a liability. That a girl didn't belong to her family so there was no need to invest in her beyond the basics. Things have changed. Your grandparents were feminist. Your grandparents never treated your mother, your aunt or your uncle any differently because of gender. Your grandfather washed dishes and cooked alongside your grandmother, while your grandmother mowed the lawn and shoveled the snow alongside your grandfather. They defied the social roles they were expected to follow. Our legacy to you is that you are valued. You deserve to be showered by our love and we promise to give you every opportunity possible to follow every dream, no matter how whimsical or grand—your dreams are our dreams.

You have the gift of life. Whether you become a mother or not, your body and soul are equipped to create the miracle of life. If you can create life, you can create anything. Always remember that your footsteps may humbly walk upon the earth, but you are Divine and sacred.

You come from a strong line of women, of Goddesses and I promise you, you will always be embraced by your mother's sisters and foremothers. You will always have their arms for comfort, and to hold you up when the world doesn't want you to stand as tall as you are. You come from a father who sees your Goddess nature, you come from a grandfather who sees nothing but brilliance in you and you come from an uncle who marvels at the miracle of you, and all of your cousins.

You are my greatest blessing. You are my miracle. Your existence makes me want to fight for justice, so that the world is a better place for you. For you, I am a radical mama, whose voice will never be silenced.

Forever, and ever, your loving mother,

Harminder Bindy Kaur

Night Terrors, Love, Brokenness, Race, Home & the Perils of the Adoption Industry:
A Journey in Radical Family Creation
Terri Nilliasca

First year together. Luis wakes up three or four times every night, in the throes of grief. The child experts call it "night terrors." He is like a wounded, raging lion. He thrashes, screams, and cries. He doesn't see me and when I try and hold him, he arches his back, goes stiff, recoils at my touch. He holds his tiny hands in tight furious fists. He is burning hot to the touch, sweat and tears course down his face, down his neck, soaking his clothes. He reaches his hands up to the sky and cries, "Mama! MAMA!"

I ache for children. I identify as a Filipina feminist, radical, and queer, but still I ache for children. Even knowing the politics of compulsory motherhood, the diagnosis of infertility was like standing at the edge of a dark, endless abyss. My spouse and I have dreams of raising radical children and passing on our values to them. I have dreams of being the mother my mother never could be and mending that torn place in my heart.

I am unable to have biological children because I have endometriosis. Endometriosis is a disease linked to environmental degradation and exposure to PCBs, an industrial byproduct. Did it matter that my mother, as a child, swam in the most polluted river in Asia, the Pasig River? What does it mean that many of my family continue to live next to that river?

Most of the time, there is nothing I can do to stop his raging, terrified moments. But I am his mother now, and it is my job to heal the wounds, to put salve on his scars. So I try. I try to hold him to my body, even though he screams "NO!," even though he pushes and kicks and howls. When I carry him, he gets quiet, his eyes wide, haunted; sometimes, he sighs and goes back to sleep, other times, he goes right back to the rage when I try and lay him down.

After much soul searching and discussion, my partner and I decide to adopt. We decide this even though we know that the adoption industry is a minefield of class and race contradictions. Next, we decide the only place that we will adopt from is the Philippines because even though I was born in the United States, I still think of the Philippines as my homeland. Many of my family still lives and struggles there. If we are not able to adopt from the Philippines, then we decide that we will not adopt at all.

I find an adoption agency that assists U.S. citizens adopting from the Philippines. She tells us about the requirements to adopt from the Philippines: we must be married and we need a letter of recommendation from a church (preferably Catholic). So we get to use our heterosexual privilege; my partner is a man and we are married. And then there are the unspoken requirements, the money to pay the agency, the airfare, and all the immigration fees. She also tells us that because I am Filipina, we get preference when the time comes to be "matched" with a child.

We need a letter from a church. How would we do that? We "join" our local church, we give money every week and we shake hands with the parish priest. We try to ignore the anti-Semitism during Easter. Since I was raised Catholic, I feel personally responsible every time the priest said "The Jews were jealous of Jesus," so I lean over to my Jewish partner and say "I am soooo sorry." After a symbolic nine months, we work up our courage and ask the priest for a letter of recommendation and then we flee the scene never to return. I can still hear an imaginary Catholic nun telling me that I will go to hell for what we did.

Aida doesn't have the dramatic night terrors like her brother. She wants to suck on a bottle all night, even when it's empty, she holds onto her bottle like her lifeline. She cries all night, softly, intermittently. If I try to take the bottle from her, she grasps even tighter. The only way she will sleep is laying on Jeff's chest, while he rubs her back all night.

Every prospective adoptive couple is required to have a homestudy, conducted by the agency's social worker. It consists of several interviews and home visits. But unlike welfare recipients, there is no searching of our house or intrusive questions about our sex life.

Cindy is younger than me and white. She is fairly kind and eager to help us adopt. She asks Jeff and I questions about our marriage, how we solve conflict, how we met. We try to keep our answers innocuous and harmless and uncontroversial. We hope she doesn't notice the giant poster of Lenin on the wall.

The other day, we went on our first visit to the twins' pediatrician. We asked her for advice, describing the tsunamis of emotions, the unrelenting frequency, our attempts to wake him up. She recalls, "You know, I moved to this country from India when I was five to live with my parents, whom I hadn't seen since I was a one-year-old. I didn't know them, I was terrified, I was lost. I think that you should stop trying to wake him up, just let him feel what he is feeling."

We ask the agency if we could adopt a family member from the Philippines. My family is living testimony that remittances don't work to break the chain of crushing poverty in the Global South. We have a least three generations who have worked overseas (called overseas foreign workers or OFWs in the Philippines). Even today, I have cousins currently employed in Saudi Arabia, Macau, Hong Kong, Vancouver, Italy, and on cruise ships. They all send money, and I send money, but still my family is what activists in the Philippines call the urban poor. I have cousins that live three feet from railroad tracks. Remittances have given them the money to buy a TV and pay for clean water that they pump and carry over the tracks to their home. We want to adopt a child from my family and share the familial responsibilities. But the agency discourages us from this route.

The agency explains that if I tried to adopt a family member, then in the eyes of the immigration system, I am subverting the immigration system. This statement casts a clear light on the adoption industry. The industry and the accompanying immigration laws, act to facilitate and accommodate the needs and desires of a privileged, first-world consumer of brown, third-world babies. In trying to adopt my family, I become an average brown person trying to get more of my family into the United States, not someone to be helped or encouraged by the adoption industry. So we go back on the path of every first-world adoption family; we wait to be matched with our children.

Informal adoption, is very common in the Philippines. My family is poor, but they often take children whose parents are unable to raise them. We are filled with children who are being loved and raised by people other than their biological family. But adoption in the western sense: formal, bureaucratized, monetized. This is not so common in the Philippines.

In the morning, Aida is hugs and smiles. She laughs and plays in the house and with us, our small family. But as soon as she leaves the house, she goes "out of service." Friends, family rush up to greet her, but she will have none of it. Her eyes slide off of the intruding stranger. She stares past them, her huge black eyes like blackout curtains. There is a permanent air raid warning, enemies flying overhead at all times, she will keep the curtains closed. At times like this, she won't acknowledge any ties to anyone. She is in overdrive, self-protection mode. She won't allow me or her father to hold her/ comfort her. She is "out of service." If I reach out to her, she will walk away, eyes large, serious, and focused on some far away point. I sit near her, until her sense of danger passes, and she can reach for my hand again. In the end, she always let's me back in, and I am so grateful and awed that she can reach across the abyss and find me.

It is early January, and I have just arrived back from five months in the Philippines. The agency calls, "you have been matched with twins!" Cindy says that their names are Leona Aida and Luis and they are twelve months old twins. That's all the information we have until three days later, when she sends us two pictures. Aida looks like an old soul and Luis looks like a new one. We gaze at their pictures and we feel terror, excitement, joy, and grief. We feel grief because we know that it was only tragedy that brought our children to us. We don't fool ourselves into the adoption narrative that we were meant to be together or that we are saving them. We know that in the best world children are raised by their biological family and in their home country. But we leap ahead, eyes open and arms wide open.

Soon the packet for traveling families arrives. The information inside is written for future white families that have never left the United States. There are tips as to how to get your passport and why they should guard their passports with their life. These are typical tips about not drinking the water and avoiding street food. The proposed timeline assumes that the adoptive family will want to remain in the Philippines for as short a time as possible; in fact, the packet states, that they can stay for only three days, if they so desire. The paperwork also tells us that it will take four more months of paperwork processing before we can go to the Philippines to pick up our children.

I call the Agency and ask if I may go to the Philippines right away, and start a slow transition with the children. I would like to go and visit them with their foster family while I stay with my family. For me, four months in the Philippines is ideal. I will spend time with my family and work at slowly getting the children accustomed to me. The Agency liaison with the Philippines is shocked by my question—no one has ever asked this before, she says. She quickly says no, she explains that they are entirely unprepared for the process I suggest, and she tries to shift the blame to the foster parents, explaining that they perhaps they would not be ready for this kind of process. Looking back on it, I wish I had pushed harder for this transition period, because it would have helped our children tremendously. While any separation from their foster family would have been traumatic, it would not have been such a giant, volcanic upheaval as the one they suffered through. But I don't want to do something or say something that may jeopardize our adoption, so I don't push back. Again, we accept the process that was created for first-world adopters, and we stay in the United States and wait.

Tonight, I just sit next to Luis's bed. He screams and reaches into the night and I try to breath calmly and slowly. This takes a real effort. Because the noise of him, the forlornness, the physical pain of it, makes the hairs on the back of my neck stand straight. My heart races, my palms sweat, adrenaline pumps through my body. FIGHT! FLIGHT! But I can't do either so I learn to sit and breathe, breathe. Deep breaths in the dark next to my poor, hurt lion cub of a son. I wonder how long will it be until I am his mother in his heart? When will I be able to comfort him with my scent, my breath, my murmuring voice? Twenty minutes passes and the lion is my sweet, sleeping boy again. I fall asleep too, on the floor, next to his bed. There will be another night terror in another hour. And I will be there to witness his heart-rending grief, his torn, flooded landscape. The doctor's advice was good. The lion wakes up less and less.

The day finally comes. The medical exams, the U.S. Homeland Security check, the Philippines passport—it's all finished. It's time to book a flight and a hotel. The Agency's travel guide says to book a room at the Intercontinental hotel. The Intercontinental is a typical first-world hotel that helps first-world travelers to maintain all of the luxury of the first world despite being in the third world. I have never stayed at the Intercontinental; in fact, I never even visited that part of Manila. I call the agency and ask if I could book a hotel close to my family, instead. Again, the Agency liaison says no, everyone ALWAYS stays at the Intercontinental, she says. She frets that the social workers in the Philippines won't be able to find me at the hotel I prefer, even though the social workers are Filipina. So my partner and I plan to arrive a week before the scheduled "turnover" in order to spend time with my family. After a week, we transfer to the Intercontinental, with the plan to go back to the hotel near my family after the transfer happens.

Suddenly, we wait in the opulent lobby of the Intercontinental hotel. Our social worker arrives and we get in a car service and go to the Philippine adoption agency office. There, we wait in a conference room for the arrival of our children. Finally, we see them, being carried by their foster mother and foster sisters, the Razon family. They are sixteen months old, they can walk with authority, and they run with a toddler's gait. Luis has a bottle in his mouth. Aida has her hair in intricate cornrows, the last time she ever let anyone put her hair in tight cornrows again. They both cling to their family. They have been loved and nurtured by their foster family since they were three months old. All the people in the Philippines that helped facilitate this adoption come to the room and greet us. We ask the foster family questions like: what are their nicknames and where do they sleep. As never before parents, we forget to ask important questions like: what is their bedtime routine. They come to us with nothing of their life with their foster parents, except the clothes and shoes that they are wearing and their bottles. The ceremony is short, we share stories, light candles, and suddenly, the children are placed in our arms, and the foster family leaves with tears streaming down their face. We bring Luis and Aida back to the Intercontinental, where they fall asleep instantly. When they wake up, they cry inconsolably for three hours until they fall asleep again.

Second-year together. They take my hand to go down the stairs, and Aida says, "It's like we are one big family!" She still doesn't like parties or crowds or meeting new people, and loud sounds will send her diving underneath a table or pulling herself inward and drawing the black-out curtains over her eyes. Luis's night terrors still happen, but now only two or three times a week, instead of several every night.

Every day, they want me to read to them the story "Owl Babies." It's a story about three baby owls that wake up to discover their mother gone. They wait and worry until the end of the story when the mother comes home. Luis and Aida wait breathlessly until she does.

At the four-hour cultural sensitivity course, required by the adoption agency, they mention with approval the adoptive mom that would have Russian borsht once a week or during "Russian day" at their house. At our house, we eat like Filipinos every day! We eat rice, sardines, dried fish, and various Filipino specialties. Our kids fight over the fish eyes and the brains.

And now they are six, which they declare proudly to any adult who will listen. My partner and I never take for granted the simple trust between us and Luis and Aida, the kind of trust that, I imagine, most biological parents take for granted. Every time I pick them up at night to move them and they melt in my arms and in my scent, I breathe a sigh of relief and gratitude to them for loving me back and trusting me with that awesome love.

The adoption agency sometimes sponsors cultural visits back to the home countries, where the adoptive children see their country as visitors and tourists. But we plan to return not as visitors, but as "balikbayan" (the people who return to their home county). Finally, after five years, we are all returning back to the Philippines, and like every Filipino/a balikbayan, we have begun the ritual of collecting food and clothes and gifts to bring back to our family. We describe the cousins they will meet and the river they will swim in and all the fish they can eat. And we are bringing back one of my cousin's children, who couldn't arrive on her petition and had to wait three years for his own petition to be approved. So our children know that, he too, was separated from his mother. We raise our children with my aunt and her daughter, my first cousin, both of whom immigrated here from the Philippines two years ago and live with us. We talk about the homeland of the Philippines with all the yearning and nostalgia of every immigrant. We Skype with our family still in the Philippines.

Will all of this help them as they grow older and understand fully the broken feeling they still have in their hearts? We have to believe that it will, because my love and my partner's love is not enough. I think they need the love of their/our people and a country to call home, and we hope we can give them that.

From the Four Directions:
The Dreaming, Birthing, Healing Mother on Fire
Irene Lara

For my daughters, my students, my teachers, and my self

My radical mothering approach to becoming and being a mami is infused with a holistic, spiritual worldview grounded in the evolving teachings of my indigenous and mestiza ancestors. To claim one's whole self as a bodymindspirit in the face of dominant worldviews that would have you split yourself is radical. To write as a mother and erotic woman, inside and outside of the university, is radical. To teach—your children and your students—from a spirit-permeated place of trust, love, and vulnerability is radical. In this piece, I share aspects of my dreamworld-life expressed through a Xicana decolonizing feminist lens that I attempt to embody and ensoul every day. I performed an earlier version of my narrative at San Diego State University, at a spring 2010 Health, Healing, and the Humanities Symposium that I helped to organize with my colleagues in the Women's Studies Department.

Drawing on the wisdom of several of my teachers, con respeto, I dedicate my narrative to the four directions: south, the place of the children, associated with the earth; north, the place of the ancestors, associated with the wind; west, the place of women, associated with the sea; east, the place of men, associated with the sun. I am still learning about the ways the directions nurture and teach me. I do know that they help me to tell these stories with integrity, and in the process, help transform and heal me and everyone who dares to radically listen with open heartminds. This is what radical mothering looks like for me, a Xicana scholar, writer, teacher, dreamer, and mami to my two young daughters, Belén and Xóchitl. A woman who works to mother my own creativity into being.[1]

---

1   Like Audre Lorde, I believe "we can learn to mother ourselves" ("Eye to Eye: Black Women, Anger and Hatred," *Sister Outsider: Essays and Speeches by*

Dream facing south—from the earth

Dear human child to be, I'm finally asking for you, envisioning you, planning for you. I've imagined you a little spark, waiting, traveling around, coming around—no, still not ready—waiting, more traveling around . . . And now I'm finally inviting you and you're actually here, meeting me all the way in Italy. But I'm getting scared and tell your papi maybe not, maybe not yet, maybe I do not want to become a mom, ever? I'm rethinking, I'm overthinking, I'm rethinking, I'm overthinking but then your papi and I open the door to our room in Florence and I start laughing: belly laughing, full of tears laughing, laughing in spite of the fear laughing, letting go of the fear laughing. My body—the earth's body together laughing, spirit-matter together laughing. I know I truly *do* want to have a baby laughing. Because Michelangelo's framed art depicting one version of the moment of Creation is on the wall over our bed and Tonantzin comes all the way from Tepeyac to remind me, "First you make the prayer, then you do your part in making the prayer come true."

Dream facing north—from the wind

Storytelling with my firstborn, Belén, on our sacred family bed, years later.

Playfully, I ask if you remember the day you were born, *el dia que te di a luz*.[2] Serious, almost solemn, you respond, "*Sí, no podía salir.*"[3] Could I have given you that memory? Or was it all your own? I do remember telling you that you emerged with your "*Sí se puede*/Yes we can!" hand next to your head. But I don't remember telling you it was the reason for the extra long pushing I did at the very end. *Sí Belén, es cierto*,[4] you couldn't get out for quite a while. Imagining that you do remember our birth-day, I can imagine that you must have known it was time to get to the light. It was your

---

Audre Lorde [Berkeley: The Crossing Press, 1984]), especially with the help of our loving ancestors, with spirit, and in community. Also see, Alexis Pauline Gumbs, "Mothering Ourselves Manifests" on the *Feminist Wire*, http://www.thefeministwire.com/2011/01/mothering-ourselves-manifests/.

2   In Spanish, "dando a luz" literally means giving to the light, and is commonly used to describe the birthing process.

3   "Yes, I couldn't get out."

4   "Yes, Belén, it is true"

time of *panoltia*—a Nahuatl word that means, "to pass, convey something [or] someone from one place to another." Your time to make the crossing. And my time to make the crossing. Like all of our ancestors. Together, *sí se puede.*

Belencita, one of your favorite games since you were about two and a half years old is to pretend that you are about to be born. "*¿Jugamos que estaba en tu matriz?*"[5] you'll often ask me as we are getting dressed in the morning. After showering, I'll bundle you up in a decades-old Mexican San Marcos blanket, a red wine and cream-colored blanket with an image of a deer that I carefully arrange around you so that only your eyes are peering out. Our ritual began as a way for me to keep you entertained so I can brush my hair, apply lotion to my legs and arms, and otherwise finish getting ready for the day. It soon became an opportunity to teach you what birthing is like and for you to remember what it was like to be in my womb and then be born.

Now, as I retell the story, *me llega el conocimiento*[6] that our game is also a ceremony that provides us both with a healing occasion to rewrite our birthing story to be less traumatic. Instead of the three *hours* of the last phase of me pushing and you trying to push through, of *panoltia*, of conveying ourselves from one place to another, you are born within three *minutes.* Yahoo! I give thanks to Tlazolteotl, the Nahua sacred energy of birthing and regeneration and patron to midwives and birthing women, who may very well have gifted us *con esta ceremonia.*[7] A playful reminder that every day we are reborn. Every day we can work toward our own healing.

As we play, sometimes I will pause between whatever I am doing to profoundly breathe, simulating the moments before you were actually born. Sometimes I hold my belly and lean back, open my mouth and my *panocha,*[8] just like the Tlazolteotl-like Mesoamerican birthing figure on the altar. "I think she's coming . . . here you come" I excitedly say as you synchronize your emergence from the tightly wrapped blanket. We always celebrate when together we make our way through *nepantla*[9] *y aterrizamos,* together

---

5 "Can we play that I was in your womb?"

6 "I receive the awareness"

7 with this ceremony

8 vagina and/or vulva

9 An in-between place, "a transitional space."

we land, body-spirit together and transformed: "¡Yay, bienvenida a la Tierra, Tonan, little one!" Welcome to Mother Earth, little one! We did it! This is you daughtering and me mothering at our best.

Dream facing west—from the sea

Soul traveling, pregnant with my second daughter Xóchitl, a year later.

Heart beating, enter my room, with walls of brick, to find two teen girls, my daughters in the future. They are waiting for me, in our room, made of brick. Sure, steady, certain, they listen. Heart beating, I say, "The water is rising, mother sea is getting closer, the surges keep coming. We must decide: do we hunker down or do we head upland, try to escape the sea. She keeps coming, the water is rising." At a crossroads, in our room, made of brick, we must decide. But I do not want to Fight or Flee. I want to Be, in our room, facing west, at the crossroads, letting go, with the sea, with my daughters. My newborn and my newborn fifteen years from now: Xóchitl and her nineteen-year-old sister Belén. My daughters now and in the future, sure and steady, filled with certainty, an ancient certainty, a knowing from the future, showing me all is fine, all will be well. The water will subside. We are here. We survive.

Dream facing east: from the fire, the sun

Sunrise, Xóchitl's birthday, months later.

I cannot stop looking. Spreading like warm red corn oil over the porcelain white tub. I cannot stop looking. Blood. Still flowing out from me. I cannot stop looking. The blood that is me, there, on the birthing tub. I cannot stop looking. The crimson current grows. I do not *want* to stop looking. I am not afraid of the brush fire of blood forming at the site of my birthing. Roberta the midwife is helping me birth my placenta and I am bleeding, profusely. Iridescent blood, marbled with sea, 3D on this birthing altar-tub. I am not afraid. And I am aware that I am not afraid. I am in awe. In awe with myself, with the unfolding of my self who is body, a birthing, bleeding body, generating heat. "Don't look at the blood," Roberta firmly urges. She speaks from the wisdom of midwifing a thousand women before me. But I cannot stop looking. I have been preparing for the blood ever since I met Fear at my first baby's birth. When I looked Fear in the face, wrestled with her, took her in and bled her out.

Look with me. Do you see her? Not Fear. Me, the dreaming birthing healing mother on fire. "Don't worry, we survive" I reassure her. This is our new beginning.

Full Circle: Center

Facing east, facing west, facing north, facing south
Moving, forming a circle
Here, in the direction of the center
Here, shaped by my dreams, the dreams birthings bring
Here, shaped by my births, the births that dreamings bring
Making Face, Making Soul[10]
Showing Face, Showing Soul
Unmasked, with you
In all my warm splendor and wet abundance
In humble gratitude

10 Drawing from Nahua philosophy, Gloria Anzaldúa describes "making face, making soul" as the process of constructing and simultaneously remembering your identity. See "Haciendo caras, una entrada," *Haciendo Caras/Making Face, Making Soul: Creative and Critical Perspectives by Women of Color* (San Francisco: Aunt Lute Press, 1990), xv–xxviii.

What Does the Daughter of a Chicana-Lesbian Teenage Mom Know About Having Babies?
Panquetzani

I was pulled from her canal, yanked into the world
bruised face
swollen eye
suction-marked cone head
eyes wide open

My undrugged mama screamed
"I wanna go HOME!"
"Why does it have to be this way?!"
two months 17
bleeding on her back, legs spread
begging Sterile men
who knew nothing of
feminine strength
maternal affection
Mexican culture
innocence butchered

We cried for days after that.

My genetic memory of FEAR
rage-shame-longing
loss of self-worth
as a young Indigenous woman
rebirth themselves as subconscious emotions
manifesting themselves throughout my life journey

A grown woman now

I inherited Strength
finding other ways to cry
giving birth
to myself:
a life partner
Mother of two
an artist

Squatting over my bedroom carpet
painting bloody pools
with a pubic hair paint brush
onto a backdrop of:
potty-training urine
Food-in-the-bedroom
size 12 muddy Lugz
Stainz.

Sending my guttural RAAARRR to all women giving birth
that fierce moment in the universe
a force my ancestors felt
from Tamoanchan
every cell in my body about to explode
flowers Bloomed
prisons went up in flames
my Compton neighborhood gossiped:
"Either someone's giving birth or getting murdered in that house"

No one called the cops
when both happened that rainy 9:55 PM
birthing my purple boy wrapped in an umbilical cord necklace
no Doctors, hospitals, pharmaceuticals, vaccines
Just me.
murdering my memory of birth as a newborn
my lineage has been cut free
with the snip of his cord
nourished with his suckle on my breast

Now, with his warm, newly born body
in my arms nuzzled tightly against me:

I want the Doctor
who spanked my newborn bottom
ripped my mother
cut her
ignored her pleading
and then FORGOT HER . . .
to look at me
A WOMAN without a degree
ASK and learn finally
what I know
about birth.

VI.
Between the Lines

Introduction
China Martens

I made my first zine, *The Future Generation*, in 1990, because motherhood was the impetus to communicate with others outside the lines like myself. I set out to help create an information-sharing network with others as we lived in this world and tried to build another world we wanted. My zine's influences grew from the Reagan era "No Business As Usual" actions and anti-apartheid divestment sit ins, Rock Against Racism punk rock shows, those concerned for ecology, gender nonconformists, and anarchism in its many forms. I watched others make subculture media in the form of flyers, zines, records, and distros so I knew what to do when it was time for me to start something of my own. I wanted to create new alternatives and seek out new ways of living as well as many of my peers. As my daughter grew, the world changed and zines went through different periods of popularity, waning and waxing. At a certain period, zines seemed to me to lose some of their radical edge of understanding independent media made from those who seized control to print what the mainstream would not, but the creation of zines was always a small connection, a letter, not always hearing back, taking some dedication to remain part of and then on other days worth it. Over time, I made more connections until I found myself; through the internet, connected to others, and then one day connected to a whole new generation of radical mother of color bloggers. I learned about networks and communities they had been building for decades. My respect for these media makers renewed my faith again in the media we make. When I met her at the 2009 Allied Media Conference, Maegan "la Mamita Mala" Ortiz (Vivirlatino) told me, "We all move towards mediums of information sharing that feel organic to us and they are all valid." Noemi Martinez (Hermana Resist) has been another influential media maker in my life, a zinester that helped me make the leap from zines to reading blogs. It is predominantly radical women of color media makers who have made the most use of the blogosphere, in my opinion, whose work has helped make greater connections as well as to give the best tools to fight against white supremacy, as well as racism, sexism, classism, and other injustices in this country. It has been women of color bloggers and other marginalized media makers who have most helped inform my rebel path, expanding clarification in continuing explorations of race and class to build the worlds we want and to reject what is killing us. So many letters and conversations, works, and efforts in a world where often for a mother there is no time to spare. No time to oneself to use the bathroom, no heaven of a morning alone, and no time to read beyond a short magazine article or online snippet.

Time traveling is a necessity. We need to tell our stories. Sometimes in a patchwork fashion like my grandmother's patchwork quilt across my parents' bed, we read each other's words in different places and times—and read between the lines. This is essential for us to communicate with each other, to break our isolation into movement as well as to fall back into the spaces between space, now and again.

The purpose of writing, the sacred nature of writing, of self-expression via print, manifesta, collective testimony or theatrical script—to witness heal, resist, and build another way; shifting paradigms and universes—of creativity in its many forms, of exploring and organizing thoughts, making discoveries about yourself and the world, growing and communicating—this is for you. Respect, dignity, justice, this is for you and for everyone. Everyone has their part to play; we can do more together than alone. Actions and words, practical deeds and dreams, this is how we build tomorrow.

Collective Poem on Mothering
Mamas of Color Rising (Austin, Tejas)

It's Hard
It's Tiring
It's Painful
But
It's Love
It's Joy
It's Peace
Mothering is an act of social justice
Creating a community of solidarity and support
That models the way we want the world to be.
Using that collective strength to challenge
Injustice
And build alternatives for ourselves and our communities.
How are the children?
How are the weakest in our society treated?
Parenting socially just people.
There is enough for each of us.
Let's share
Stories
Food
Hugs
And laughter.
If we can embrace
Ourselves
Our children
And our community
Give and find comfort and safety
Without hiding truths.

Mamas of Color Rising
Our Core Values
January 25, 2009

This poem was created through a collective process in which the members of Mamas of Color Rising individually and without knowing what the Mama before her had wrote, expressed what Mothering is.

Telling Our Truths to Live:
A Manifesta
tk karakashian tunchez

---

1. Telling our truths to live

In telling this, I am bearing witness to my own experience as a single, teen, welfare, queer-femme m/other at a private, liberal arts college, and I am bearing witness to my own experience as a student at a community college, because both of these experiences are equally important and valuable and are pieces of a larger, universal narrative. In telling this, I am bearing witness to mama-love, to days spent behind books and hands wrapped tight on steering wheels while the sun burns down, building worry filled pockets on foreheads cuz you can't afford to pay the late fee at the childcare and your professor won't let you leave that class early and the electricity got shut off because your student loans ran out and you got just enough money to afford some gas to get to class today but not enough for heat this month.

I am bearing witness to the joy that comes from finally telling our truths; to sisterhoods and brotherhoods that form coalitions; to phamilies with a ph, that are chosen and stronger than blood; to life-sustaining networks full of our tribes, our communities, our peoples, the ones who "get" it and don't need no theory based language to express it cuz they can say it with their eyes.

2. Offering recognition

I sing praises and thank the sisters and m/others and mamaz who have paved our way, because they are so often overlooked, silenced and written out of our institutionalized histories.

Yet they haven't given up, and refuse to hold their tongues at institutions that will use voyeuristic lenses to construct elaborate ethnographic (read: anthropological) studies of "single-mother subcultures," rather than support the actual m/others that are part of the institution and then question why retention rates aren't higher.

I give praise for mamaz, because we keep on "showing up" with our kids. We do more than discuss the theoretical value of liberation. We practice lived, beauty-full and fragile liberatory models in our daily lives, constructing curriculums far more intricate than anyone will ever use in any classroom and practicing on the very most precious relationships we hold, our families, our communities.

3. Honoring our collective histories

We know that many of us come from long-lines of storytellers and folklorists and artists and community builders who used popular education models, long before that phrase even existed, to subvert and resist. We come from a long legacy of community and individuals who knew how to survive. It is in our blood. We are prophets, future-readers, story-keepers, media-makers, and builders of schools with dreams. We hold graduations through ceremonies under stars, and in our legacies we are educators that hand down centuries-old knowledges.

4. Naming the ongoing work that m/others and mamaz are doing wordwide

We believe education is liberation.

We work to free ourselves.

We create our own models of lived educational structures.

We encourage and support each other and create communities and movements that include crafting, healing, transforming, liberating, and reclamation of agency through truth telling.

We do not distance ourselves from our personal truths while in academic settings because our personal is beyond political, it is quintessential.

So, we craft community classrooms, and serve as mentors, recognizing there are so many of us participating in these educational settings and that we won't allow "opting out" to be the only option. We won't be squeezed out or silenced anymore.

We embody and model our vision for shared power and equity through being our sisters' (and brothers') keepers. We create our own grassroots childcare systems, caring for each other's children and bearing witness to our sisters and brothers struggles. We accompany each other to medical, advisor, welfare, housing, court or any other form of bureaucratic appointments to advocate *with* each other and then provide each other the space to tell our truths and heal afterward.

We stand up for each other, straight, queer, gender variant, and trans when we are harassed by campus police who frequently are not held accountable for their actions and mirror the city and state police brutality that is so often found in our communities.

We fight for welfare rights AND create candlelight dinners for our loved ones, creating tables filled with feasts at which to celebrate our joys and challenges, and bring our families into kitchens full of laughter when there is no food to share.

We recognize and value space for self-care, lived and fully experienced sexuality and gender exploration as acts of resistance by consistently investing in and creating spaces where we love ourselves, despite the fact that we know our society has criminalized our sexualities and devalued our self-care for centuries.

We recognize that our differences, including our disabilities, may be sources of strength, beauty, and change and we recognize that ableism disproportionately affects communities of color and working-class communities.

We celebrate immigrant rights, workers' rights, indigenous resistance, disability justice, and educational rights, because mamaz have always been involved with (if not at the forefront) of these movements.

We support self-determination models of care for our communities and share resources from institutions for the good of our greater communities. We have created and are organizing (both in and out of academia) organizations and movements that are by us for us, from Gris Gris Lab (New Orleans, LA), to Mamas of Color Rising (Austin, TX), to POOR NewsNetwork (San Francisco, CA), and INCITE! (a national organization). We value our ability to educate ourselves, leaving space for learning, mistake making, and growing; because, after all, we are mamaz and realize that this is part of our own growth cycle.

We provide health-care, self-defense classes, and counseling services for families and sisters who cannot afford overpriced institutional and privatized health-care, and we honor traditional knowledges and forms of healing, such as acupuncture, homeopathy, doula services, curandismo, etc.

5. Affirming our vision: A call to action

We know that academic institutions are built on our backs and continue to profit from us, and therefore we have the right, responsibility and obligation to influence and impact them: Re-forming, Re-mapping, Remembering! As leaders and members of international movements we demand institutions that support our work while honoring and supporting us as the complex individuals that we are.

We are not interested in pursuing academic gain at the expense of sacrificing our financial stability or personal growth.

Do not ask for us to sacrifice, hide, or otherwise deny our valuable mama out-of-home-AND-in-home work. We recognize that attacks on this mama work are grounded in anti-feminist, classist, racist, and sexist ideologies.

We are aware that the double standards that permit and support academic institutions to maintain firmly grounded positions that do not service or accommodate their student bodies are the same double standards that coerce our nation's citizens into believing we live under a democracy. The power-down, two-partied systems that share similar values and support patriarchy are NOT intended to support OUR liberation. Furthermore, we recognize oppressive institutions and systems when we see them, and we are not afraid to name them. Let's get real clear about how we, single/teen and welfare mamaz, are not encouraged to pursue higher education degrees systemically, by institutions and by teachers, administrators, and the workers of the welfare system. Through our labor and off our backs hundreds and thousands of lower-income positions are filled. Our children are pipelined into low-paying jobs to keep our country running and our jails filled, while we continue to be criminalized and portrayed as welfare-abusers. We work systems like webs and weave ways for each other, and ourselves, to make it, even when we're told we shouldn't because WE ARE WELFARE QUEENS AND WE AREN'T ASHAMED TO OWN

IT. And so, NOW MORE THAN EVER BEFORE, WE DEMAND EQUITY AND SHARED POWER IN OUR SCHOOLS AND COMMUNITIES.

To this effect, we declare our need for childcare, health-care, and reasonably paying jobs.

We demand the right to unionize our labor, demand access for all class levels to ALL institutions of higher education and call for experiential learning credit to be given to us for our unique life experiences.

We demand professors who are eager, not just *willing*, to work with us. We honor those professors who work endlessly to support our work and create spaces for our voices.

We demand safe campuses and communities for all.

We will no longer be the silent partners in the telling of our histories by others. We demand representation of us that is created by us and for us, locating ourselves in our own histories. We have harnessed the media's power to tell our own truths.

To fortify, empower and strengthen ourselves, we search each other out and, upon finding each other we create communities and participate in ongoing conversations so that we may learn and grow with each other; locally, nationally and internationally, online, and through convenings.

We know we are valuable. We aren't waiting for you to recognize it. WE WILL, AND DO, CREATE OUR OWN INSTITUTIONS and we will continue to tell our truths to heal, vision, and live.

Love Balm for My SpiritChild
Arielle Julia Brown

"People might think that things happen by chance or accident, but God knows the truth."
— Bonnie Johnson, Grandmother of Oscar Grant III,
Love Balm Collaborator

When I disembarked from my RwandAir flight on June 16, 2010, in Kigali, Rwanda, I was completely naïve to the fact that this trip would trigger a soul revival for my artistry, community alertness, and love for justice. I traveled to Kigali, Rwanda as a part of an international delegation of artists and scholars led by American playwright Erik Ehn. The 2010 Rwanda/Uganda trip was in its eighth year. Each year the delegation goes to the Interdisciplinary Genocide Studies Center in Kigali to bear witness to the 1994 Rwandan Tutsi genocide. The delegation also travels around the country, witnessing for survivors who need to share their stories. We also went to witness for the dead, those victims of the 1994 Tutsi genocide whose bones, in some places, still lay out for public viewing. The act of witnessing on this trip works against a consumption-based, cannibalistic voyeurism working instead to create a greater listening space within each of the artists in attendance. The act of witnessing on this trip also works to combat genocide denial in Rwanda and internationally. For the witness, this trip requires committed physical, intellectual, and spiritual presence with life and death, injustice and justice, oppression and hope.

While in Rwanda, one of the collectives of survivors for whom we witnessed is Ineza. Ineza is a sewing cooperative of women survivors of the genocide. All of the women in Ineza were raped and intentionally infected with HIV during the genocide. They now work together to create clothing and accessories that they later sell on the international market to earn money to pay for their HIV treatment. This collective is not only for sewing but also for witnessing and holding. These women are each other's family. They are each other's support system. In finding support, empowerment, and hope in each other, they are empowered to share this revolutionary love with their children. Many of the women of Ineza have adopted/claimed several children that were orphaned as a result of the genocide. These women, as they boldly rear their children, are radically, physically, communally, emotionally, and spiritually fighting in resistance to death.

The Rwanda trip triggered in me a greater alertness to the interconnectedness of the unhealed hurt and oppression in Rwanda and in my own communities in America. The 1994 Rwandan Tutsi genocide was the most recent of several Tutsi massacres that have occurred in the last sixty years. In the Tutsi genocide, an estimated eight hundred thousand Tutsis were murdered in a period of a hundred days. Every year since this genocide, the month of April is reserved for mourning and commemoration of the dead. Witnessing Rwanda sixteen years post-genocide was an honor and a charge. I was charged to share the testimonies, spirits and hope that I was privileged to witness.

The art that I witnessed in response to the genocide was very community-rooted and impactful. One of the national artistic themes in reference to the genocide was articulated as "Never forget, nor (re)member." These artists in Rwanda seemed to fight to find a balance between addressing the resurging trauma of the genocide and imploring their communities (and themselves) to be present in hope and grounded in their aspirations for the generations to come.

During the course of my trip, preparations were underway in Los Angeles for the trial of Johannes Mehserle, the Bay Area Rapid Transit Police Officer who murdered Oscar Grant III on the Fruitvale BART platform in Oakland on New Years Day 2009. Mehserle fatally shot Oscar in the back, execution style, without true apparent cause. Oscar was a childhood friend of mine. We grew up in church together and our families are close. His grandmother, Bonnie Johnson, is my godmother. Oscar's death was a personal loss for us who knew Oscar. It was a loss on so many levels of community for us to traumatically witness yet another Black youth unnecessarily discarded by the police in Oakland, California, the United States of America, North America, and the world. Witnessing in Rwanda provided me with just that prism through which to see how communal memory operates on personal, local, regional, national, and international levels.

As Oscar continued to come up in conversations among the delegation in Rwanda, I correspondingly began to see how in this African country many people are able to find space to honor the living memory of the loved ones that they lost in the genocide through cultural commemoration. In Rwanda, there were not the resources to try all of the genociders in the national courts, so the ancient Gaccaca system was reinstated to enact justice throughout the country. The Gaccaca courts are local courts where communities meet on an individual basis once or twice a week to witness and lend testimony regarding various acts of genocide. The traditional sentence for a genocider under the Gaccaca system is six years in prison with seven years of community service. Needless to say, many (if not most) genociders in Rwanda have been released and are now back to being neighbors with survivors of the genocide. However problematic the Gaccaca system was, it did work to ensure that the process of enacting justice worked on a local community level. Community members witnessed for each other while grief found a collective space.

In the case of Johannes Mehserle murdering Oscar Grant III, however, the trial was re-located from Oakland to Los Angeles. Subsequently, Oscar's community was not even afforded the basic right of being able to witness this trial locally. Perhaps one of the greatest crimes in the murder of Grant was that his memory had been relegated to merely that of "the twenty-two year old Black male shot on a BART platform" by the media. There was no communal space in the judicial process for grief or community witnessing. There was no space to share or convey the value of Oscar's life before and beyond the moment in which it was taken. There was no room for the memory of Oscar to be full and comprehensive. Perhaps a more comprehensive national memory of him would have signified the true weight of his murder.

The final systematic stage of genocide is genocide denial, just as the final steps in the murder of Grant were apparent in both the systematic belittling of his memory and the judicial injustice. Genocide denial and counter-memory work hand-in-hand to erase any historical document of the value of the murdered person(s). After seeing the verdict of involuntary manslaughter, I began to consider justice for my communities as something much more expansive than the American judicial system could afford. I began to consider commemoration and memory as conduits of justice.

Mothers, I find, both in Rwanda and in the United States, are among the greatest conduits of commemorative justice. So after arriving back in America, I took the first opportunity I had over the summer to go to Oakland and spend some time with my Godmother. I spent a couple of days at Oscar's family's house in Hayward. I took the time to fellowship with the family and collect Bonnie Johnson's personal testimony. Her testimony, however humble in tone, screams of the radical love she employed in the raising of her grandson. This testimony, along with transcriptions from the Rwanda community journal, would later become the root and inspiration for an original theatre of testimony workshop series I created for mothers entitled *Love Balm for My SpiritChild.*

The inaugural *Love Balm for My SpiritChild* workshop series began in December 2010 with a total of six mothers/collaborators. The Atlanta workshop series took place between December 20, 2010, and January 2, 2011. The four part workshop series created the space and creative framework for the women to construct their testimonies grounded in their own lived physical, spiritual, and activist-inspired memories. The series concluded with a reading of the mothers' testimonies on January 2, 2011, at 7 Stages Theatre in Atlanta. The performance date was chosen to commemorate the two-year anniversary of the murder of Oscar Grant III. Following the reading, we held a candlelight vigil for all of the community children who have fallen victim to systematic violence and police brutality in our communities. All of the proceeds from the reading were donated to the women/mothers of Ineza in Kigali, Rwanda.

Since this workshop series and performance in Atlanta, the Love Balm Project has grown to engage with mothers based on the San Francisco Bay Area. In the Bay Area, the Love Balm Project has hosted workshop series for mothers and youth, performances in traditional theatre spaces and cultural centers and site specific performances in the spaces where youth were murdered.

Excerpt from Atlanta Love Balm Testimony Series

*(On stage, the women are sitting in a
circle. The audience forms an outer
circle around the women. The women
share their personal testimonies as well
as some testimony written by Arielle Julia Brown,
including "Straddling Two Coasts" and
"A Tribute to The Virgin Mary of Nyamata Rwanda."
All of the mothers are in a praying position.)*

SELENTIA

When I was a child, Mama used to pray in a language I did not understand but I could feel its power.

You have another chance at this
Life
Inside
It's giving you another chance

To right the wrongs
To learn more of yourself
You're birthing a mirror
Look into it and thank God
For another chance

SHEILA
(Straddlin' Two Coasts)

I swear some days I feel like Im straddlin' two coasts
Murky muddy waters rush 'tween my legs
Warm and violent —Ruled by the moon
Bloody sediment runs up and down my ankles
It exfoliates my toes.
I'm ashamed. Standing here lookin' like this
Vulnerable like this
Soakin' in my own filth
Heavy hot(n)hurtin like this

Papa said "close yo legs"
Mama warned I'd loose alla my eggs

And all old church ladies cud do was hummm
Mmmmhhmm — Tryna give birth in the middle o de Atlantic, I
'ono who
She thank she be?

Wit my hips swayin in misty salt-water tide.
Aint I, caint I be a mama too?
Wit babies born of outstretched flesh
Free as they WANNA be,
Wit bloody red sediment creepin up they toes . . .

I Sheila pledge to Love this boy child raised by a 27 year old with
nowhere to lay her own head. My mama told me all my life "you
gonna learn things the hard way."
Why I gotta learn the hard way, why you didn't teach me how to
LISTEN.
No you just left it up to me to pass this mess to another innocent
SOUL. I can't teach what I wasn't taught . . .

And I guess I had not explained all the RULES, but I know I DID . . .
Never answer the door when Mommie is not Home.

I am working
Child Is Home Sick
I can't miss work Its Only
My INCOME we live off of.
And I can tell you the prices I have paid.

I've moved from the hood to the suburbs tryn to make sure he had a
better understanding of LIFE than I did so hopefully we could stop
the CURSE—

My Son is home alone at the tender age of 8
A Man comes to the door
he does not know quite what to do

he finally got scared and slammed the door.

The repo Man called me and said he will be calling DeFACS since I don't know how to pay my bills or raise my Son.
But I have earned the title of MOM. What is Mom? A Maniac on a Mission to raise my son with wisdom, love, and understanding.
A mother's memory is sometimes sweet and sometimes bitter, but Christopher, he makes me laugh, cry, strive.

SELENTIA

A Tribute to Mother Mary and all of her fallen children in Nyamata, Rwanda.

SIMONE

resistance
proof of what happened in the presence of God
Inside they came
blew open the door
thrust
in
Murdered all
Now all of my children's clothes lay dripping
on the pews
where people could have prayed
the altar
stained with their blood
Is too literal
For anyone's use
And against my eyes,
I play it over and over again.
My malignant iris'
Are worn from over use
And My house
still smells like death after 16 years
And I heard my children
Hollar in the
Heat of a distant afternoon
I can still hear them in the
Yonder

Low down
these secrets
dropped under layers of green
where life is abundant
I greet a baby still inside her mother's stomach
both of them decomposed.
These children of mine,
they are survived by me,
and I hold them
even in death
flesh of my flesh
suckle at my breast
for
peace
while heaven infiltrates heavy clouds
for justice

*(All mothers assume a praying position.
As they complete their prayers, they pass
the candle to the next mother.)*

LOREEN

When I was a child, my mama used to pray "lord bless me to live long enough to get my children out from under the feet of others.

SIMONE

"Father, please cover my children and give me the strength to be a good steward for You. Bless them; cover them; watch over them and grace them with your presence and your instruction. Amen."

SHEILA

Gotta give those babies a safe haven. Gotta give those babies a safe haven . . .

This too shall pass. God never gives us anything without providing for it.

SANDY

Now Lord beholding my children, I am thankful every day that you have given me this honor to be a mom. For now, I behold the 'Lambs', the precious Lambs of God. My children who I sacrificed myself daily just for the honor of beholding 'My Precious Lambs Of God'.

When I think I have done all I can
I have been the best mother I could be
Yet my child is *still* taken from me
Lord, I ask that you let me just 'STAND'

LOREEN

Lord bless me to live long enough to get my children out from under the feet of other people.

All mothers are powerful.

SELENTIA

When I was a child, Mama used to pray in a language I did not understand but I could feel its power.
Now beholding my children, I have interpreted that language and now know it has power.

Love never fails.

END OF TESTIMONIES

Love Balm for My SpiritChild Manifesto

Love Balm for My SpiritChild: Testimonies of Healing Justice through Mothers' Memory is a workshop series that was constructed out of a need for a space in which mothers who practice revolutionary motherhood in the rearing of their children (as they were spirits yet to be born, as they live/lived and as they are spirits yet passed on) can share in creative communion with one another.

Love Balm for My SpiritChild was inspired by the revolutionary acts of mothers fighting for justice for their children after their children were murdered. It was specifically inspired by how mothers' memory has served as a vehicle for justice in the cases of the Rwandan Tutsi Genocide, Oscar Grant III, Amadou Diallo, Emmett Till, and so many more. The performance workshop is rooted in testimonies and monologues from the revolutionary mothers of these children.

Revolutionary mothers employ everything from radical teaching pedagogies to empowering spiritualities in the raising of their children. Tapping into these epistemologies, this workshop series explores mothers' memory as a political/spiritual/creative force, energy and historical document that works in resistance to systems of domination and fights for a healing justice that only these women givers of life can reclaim. This workshop series works to inspire internal healing for mothers in personal and communal mourning. This workshop explores the ways in which mothers' memory is used on personal, familial and communal levels to enact justice. The series works to honor and nourish the spirit of loving and healing justice for mothers.

Love Balm for My SpiritChild engages mothers in the community who identify with having been affected by the murder of personal and communal children. Women in the workshops are asked to bring in their own experiences as mothers fighting for justice for their children. Workshop activities include creative writing, the reading of testimonies and monologues, performance building and constructive dialogue. Through this process of communal creativity, participants in this workshop share with each other the love balms of healing justice that they gift to their children in their fight for liberation. The performance of these testimonies work to infuse the collective consciousness of our communities with a new sacred awareness of the precious healing found in mothers' memory.

"You Look Too Young to Be a Mom"
Excerpts from *Girl-Mom*, a Play Created from Posts to GirlMom.com 2001–2003

Lindsey Campbell

Projected above the stage:
GirlMom.com is designed and moderated BY and FOR young mothers. GirlMom.com is a politically progressive, left-aligned, pro-choice, feminist website. GirlMom.com intends to support young mothers of all backgrounds in their struggles for reproductive freedom and social support. We believe that all teenagers are sexual beings with the ability to love, procreate, and nurture. We believe that teenagers have the innate ability to parent well but are socially conditioned to believe that they are irresponsible and reckless. We believe that such social conditioning often creates a self-fulfilling prophecy, in which teenage parents believe that they cannot parent well and move on to not parent well. We believe that in order to solve the "problems" associated with the "epidemic" of teen pregnancy; we must reassess and change our collective social attitudes toward teenage childbearing. We believe that in order for teen parents to succeed, they must be encouraged to do so and assured that they are capable. Degrading, vilifying, marginalizing, and rejecting teen mothers (as is customary in our society) is counterproductive and illogical. Teen mothers will succeed if allowed the opportunity. When a teenage girl finds herself pregnant, it is one of the few times during her life course where she will not only be expected to fail, but socially encouraged to fail. We believe that encouragement and support beget success. (Allison Crews)

The screen changes, it now reads:

Girlmom.com
Our users have posted a total of -73460- Messages.
We have -1723- Registered Users.

This play is based on actual posts to that message board between 2001–2003.

"You look too young to be a mom"

GM2: See, 22 isn't really young for having kids. Really it isn't. But I found myself quickly saying to complete strangers "Oh I just look 18, really I'm 22." Like, explaining that would make them like me more. And not think poorly of me. Me? Oh, no, I'm not a "teen mom." But then I realized how stupid that was. Cause who cares if I'm 15 or 25? I am a great mom! And what the hell did they mean "oh you look *almost* too young to be a mom"?

GM9: I stopped caring what people thought at some point and it seems the message has been sent out to everyone.

GM36: I am 20 now.

GM9: I remember points where someone would say something rude to me because of my age, or give me a look that hurt.

GM62: People look at me like I committed the biggest crime. I hate the looks that I get.

GM36: By no means do I feel too young. Like I need to be ashamed. Like some people try to make you feel out there, being young and pregnant.

GM9: I didn't know what to do; I usually just stood there and tried to fight crying. But now, it's different.

GM3: I think we get those looks because we are so damn gorgeous! We're in a youth worshiping culture after all.

GM9: I don't know if I look slightly older than I did when I was 15 and pregnant, probably not. Still look young just don't have the braces.

GM36: I would rather have a baby while I am young anyway.

GM9: My daughter is 2.5 now and I am 19 and I rarely get comments or stares. Like, hardly ever.

GM31: When someone asks me my age, I answer . . . And then, I ask them theirs.

GM62: No one understands the situation, and no one bothers to ask either.

GM9: I don't really think this sudden change in people is because I look a tad older, more the way I act.

GM31: Ignore, ignore, ignore. But if you can't do that, rude comments work great too.

GM21: *(giggling)* Alli always says:

GM1: *(raising her fist proud)* Fuck all y'all. I'm from Texas!

GM57: *(laughing)* Yeh! Fuck. This. Shit.

GM36: Although finances aren't as stable as one would hope, this way she will learn that you have to work for things. That not everything is handed to you on a silver platter.

GM5: I'm fortunate enough to be Black. It's something that I can't hide (To many, I'm just a n*****.) Because, others went before me with their heads held high and asserted their right to be, so can I.

GM9: I don't hold my head down when I am outside. I play with my kid and act however the hell I want.

GM5: I extend that to my sexual identity, my religious affiliation, my socio-political beliefs, my parenting style and the abbreviated age difference between me and my daughter. Just one of the aspects of my life that flies in the face of the judgmental, control-freaky, moral right.

GM9: I guess it comes with time. Maybe it depends on your community too. I moved from a mainly upper class, rich-as-fuck town, to a big working class not-so-rich place. Maybe that is part of the difference.

GM74: Bella is 4 and in pre-school. The parents always want the kids to get together and have parties and the like.

GM3: I think I was lucky to find a few people that were open minded enough that I could relate to.

GM74: I am so painfully uncomfortable at them.

GM3: I feel uncomfortable at soccer or baseball game get togethers. It's funny how the kids that he becomes close friends with, they DON'T have certain normal, typical, two parent, "accountant type parents." Our kids have more in common.

GM74: They are all in their 40s.

GM75: All of T's friends have parents that are these middle aged married people.

GM74: Even though they probably aren't. I think that they are just sitting around, judging me.

GM75: They intimidate me. They also seem to have money. I'm embarrassed to have them over to my one-room apartment.

GM53: I think I'm doing a great job; I am so content being a parent. It's not easy and sometimes I question my sanity. But it wouldn't be any easier for me at thirty-five years old. Money is tight, but love is abundant in our home. And that's a lot more than some rich families can say.

GM5: The first time I ever talked back to my dad was when he accused me of thinking my baby was just a doll to play with and put away when I was done. I asked him if he ever got up every two hours with any of his kids. Changed a diaper. Washed vomit out of their AND his hair. Woke up with their pee soaked into his mattress. Wrote a six page analysis of *The Color Purple while* breastfeeding. Or had to sit by the door in all his classes, so he could go into the hall when his teething baby cried. My dad has the utmost respect for me.

GM77: You know nothing about me, and I am a great mother. And I am very proud of my child and I am not going to act ashamed of the fact that I brought a person into this world. Flaunt it; be proud of your amazing child!

GM78: You created a miraculous life. Show that kid off damn it! Don't let anyone bring you down!!!

GM63: I do not ever feel ashamed. I could never feel ashamed.

GM9: Ashamed? No. Angry? Yes.

GM52: We will not be ashamed of our choices, our kids, or the way we're living our lives.

GM76: No, I don't feel ashamed. It was my decision to keep my child. I refuse to be ashamed of my decision.

GM9: I am an eighteen-year-old girl.
I am a mother to a 2-year-old girl.
I am a college student.
I am a single mother.
I am breastfeeding my toddler.
I am so thankful that my child chose me to be her mother.

The girls all begin to repeat lines over top of one another overlapping their "I Am" poems. Depending on cast size actors can choose their own favorite "I Am" poems and read overlapping. Just play with it! The last line heard should be the last few lines of GM31's "I Am" poem.

GM36: I am 20
I am gay
I am expecting my first born child this October
I am a high school dropout
I have lived through tough times
I use every good and bad experience to grow
I am constantly changing

GM65: I am 20, soon to be 21
I am a mama to Juliet who is my daughter and my closest friend
I am a writer
I am a bleeding heart
I believe, I dream, I hope

GM33: I am a womyn.
I am mother to a beautiful little person.
I am strong, and my voice is loud and clear.
I have a body, which produces children and food.

GM11:   I am a Mommy
I am 19
I am gay
I am happy my children are healthy

GM31:   I am single
I am strong
I am stronger for leaving him
I doubt myself
I laugh at myself
I hope that my daughter will always look up to me and know that what I did,
I did for her
I regret not breastfeeding
I am a high school graduate
I am in college
I am NOT a statistic and don't think any of us are
I am me and
I am fine with who that is.

Letter to Aymara

Micaela Cadena

Aymara Nayeli.
tu eres la mas loca del mundo.
tu eres mi vida. y te quiero muchiiiiisimo.

Having you made me who I am. You have brought me beauty and balance and keep me believing in a better world. I didn't plan to be pregnant when you happened, but I was meant to be your mama.

In the circles and communities of women we live in, I've learned so much about creating families and raising children. A few months ago we were at a Promotoras del Parto Natural training (natural birth promoters) in Albuquerque's South Valley. It was part of the Young Women United (YWU) / Kalpulli Izkalli Promotora Apprenticeship. So we were hanging out with lots of mujeres, women of color learning about pregnancy and birth and caring for each other and community through these reproductive cycles. Many of the "regulars" in our life were there: Nandi, one of the amazing midwives close to my heart, your tia Boo of course, Sylvia, Aysha, Adriann, Andrea, Syrena, Jocepha, Kirbie, Caitlyn, and probably a few more.

But to say a little more. I believe you are a brave soul in picking me. I drive myself crazy with the little I know about all the things going wrong in the world. Basically, you are brave because to wake up reflecting on an unjust world is not easy, and you wanted to join my journey anyway. I say you are brave because in choosing me you will by default be exposed to lots of reality that with our social privileges could easily be avoided. So you will wake up with me, holding stress and responsibility and obligations to doing our piece, being part of movements to a better world. And to be real: I had you when I couldn't handle the rest anymore, you brought me center and grounding. Right before you came around, I realized that I couldn't keep doing social justice work without solid/deep/

extended community and love . . . an abundance of love that makes things good in the moment and always. So much of community that I was seeking, I was already building, but you are the piece that makes it real, and makes it work. You make it so that wherever I exist, I carry enormous/grand/unconditional love.

You were born at home. This experience changed me and shaped what I want to do with the rest of my life. Our homebirth happened with Luna y Sol midwifery, with Ruth and Terri, two of the most conscious, radical, and giving white allies I've come across. From there, my belief in homebirth (as a valid, safe, legitimate, AMAZING in a million ways) birth option grew. I wholeheartedly believe that every woman should have access to this option. Of course, as so much else in the world, a woman's access to birth options is shaped by race and class identities, among other things. I started to think more and more about all the ways pieces of identity, like race and class and sexual orientation shape the way mothering happens. And through YWU, I've been blessed to be a part of national conversations about these things. We've been calling ourselves Revolutionary Mamas, and have begun identifying issues affecting our lives, finding common experiences and collectively organizing as Mamas of Color. Being your revolutionary mama is the way all the parts to my life come together . . . in love and struggle, beauty, and solidarity.

And there is one more thing. As usual, because with me, there always is. I always thought I would have more than one child. Once I had you, I realized that wanting more wasn't about me, but about what I wanted to give you. You are all I would ever need, you complete me, make me happy beyond imagination . . . so it's about giving to you. I can't imagine my life without my sisters. They are dear friends, and confidantes, and would stand by me in any situation. They are the people who get where I came from and will continue with me to care for our parents and other people that matter. They are people whom I love and get love from regardless of what I'm doing or where I am at. They very much matter in my life.

Lots of people tell me that brothers and sisters are not always like this, and so many people have siblings that carry different roles . . . and while I understand and respect those stories, I wanted to give you a shot at what I have.

I set out to make that happen. I thought and reflected and prayed about my options. I talked to my mom and sisters and other people whose hearts I trust. After all of this, I decided to use a known sperm donor to try for another baby. This basically means that I asked a dear friend/good soul to give me this great gift. To be part of making a baby for you and me to build our family. He and I shared and opened and talked about all the ways this might work and what it might look like. Just after your second birthday, I got pregnant. I was thrilled, but also blown away. Someday you can ask for details, but the actual getting pregnant was based on a crazy plan with lots of what-ifs. And that was part of the whole thing—going into it, I said that our lives would work in so many ways. The two of us, a bigger family, maybe something else that I didn't even see at the time? I put my energy and intentions into the world and felt that if this was meant to happen it would, and if not that was okay too. And then I was pregnant . . . I talked with you through all of this, and you seemed to know what it meant. You seemed to know that we had a little being in our company. The first few days, I was still sort of shocked that I actually made it happen and you were making it real for me. You and I went for a walk by the river and out of the blue you stopped your exploring, turned to me, and started talking to the baby. You said hello and we had a serenely calm, at peace, unforgettable moment. We then continued our walk and I was ready to be a mother to you both.

The next week I started bleeding. I was losing the life that had started growing inside of me. I sort of knew what was happening and although I didn't want to believe it, I emotionally began working through things. I knew a lot of my women were out and busy and in the middle of hectic days . . . and I didn't want to freak myself or them out. I called one of my midwife friends. She was over within hours. She was calm and thoughtful, and sat with me. She explained different things that could be happening and immediately reached out to other midwives for advice. As my friends and family came home, I felt safe knowing that you were being taken care of as I got through whatever was happening. I was emotionally hurting in crazy ways but very much felt love and support. Our friends and family and dear midwives got me through this in a healthy way.

As I began to heal physically, you and I again were on a walk. I was pulling you on a wagon through the neighborhood. I knew you felt something big going on, and knew I needed to tell you what had happened. I was at a loss for words, in English or Spanish. While explaining the coming of a baby had been pretty easy, I didn't know how to tell you the baby was no longer. As I started to try and say something, I said that the baby was lost, because miscarriages are commonly explained in that way. But you understood the concept of lost and as soon as I said it, I realized that I needed another approach. (You kind of gave me a look that said: well then, why don't you go find the baby?) As you turned up at me with a confused but caring expression, I went on to tell you that a soul had come to be with us for a short time, but that for reasons I didn't quite understand, the baby had not been here to stay.

This whole experience terrified me, it shook me to the core. Planning a pregnancy, I expected my emotions to be about not getting pregnant. I didn't consider that I would get pregnant and not birth a live baby. All of this made me doubt who I was and the ways I was trying to live. It made me wonder if my lifestyle was too radical, I started thinking that maybe if I could "settle down," things might work out differently.

I came back to myself by turning to the knowledge I've picked up as a daughter, and as your mother. My mother raised Mireya, Denicia, and me with an almost daily affirmation that we were "macho, chicana women," before we knew all the complexities and contradictions of what that meant, or could mean; we just understood it to be the center to the story of our lives. And we've all taken this affirmation in our own ways to do and be all that we are: bad-asses, basically. For me, it means that life is crazy but we are solid. That we live in compassion and that we do what we believe to be best, wherever we are. and that is how I raise you, doing the best I know how, radical as it may seem. So I will probably never "settle down," because that isn't how I know to live. My intention as a mother is to raise you in love and light.

This is all part of your story, of our story, and the ways you have made my life what it is. You are part of my understanding and appreciation of homebirth midwives; in new life and in loss they are competent, kind and generous people. Our shared birth experience made it so that my life's work will be about improving access to homebirth for low-income women and women of color. You and I are blessed to be living and loving with the fabulous women of

YWU. In all that we experience, we have communities to turn to and be a part of. Whether or not you and I have another child in our lives, we have so many people to build and grow all sorts of relationships with.

So thank you Aymara. Thank you for coming to me. And thank you for all that you already are and all that you decide to be.

Peace homie.
Mama

My Birthday Present

Karen Su

"It takes courage to grow up and become who you really are."
    —E.E. Cummings[1]

"Tomorrow is a mystery, yesterday is history and today is a gift. That is why it is called the present!"
    —Master Wu Guei in *Kung Fu Panda*[2]

My six-year-old son bounces into the kitchen where I am cooking dinner and announces, "We don't have money to buy you a birthday present so we're going to make you something awesome, okay?" I say "Sure!" without turning around from cutting broccoli. This sends him rebounding back upstairs to report to his sister, "She said 'okay'!"

My daughter is taking a bath. My son is keeping her company. Because she's ten years old and her body is changing, they have worked out a new routine for this, which I got to observe just before coming down to cook dinner. My daughter closes the door, undresses, gets in the bath, pulls the shower curtain shut, then tells my son he can enter the bathroom. He sits by the sink on the footstool, which he's just about to outgrow, and they talk about their toys as if the toys are family members or invent games like who can say the randomest thing that will make the other laugh. I'll usually hear my daughter groan, "OK, you can't say purple monkey poop again!" Apparently today they are scheming to make me a birthday present.

I open a package of tortellini and suddenly remember how I'd really like to write something for the *This Bridge Called My Baby*[3] anthology. The deadline is five days away. I've sent the call for sub-

---

1   Thanks to Stacey Horn for sharing this quotation at an anti-bullying event on campus.

2   Thanks to Anna Guevarra for mining KFP for the best secret ingredients to share.

3   The original title of this anthology when the call for submissions went out.

missions around to many friends after a friend sent it to me on Facebook. Someone immediately emailed back that she'd definitely whip up something to submit. It made me feel sheepish for having already thought about giving up since there was hardly any time.

Last week, I had started typing a list of random jottings about parenting experiences into a file I simply named "This Bridge." With a hugely hectic workweek, trying to move my divorce along, and the usual kid commitments, I have not managed to turn any of the jots into paragraphs or even full sentences yet. As I start dropping tortellini into the pot and stir-frying broccoli, I think back on the Asian American women's essays in the original *This Bridge*. A surge of inspiration tries to gain some traction . . . maybe tonight, after the kids are asleep, I can write a letter to them, something like "On the eve of my 49th birthday"—think Nellie Wong's letter to herself and Merle Woo's letter to ma, but it would be an open letter to my kids. Or maybe I should write about how there are so many things that make us angry as Asian Americans and yet we are still so unrecognized as a people even though Mitsuye Yamada wrote "Invisibility is an Unnatural Disaster" so long ago. Has anything changed? What are my parental concerns about how this affects my kids?

The kids come tumbling down the stairs, my daughter dressed like it's summer in a short-sleeved T-shirt and jean skirt. I say nothing—it's March in Chicago and still 35 degrees out. I'm trying to work on that parenting approach where I let my kids be in tune with themselves and let their own instincts guide them. If they are cold, they will put on their snow jackets; don't tell them, "Zip up, it's cold!" (I do this all the time.) Don't second-guess them. Let them be their own people.

As I start a salad for my son (who stopped eating broccoli recently), ripping the lettuce veins off into a separate bowl so he won't get any "crunchies," I try to stave off a familiar feeling of resentful anger over the fact that a good past decade of my life went to supporting my husband's university career—his book to secure tenure—while I gave up the faculty track and most of the intellectual stimulation that I found hard to sustain while holding down the academic wife fort, the parenting fort, the administrative student affairs job fort. I stopped using my academic brain and I struggled to clear time and space for my creative brain. Any energy or emotion I could muster during the lost decade seemed only to be a green rage of not being able to get past the enormous shock of finding out that mothering in the 21st century was still a completely unequal enterprise for most women. Here I am now on the brink of being divorced, finding myself thinking: if I had been better disciplined and just pushed myself more, wouldn't I have something to dust off and be able to send in to lots of calls for submissions? Wouldn't I have something more to show for myself than just being on the cusp of getting my "own" life back at age forty-nine? I struggle with the immensity of feeling wronged by my ex-husband and by society as a whole. I hate that it feels embarrassingly self-pitying; that it's somehow wrong to feel wronged. So I end up blaming myself; that somehow, I just wasn't productive enough.

But, okay. In the past year since starting the divorce process, I have jumpstarted a process of coming more into my own. Last March, I began to draw a coffee cup a day. I decided on coffee cups for no other reason than the fact that I love coffee. It was a way to remind myself to let my own desires and needs guide me for once, at least once a day, everyday. It was a commitment to creating the life I want to live and being the me I want to be—dare to claim I have aspirations of being an artist, a children's book writer, and illustrator, of doing more creative writing generally or maybe even reviving some academic writing if I have something to say. Besides doing a daily coffee cup drawing, I connected with other women artists and writers, art buddies with whom I formed pacts to root for each woman's artistic actualization.

Gaining back the advantage of sheer time and brain space has allowed me to navigate my way out of the sexist marital labyrinth that I never thought I'd get trapped in. Yes, I was one of those women who thought I would have an enlightened and therefore equal marriage, one in which my partner and I would each support the fulfillment of the other's true potential. I still ended up The Wife who waned into a non-person while helping to establish The Husband's life.

My kids, though, they are my north stars. My daughter has asked me point blank a few times in her life, "Why didn't you become an artist? If you had, you'd be famous by now." When I shrugged, "Well, I want to do art, yes, but I don't have to be famous," she would roll her eyes at me with an *okay, just completely miss my point, why don't cha* sigh. "What I mean is you are an awesome artist, so you should be an artist." I finally listened to my daughter. She propelled me to try and be a learn-from-my-example-not-from-my-mistakes kind of parent. I want my kids to have the courage to pursue their dreams no matter when in life. They have given me courage in the ways they have embraced my new endeavors without even a blink of an eye. I am surprised by this ease and their unconditional acceptance. I draw coffee cups; my kids think they're cool. They offer me ideas: draw a coffee cup monster! I read them a story draft. They act it out and recite lines from it. They offer me plot details: make the boy break his arm and wear Mommy Pajammies as a cast!

The divorce process has been good for me. Freed from a structure of shoulds that I used to define myself by, I've begun to follow more what I want. It's been a catalyst for sowing seeds of myself that need to grow: my art and my desire. I have come out to myself not only around art but also around growing attractions to women. I am feeling out how to be me in ways I've never known before, but in ways that feel more right.

"Dinner's ready!" I call to the kids. I start putting food on the table. My daughter offers to pour drinks. When I say, "I think I'll have some wine," both kids clamor for wine glasses too. My daughter fills theirs with water. My son brightly pronounces, "We should clink to Mommy's birthday and the awesomest birthday present we will make for her!" We all clink. My son goes to get *Highlights* magazines for a dinner ritual he invented: joke time. We each take turns sharing either a joke or riddle. Now that he can read, he's really proud of this dinner activity. We all get a good laugh over one of his: "What's a ten-letter word that starts with gas? a-u-t-o-m-o-b-i-l-e!" We get thrown off by one about an ogre that shops at a grossery store because he doesn't know g-r-e is pronounced 'ger' and that gross is a long 'o'.

After dinner, it's my son's turn for a bath. Before going up to run his bath, I ask my daughter, "Wanna do the dinner dishes?" This is the first day my daughter has officially helped to wash dishes. She asked to do them and proudly washed the breakfast and lunch dishes in the afternoon.

"What?! I just did the dishes!" she indignantly retorted. I can't help laughing at her innocent, dismayed response. I also cringe inwardly—even when doing the dishes is still a novelty, the reality of *the work that's never done* immediately hits home to her on day one.

Still eager enough though, she puts on the rubber dishwashing gloves as my son and I go upstairs to do bath time. I make a mental note to add dishwashing to his list of chores too when he turns ten. No son of mine will be dead weight when it comes to housework, damn it.

As I rinse shampoo out of my son's hair, I think about how it has taken divorce to equalize childcare more—well, almost equalize it. My ex-husband picks up from after-school care, gets dinner, keeps track of homework, picks up from dance class every other week when the kids stay with him. But their nails still get clipped more when they are with me; the caregiver schedule is set by me; the play dates, sleepovers, birthday parties, the dance and music recitals, special school performance dates, the parent-teacher conferences, doctor appointments are still all coordinated, remembered, managed by me. Almost all of the emails, phone calls, permission slips, RSVPs, and registrations this requires are all handled by me. Yesterday when he was responsible for getting a gift and dropping my son off to a birthday party, he came over to my house to wrap it. I was out with friends when he called to let me know this. I found the tube of giftwrap he used still in the kitchen when I got home.

When my son and I come down from his bath, my daughter has finished the dishes and is setting out art stuff on the kitchen table. They shoo me out and declare the kitchen off-limits so they can make my present.

I'm happy to settle into the living room with my laptop—maybe I *will* submit something for *This Bridge*, yes, I should at least try. I look for the file to see what I have so far. I overhear my kids exchanging plans in loud whispers, "No no, draw the coffee cup this way." I chuckle as I double click on the file icon. I see I started something on 3/24/11. Only three days ago? It feels like at least two weeks ago. What were all the random jottings I typed up? There's a page and a half of bullet points. At the top, I am surprised to find I had actually written out a paragraph:

> I am an Asian American mom in Illinois in the year 2011. Having just seen the call for This Bridge Called My Baby, I'm sitting down to write. Even though I have only a week until the deadline, I cannot forgo this opportunity to sit and dwell, cull together, conjure up, plumb the depths of my soul around what mothering two Chinese American kids in the

Midwest has been like, how to describe the gap and the con-
tinuities between the work I do in the university around race
and Asian American issues in higher ed and the world of my
kids, their school, teachers, friends . . .

Eek—an attempt to just get anything down on paper. I cringe.

My son runs out with anticipation. He asks me whether they
should give me their present tonight or wait until tomorrow. I
muse, "Well, my birthday is tomorrow, so maybe you should hide
it and I'll open it first thing in the morning." He cocks his head to
the side and thinks about it. "We don't have a tree to put it under."
My daughter yells exasperatedly from the kitchen, "It's not like it's
Christmas!" He runs back in to consult with her.

I return to my file. What comes after the paragraph is just a list
of more or less shorthand codes to jog my own brain to fill in what
it is I have to say or recount about these items.

Chinese! kids say with surprise when we open the door to trick
or treaters

daughter announcing she will become vegetarian, son announcing then he'll become Mexican

daughter telling me about the boy she likes—her twinkling eyes
and mouth—they are fifth graders!

asking my daughter if she's ever had a crush on a girl

son sword-dueling, son gun-shooting with pointed finger. how
to stop him?

Which ones can I develop? What can I write out before Friday?! I
try to quell a sense of panicked longing.

All of a sudden, my kids appear and show me what they have
constructed—
"Ta da!"
I marvel at their creation, moving back to admire their ingenuity as they hold it up too close to my face. It is a paper cylinder "cup,"
with a circle of brown paper "coffee" on top. It is decorated with little

pictures of coffee cups taped all around it. A brown satin ribbon at the top holds a tile with the letter K on it and a brown wooden bead.

My daughter confesses that the gift isn't done yet though. "Can you help? How do I make the handle?"

"I told you! You can do it with a paper handle," her brother says impatiently. My daughter doesn't listen, instead picking a stick from her brother's collection of outside treasures to see if it might work. I suggest punching holes in the cup and using twisty ties to attach the stick. My son says too bad we don't have pipe cleaners. They disappear back into the kitchen again. I'm not sure what solution they will try.

I go back to looking over my jots. I find certain ones that begin resonating with me tonight as I scan the long, random list:

artist—my daughter sees me

i had kids and experienced the traditionals of marriage in all the ways that I thought I would avoid—I "gave up" my career. i hate the response: but at least you have your kids.

daughter spilling all the new paint to see the colors all over the floor! —2 yrs old

post-it one-upping contest:
yesterday my daughter left a post-it note on the kitchen table— scrawled with I AM AWESOME and two hearts underneath— tonite son wrote in his neater first-grade handwriting a line of post-its—I'm awesomer, I'm awesomer then [sic] anything, I'm awesomer then anybody, I'm awesomer then my sister
—i am surprised at their self-confidence—something I definitely had trouble with as a kid

process of coming out, coming into art, and parenting—converging into the process of becoming me

my children make me art, my children make me artistic

They dance back into the living room and wave the finished coffee cup too close to my face again—a paper handle has been attached with tape. I hold the handle and pretend to take a sip. "Now I have

birthday gift
kids made for me
3-27-11

a coffee cup to draw tonight!" They beam. My daughter gestures for me to hand it back over again. She disappears to the kitchen. "What do coffee beans look like?" she yells. I say, "Look at the coffee bean magnets on the bulletin board." After a minute, she skips back to show us how she drew some coffee beans on top. My son peers over at her finishing touches. "They look like squished butt cheeks!" We all laugh.

As my kids giggle on the couch and resist bedtime, I cuddle with them and decide I will write about our night together.

After they go to sleep, I draw their coffee cup. As I write *birthday gift* at the bottom of my drawing, I savor how much there is to celebrate during this time of transformation.

March 27, 2011

Notes: A huge nod of thanks to my art and writing buddies who gave me invaluable input and support as I wrote this essay after drawing my year of coffee cups.

Editor Bios

Alexis Pauline Gumbs was the first person to dig through the archived papers of several radical Black feminist mothers including June Jordan, Audre Lorde, Lucille Clifton, and Toni Cade Bambara while writing her dissertation, "We Can Learn to Mother Ourselves: The Queer Survival of Black Feminism," a 500-page work. Alexis is shocked when she travels the country and organizers, artists, teachers, students, and established academics confess that they have actually downloaded that massive dissertation document or are reading it online and even out loud in groups. Alexis is the instigator of the Eternal Summer of the Black Feminist Mind Educational Movement, which includes local events in Durham, NC, workshops around the United States, a public-access TV show, a series of podcasts, and a broad online audience. Events using Eternal Summer of the Black Feminist Mind materials take place across the United States and the world in queer and feminist organizations including Fahamu in Nairobi, Kenya, Meem in Beruit, Lebanon, and the Shakti Center in Chennai, India. Alexis was named one of *UTNE Reader*'s 50 Visionaries Transforming the World in 2009, a Reproductive Reality Check Shero and a Black Woman Rising nominee in 2010, and was awarded one of the first ever Too Sexy for 501c3 trophies in 2011! Alexis's work as co-creator of the MobileHomecoming experiential archive and documentary project has been featured in *Curve Magazine, Huffington Post, Durham Magazine,* and on NPR. She is also the author of *Spill: Fugitive Scenes,* forthcoming from Duke University Press in 2016. As Alexis grows into caretaking roles with elders and youth in her radical loving community in Durham, she is crafting herself into a mother in every sense of the word that she can imagine.

China Martens is a writer, glamazon, and empty-nest low-income anti-racist white radical single mother. Born in 1966, she had her daughter in 1988, and started her first zine *The Future Generation* in 1990. She is the author of *The Future Generation: The Zine-book for Subculture Parents, Kids, Friends and Others* (Atomic Book Company 2007), and the co-editor of *Don't Leave Your Friends Behind: Concrete Ways to Support Families in Social Justice Movements and Communities* (PM Press, 2012). She was also the submissions editor for *Mamaphiles #4* "Raising Hell" a mama and papa zine anthology (2009). China's short story, "On the Road (with baby)" was published in *Breeder: Real-Life Stories from the New Generation of Mothers* (Seal Press, 2001) and she has had various other essays printed in publications such as *Baltimore Indypendent Reader*, *HipMama*, *WIN Magazine*, and *Revolutionary Motherhood*. She also was a columnist for DIY newsprint publication *Slug and Lettuce* (the column was also called "The Future Generation") from 1994 to 2004 and won Baltimore City Paper "Best" Award for "I was . . . a Student Nurse!"

Work written about her zines appears in Alison Piepmeier's *Girl Zines: Making Media, Doing Feminism* (NYU Press, 2009). Segments of an interview with her also appears in Heather Bowlan's article in *make/shift* magazine about radical childcare collectives in the United States (Fall/Winter 2010) that was reprinted in *Utne Reader* (Jan.–Feb. 2011).

Since 2003, China has co-facilitated numerous workshops to create support for parents and children in activist and radical communities at universities/conferences/healing spaces across the United States and Canada including the Civil Liberties and Public Policy Conference, Allied Media Conference, and bookfairs from Montreal to New Orleans; Minneapolis to Santa Fe; and New York City to San Francisco. Along with Sine Hwang Jensen and Harriet Moon, she was a co-founder of Kidz City, a radical childcare collective in Baltimore (2009–2013) and is connected to the Intergalactic Conspiracy of Childcare Collectives (http://intergalactic-childcare.weebly.com/), a national circle of radical childcare collectives established at the 2010 U.S. Social Forum in Detroit. She is currently enjoying exploring middle-age self-actualization and writing with hardcore dedication. She also enjoys family time with her daughter, who lives in the next neighborhood to her in Baltimore and calls her own mother more than once a week.

Mai'a Williams is a writer and poet and lives in the United States with her daughter, Theresa. She worked in Quito, Ecuador, in 2014 and 2015 as a journalist for teleSUR English, the global Venezuelan revolutionary news agency. In 2013, she lived in Berlin, Germany, and worked as a writer and editor. From 2009 through 2013, she was a community organizer and journalist before, during and after the Egyptian revolution. In January 2009, she spent three days in Israeli detention with her one-year-old daughter, during the bombings on Gaza, and after being freed from Israeli jail, she moved to Cairo and organized outreach programs with Sudanese teenage refugees/gang members. She lived and studied in Chiapas, Mexico, in 2007–2008 for six months and attended the Zapatista Women's Encuentro with her baby daughter. In Minneapolis in 2007, she worked as a doula (birth assistant) for working poor Black American and recent West African refugee young mamas. In the summer of 2006, she was a print and radio broadcast journalist for International Middle East Media Center, during the Israeli-Hezbollah war. In the autumn of 2005, she researched the effects of war on local communities, especially on woman, in the eastern Democratic Republic of Congo. That year, she also worked on staff as the anti-oppression consultant and training director for Christian Peacemaker Teams (CPT). In 2004, she lived in Jerusalem, Hebron, and the village of at-Tuwani in the southern Hebron hills, Palestine, accompanying communities under the threat of Israeli military violence. During 2002–2003, she founded and directed Cosmic Sun Theatre, an experimental community theatre and gallery, in Roanoke, VA. The theater became one of the primary loci for anti-Iraq war organizing in southwest VA. She participated in a delegation to Guatemala and Oaxaca, Mexico, investigating the effects of the Plan Puebla Panama on local indigenous communities in 2001. Her work with Palestinian, Congolese, and Central American indigenous mothers in resistance communities initially inspired her to become a mother and continues to guide her as she practices this life-giving work, called radical mothering.

She is author of two books of poetry, *No God but Ghosts* and *Monsters and Other Silent Creatures*. She is the instigator of the *Outlaw Midwives* movement, zines, and blog which shifts the discourse around birth, life, death and healing by offering a vision of radical empowerment and accountability. In 2008, she published the *Revolutionary Motherhood* anthology zine and the corresponding group blog, a collection of writing and visual art about mothering on the margins, which became the inspiration for *Revolutionary Mothering: Love on the Front Lines*.

Contributor Bios

Claire Barrera is a movement artist, writer, and educator based in Portland, Oregon. She has performed and presented work at a variety of local venues. She co-edits the zine *When Language Runs Dry* to be released as an anthology through Mend My Dress Press in 2016.

Loreen Booker Brown is a Revolutionary Mother and advocate, community activist and professional in the field of developmental disabilities. She is the proud mother of Arielle Julia Brown, folk artist Julius Langston Brown, and U.S. Navy Active Duty Serviceman Tyler Trevor Brown.

Loreen holds a BS from Southern Illinois University–Carbondale in social work, a master of art in organizational management, and is in progress to complete her second master of science in psychology in December 2016. She continues to work hard to achieve positive solutions for individuals and families with disabilities. In 2006, Loreen was recognized for her commitment to seeking the truth by the *Atlanta Journal Constitution*. The Sunshine Award is afforded to community activists who have made positive impacts through the utilization of government records to address issues and concerns. Loreen earned her award for addressing overcrowding issues in her school district that were negatively impacting predominately African American schools in her district.

Cheryl Boyce-Taylor is a poet, educator, and founder of the Calypso Muse Reading Series, and the Glitter Pomegranate Performance Series. She is the recipient of the 2015 Barnes & Noble Writers for Writers Award. The author of three collections of poetry: *Raw Air, Night When Moon Follows*, and *Convincing The Body*. A VONA fellow, she has curated readings and taught poetry at: The Nuyorican Poets Cafe, Bowery Poetry Club, Poets & Writers, and Poets House. Her poetry has been commissioned by Jacobs Pillow, The Joyce Theater and the National Endowment for the Arts for Ronald K. Brown/Evidence, A Dance Company. Cheryl's poems are currently installed in a permanent exhibit at Brown University in Rhode Island titled "LINES OF SIGHT" by artist Diane Samuels. Her poetry has been published in numerous journals and anthologies including: Prairie Schooner, *PLUCK! The Journal of Affrilachian Arts & Culture*, *The Mom Egg Review*, *ALOUD: Voices from the Nuyorican Poets Cafe*, and in *Adrienne: A Journal of Lesbian Writers*. She is a founding editor at *The Wide Shore: A Journal of Women's Poetry*.

Esteli Juarez is a Chicana, lawyer, and a sola mother to four outstanding young men. She owns a small law firm in Albuquerque, New Mexico, where she is a fifth-generation New Mexican. Esteli's law practice centers on family law, with specialization in mixed immigration status families and LGBTQ families. Writing and teaching are her passions but lawyering isn't a bad gig.

Rachel L Broadwater is a freelance writer whose work has been featured in *The Feminist Wire*, *Love Isn't Enough*, and *Cocoa Mamas*. She is currently finishing up her first play, *Fumbling Towards Ecstasy*. She resides in Wilson, North Carolina, with her husband and two girls.

Autumn Brown is a mother, organizer, theologian, artist, and facilitator. She was a founding member of the Rock Dove Collective, a radical community health exchange that was active from 2006 to 2012, a member of the Board of Directors of the Common Fire Foundation, and a co-founder of the North American Healing Justice network. Autumn facilitates organizational and strategic development with community-based and movement organizations, and leads trainings in Consensus Process, Facilitation, and Healing Justice. Autumn is a recipient of the 2009 Next Generation of Leadership Fellowship through the Center for Whole Communities, the 2010 Creative Community Leadership Institute Fellowship through Intermedia Arts, and the 2013 Innovation Award from the Center for Nonprofit Excellence and Social innovation. She lives in the Avon Hills of the great state of Minnesota with her partner, three brilliant children, a large and ridiculous dog, and many birds and other forms of wildlife.

Arielle Julia Brown is a cultural producer, theatre practitioner, and curator. Arielle is interested in how cultural institutions and arts initiatives can inspire social justice through the presentation of work by artists from Africa and the Diaspora. Arielle began her career over ten years ago at 7 Stages Theatre in Atlanta. She is the founder of The Love Balm Project, a workshop series and performance based on the testimonies of women of color who have lost children to systemic violence. The Love Balm Project has been developed at cultural institutions throughout the San Francisco Bay Area and in Atlanta: www.lovebalmformyspiritchild.tumblr.com. Arielle's theatre experience as a deviser, playwright, and producer is rooted in social and civic practice work on both local and international levels. Her international theatre experience includes work and study in Jamaica, Senegal, and East Africa. She has worked closely with Theatre Without Borders and is the former fellowship director for SF Emerging Arts Professionals. In 2014, she served as a Mellon Artistic Leadership Fellow with the Los Angeles Theatre Center's Encuentro Festival. Arielle is currently completing her MA in public humanities as a graduate fellow with the Center for the Study of Slavery and Justice at Brown University. She received her BA from Pomona College.

Micaela Cadena is a chicana New Mexican from a family/chosen family of resilient mujeres. Micaela is raising two funny, kind, knowing, and bright daughters with her best friend/partner. For several years, Micaela was honored to serve as the Policy Director at Young Women United. Micaela has a Masters degree in Community and Regional Planning from the University of New Mexico.

Note on YWU: It has been among my life's greatest honors to serve as the Policy Director at Young Women United. Young Women United (YWU) leads community organizing and policy initiatives by and for young women of color. YWU works to build communities where all people have access to the information education and resources needed to make real decisions about their own bodies and lives. YWU moves work through policy change, community organizing, cultural shift, and strategic communications. YWU is proud to be building educational equity for young parents while pushing back on teen pregnancy prevention, leading Criminal Justice Reform with a gendered analysis, improving access to a full range of birthing options for women and people of color while centering midwifery models of care, improving access to reproductive health including abortion and contraception in New Mexico, and embodying a warrior state of mind: de-stigmatizing mental health alongside LGBTQ youth of color.

In the last several years, Young Women United has become one of the most powerful and impactful change making organizations in New Mexico and across the country. I am proud that the work I've shaped at YWU has also shaped me. In my time at YWU, I have witnessed the resiliency of women and people doing the best they could to care for themselves and their loved ones amid systems that are failing. Most importantly, during my years at YWU I have learned that the greatest opportunity for meaningful change comes from recognizing the expertise that exists in women and families across our state. I am continually inspired by the humility, heart, and deep commitment to justice that shapes this special organization. Thank you each for trusting me to do this work and for all that you do to create a more just and loving world.

Lindsey Campbell is a single mom grad student living in Edmonton, Canada. She has written for *HipMama*, *Mothering Magazine* and Mamaphonic.com, was co-editor of *Synoptique* online—an academic film studies journal. Lindsey also previously served as co-editor with a quarterly column, "Sunny Days," for *Birth Issues* magazine. Her bi-weekly column "My Little Eye" ran in *SEE* magazine in 2008. The *Girl-Mom* play has been produced as a staged reading at several festivals across North America and was subsequently produced as a radio play in 2006.

Vivian Chin lives in Berkeley, CA.

Simone Crawley is a lead software analyst by profession, but can claim being mother of three outstanding sons as her proudest experience. In 1985 Simone graduated from Georgia State University with a BBA (Management). She has since gained working and community experience in several roles with private industry, public education, civil service, and taking on leading community roles including a four-year period of elected service on the DeKalb Board of Education. Simone has always believed in upholding children and community. She has served on the Board of Directors of a local Boys and Girls Club, on the Board of Directors of the Hidden Acres Alliance, as PTSA Legislative Chair for three schools simultaneously, and on the Board of her homeowners' association. She has advocated on behalf of her community for greenspace and quality of life improvements and served as an appointed Neighborhood Planning Unit representative. In 2006, Simone was bestowed the humbling honor of one of Georgia's Outstanding Citizens. Simone has three amazing sons, C Phillip Moon, Jason Manning, and Brandon Manning. She is the proud grandmother of James, Isaiah, and Jaden.

Malkia A. Cyril is the founder and executive director of the Center for Media Justice in Oakland, CA, a national media strategy and action center building a powerful grassroots movement for racial and economic justice through media change; and home of the Media Action Grassroots Network. As a queer, working-class African-Am/Caribbean born and raised in Brooklyn, NY, Malkia's belief in cultural change as a core strategy for social justice is based in her experience as the daughter of a Black Panther mom. "I watched how news coverage helped destroy a movement, and I believe in the power of strategic stories, art, and organizing to help raise it again." Malkia is married to Alana Devich and lives in the SF Bay Area.

Christy NaMee Eriksen an award-winning Korean Adoptee spoken word artist, activist, and educator based in Juneau, AK. Her work is grounded in social justice and community engagement. She is the co-founder and president of the nonprofit, Woosh Kinaadeiyí, a community arts organization that hosts monthly open mics and poetry slams, committed to "diversity, inclusive community, and empowering voice." She has performed at art centers, universities, and theatres, including The Roundhouse in London and Equilibrium's spoken word series in Minneapolis. She has been published in a variety of online and print publications and leads spoken word workshops and residencies for diverse groups. Christy received a 2011 Juneau Arts & Humanities Council Individual Artist Grant, was awarded the 2013 Mayor's Award for Artist of the Year, and is a Rasmuson Foundation Individual Artist Award and 2013 Loft Immersion Fellowship recipient. She has a BA in social justice/racial justice and a certificate in conflict studies from Hamline University.

Lisa Factora-Borchers is a Filipina American writer, poet, and editor of *Dear Sister: Letters from Survivors of Sexual Violence*. Lisa is a long-time contributor and editor with *make/shift* magazine and has also worked as a nonfiction editor with *Literary Mama*. Her work can also be found in online publications such as *Refinery 29*, *In The Fray*, *TruthOut*, *The Feminist Wire*, and *Bitch* magazines. Her work in spirituality, racism, and sexual violence has been cited in academic texts and her poetry was anthologized in *Verses Against Haiyan: A Storm of Filipino Poets*. At the time of this publication, Lisa has birthed a new generation of Pinay feminism with the arrival of her second child, a daughter, Rosario. That essay is forthcoming.

Fabielle Georges is a Haitian-American woman, writer, visual artist, and creator. She holds a bachelor's degree in English from the University of North Florida and is working toward her MFA in creative writing from the University of San Francisco. She is a happily single mother to a precocious toddler. She has had her poetry published in *Mujeres de Maiz*, issue #9. She spends her free time working on her first novel, *Las Hormigas*.

Ariel Gore is the founder and editor of *Hip Mama* and the author of eight books. Her new memoir is *The End of Eve*.

H. Bindy K. Kang joined the wonderful world of motherhood with the birth of her daughter on October 7, 2010. Bindy is currently a PhD candidate with the University of British Columbia's Interdisciplinary Studies graduate program. Her research is focused on evaluating health inequity through a critical race, post/colonial, and feminist lens. Always dancing with the hope of making the world a better place, Bindy is blessed to have a sacred toolbox alongside her critical work. A vibrant network of loved ones keeps her grounded while Bindy's mighty five-year-old reminds her to jump in muddy puddles, paint recklessly, sing loudly, and honor the art of storytelling.

Katie Kaput is a queer radical transsexual single mama writer. Her worked has been published in *Mamaphonic* (Seal Press), *It's a Boy!* (Seal Press), and *The People's Apocalypse* (Lit Star Press).

Irene Lara is a Xicana scholar, writer, teacher, femtor, dreamer, and mami to two amazing daughters, Belén (age twenty in 2016) and Xóchitl (age eight in 2016). She is a tenured professor of women's studies at San Diego State University who loves to teach and write about women of color in the United States, women in las Américas, holistic health and healing, decolonial feminist spiritualities and sexualities, and the art of social justice teaching. She also enjoys "femtoring" her CuranderaScholarActivist students and co-facilitating the spiritual activist/reproductive justice workshop "Panocha Pláticas: Healing Sex and Sexuality in Community." Irene recently co-edited *Fleshing the Spirit: Spirituality and Activism in Chicana, Latina, and Indigenous Women's Lives* and, with her colleagues at SDSU, *Women in Culture: An Intersectional Anthology of Gender and Women's Studies*.

Victoria Law is a mother, photographer, and writer. She is the author of *Resistance Behind Bars: The Struggles of Incarcerated Women*, which won the 2009 PASS (Prevention for a Safer Society) Award, and a co-editor of *Don't Leave Your Friends Behind: Concrete Ways to Support Families in*

Social Justice Movements and Communities. She writes extensively about the intersections of incarceration, gender, and resistance.

Mamas of Color Rising is a collective of working-class and poor mothers of color based in and around Austin, TX. We are interested in organizing ourselves and other women/mamas of color around issues with accessing needs like food, housing, education, and safety, finding out together what our larger ideal community looks like and building it together. We are living in a world where the labor of caretaking is INVISIBLE socially and economically. It's no surprise that most of the world's poor people are mothers and their children. Imagine all the hours of UNWAGED work that is not counted in the Gross Domestic Product (GDP). The GDP would almost double if unwaged domestic work were counted. Working-class mothers, particularly single parents and women of color are caught in low-wage work that barely provides enough income to cover childcare, much less other basic rights. And the welfare "social safety net" scrutinizes and polices poor mothers instead of providing support to all families and recognition that "mothering" is work.

In this country, most interactions with social services and institutions have become a WEB of discrimination and humiliation, a WEB difficult to get out of. Our vision of organizing around motherhood is not a biological one, it's not just about bio moms, or even moms, but about all of those members of a community who share in the often undervalued and invisible work of caretaking and parenting. But it's not just symbolic either, because unfortunately right now its mothers and other women who do the vast majority of the work of taking care of children, elders, and sick folks who cannot take care of themselves. As Mamas of Color Rising, we want to bring out these issues to public conversation and struggle. We see this work as a way to challenge the patriarchal and isolating model of nuclear family units AND as a way of creating social justice for everyone because a society is only as good/strong/just, as how it treats its children and elders. We are currently documenting stories of welfare abuse (from Medicaid, to Subsidized Childcare, to Child Protective Services, to Birthing while Low-Income). Check out our zine, Revolutionary Motherhood, which we wrote in collaboration with Young Women United. With the Revolutionary Mamas of Color National Survey we will continue to gather and document these stories in order to build our local membership base and identify a local organizing campaign.

Norma Angelica Marrun was raised by strong and resilient mujeres. She was born in Durango, Mexico, and immigrated to the United States with her mother. She grew up in Fremont, CA, and attended San Jose State University. She majored in sociology and enrolled in Mexican American Studies courses. It was in these courses where she developed a strong desire to unlearn twelve years of patriarchal white supremacist education. Norma Angelica Marrun is currently a postdoctoral associate in the Program in Education at Duke University. Her research interests focus on Latina/o education, immigration and education, ethnic studies, and critical pedagogy.

Noemi Martinez is a writer, poet-curandera and media myth maker with Mexican and Caribbean roots living in the militarized borderland of deep South Texas, birthplace of Gloria Anzaldúa. She is a radical single mami with punk tendencies. Martinez is a long time zinester, starting her first zine, *Making of a Chicana* in 2000 and *Hermana, Resist* in 2001. She has also written the zines *Aged Noise, Homespun* and *Sofrito Pa' Ti*. She edited the collections *Voces, MAIZ* and was co-editor of the collection *For Colored Girls*. She creates workshops and distros and has been a part of larger collaborative networks to share independent media and activism. She founded and directed two community groups, Café Revolución and Voices Against Violence. She is a co-founder of the Gloria Anzaldúa Legacy Project. Noemi ran a distro for zines and work created by women and people of color (Chicana Stuff then later named C/S Distro). She was involved in the Allied Media Conference, in the years that they first started having childcare on site. She was also a presenter on zines and media and women of color created media. As part of SPEAK! a group of radical women of color composed of mujeres from different states, they created zines, curriculum, and a spoken word CD. Some of her poems can be found in *¡Ban This! The BSP Anthology of Xican@ Literature* and essays in the following collections: *Don't Leave Your Friends Behind: Concrete Ways to Support Families in Social Justice Movements, Communities, Labor Pains and Birth Stories: Essays on Pregnancy, Childbirth, and Becoming a Parent*, and *Just Like a Girl: A Manifesta!* Recently her poems and photos have been published in *make/shift, Hip Mama, Xicana Chronicles, Pentimento: Journal of All Things Disability, The Perch* and **82 Review*. She has an undergraduate degree from the University of Texas–El Paso and a master's degree in writing and history.

Jonathan River Martinez-Hernandez is an aspiring teen photographer from South Texas.

Lola Mondragón is a Chickasaw Chicana veteran. She is a student of indigenous healing, militarism, and WOC scholarship both in and outside the classroom. She is currently at UC Santa Barbara finishing her studies toward her PhD. Lola's most important identities/bio is of being the mother of two military children and the grandmother of Lolito.

Selentia Quintessa Moore is a theatrical director, teacher, playwright, choreographer, motivational speaker, and visionary who grew up in Washington, DC. Mrs. Moore graduated, with honors, in Theater Arts from Brandeis University. In 1991, she married her friend and soul mate, educator and musician Anthony J. Moore. In 2000, they moved to Atlanta and in 2003 they co-founded the Moore Arts Movement Inc., a theater company that professionally trains youth and adults in all genres of the performing arts including, acting, dance, instrumental, and vocal music. Using character development tools, largely based on Christian principles, they are on a mission to teach the community and the world what it takes to survive in these desperate days of this world's darkness Mrs. Moore is known for her inspiring writing skills, directorial skills, and her innate ability to bring out the very best of everyone she teaches. The youth of the community are her children, and her mission to support promising futures. Mrs. Moore has won and was honored to receive several national, regional, and local awards and commendations for her service in the performing arts as a teacher and leader. Her highest honor is being a wife and a mother of five beautiful, intelligent, energetic, gifted, and talented Moore children: Fadhal Anthony, Birane Redeem, Josca Selentia, Rhema Quintessa, and Josiah Deacon.

Terri Nilliasca grew up in Richmond, VA, as a child of a Filipina immigrant and an Anglo-American father. Race, racism, displacement, and loss of culture had a profound, radicalizing effect on her and she began organizing around issues of race and gender while a college student. After graduation, she organized welfare recipients to resist Clinton's attacks on government entitlements. She then spent nearly a decade as a labor organizer at UNITE (Union of Needletrades, Industrial and Textile Employees). She organized low wage workers employed in textile mills, warehouses, and industrial laundries throughout the South. Terri also spent five months in the Philippines with the progressive labor federation, Kilusang Mayo Uno (May 1st movement). While in the Philippines, she saw first hand the devastating effects of the global economy and the U.S. War on Terror. She is now the proud and exhausted mother of ten-year-old twins and a graduate of CUNY School of Law in Queens, NY. She has been very active in several grassroots Filipino/a groups, including Damayan, a migrant workers assoc., and Gabriela Network, a transnational, multi-racial, militant feminist organization. Her publications include "Some Women's Work: Domestic Work, Class, Race, Heteropatriarchy, and the Limits of Law Reform," *Michigan Journal of Race & Law* 16, no. 2 (Spring 2011). She writes in her own blog: Brooklynbarangay, and as a contributor at LawattheMargins.com

Cynthia Dewi Oka is a Chinese Indonesian poet, community organizer, and former teen mom. A 2015 Pushcart Prize nominee, her poetry and essays have appeared in *The Wide Shore, As/Us Journal, Black Renaissance Noire, Kweli Journal, Obsidian, Apogee, Dismantle: the VONA Anthology, Briarpatch Magazine*, and other publications. The second edition of her book of poems, *Nomad of Salt and Hard Water*, is forthcoming from Thread Makes Blanket. She currently works at Grassroots Global Justice Alliance and resides in New Jersey.

alba onofrio Radical Queer Brown Nonmonogamous English-Teaching Appalachian Mystic Mother Activist Missionary. Old-School Femme, Lover of Gender Nonconformists, including the inspiration for this poem, "Adelani."

Panquetzani is an Indigenous wife and mother, musician, student midwife, doula, and community educator. She was born in Echo Park (Los Angeles) and has been living in Compton, CA, for the past few years as a result of gentrification. In early 2009, she helped found Ticicalli Yahualli, a female healers' collective dedicating to improving the health of families and community from preconception and beyond.

Sandy Purkett is a retired federal investigator for the Federal Department of Education–Office for Civil Rights and has dedicated her life to helping students achieve academic excellence. She received her bachelor of science degree in business education from Elizabeth City State University in North Carolina. Sandy is the Founder and Program Coordinator for an extra-curricular activity known as the PILOT (Preparing Innovative Leaders Of Tomorrow) Program. This program was designed to empower youth to become marketable citizens, promote leaders while developing skills to ensure students are marketable and adequately prepare themselves for post-secondary education study or vocational fields of study. The PILOT has been operative since 1997, serving students throughout DeKalb County and Metro Atlanta communities. Sandy has established the William E. Purkett II Memorial Scholarship in memory of her son Billy, a 1999 graduate of Redan High School, who was killed in an automobile accident in August 2000. The scholarship fund was developed to ensure that her son's legacy "Marches On." Annually, the seniors in the program graduate with Leadership Collars showing they excelled in Leadership and Legislation. Approximately twelve to twenty seniors graduate from the program earning over $2 million in scholarships and awards, collectively.

Layne Russell is a writer, a student, and a mother of three. She has volunteered and helped organize for peace events, churches, as a community moderator at HipMama.com, and at homeschool coops as well as at schools when her kids have attended them. Her work has appeared in several Mama calendars, *Rag*, and student magazines. In her free time, she has held a number of crap jobs and washed a lot of dishes. She currently lives in a tiny house in Denton, TX, with an unseemly number of people, books, and pets.

Fabiola Sandoval lives, works, and plays in Los Angeles with her daughter Amaya and three pets. Since this essay was written they have moved from Lincoln Heights to another neighborhood in Northeast LA. She's originally from South LA and mostly understands that home is in communion and connection. Amaya is now eleven and continues to dance, sing and no longer likes long dresses. A poet, she has an essay published in *Don't Leave Your Friends Behind*, and has been a regular contributor for *make/shift* magazine. She blogged at fabmexicana.com (her own site) actively from 2004 to 2013. Being a part of the communities: Radical Women of Color blogosphere, and SPEAK! Radical Women of Color Media Collective was instrumental in shaping her writing life.

Gabriela Sandoval is a queer, Chicana, choice mom. She works as a researcher examining the role of wealth in family well-being. She used to be a professor of sociology at the University of California, Santa Cruz. She is becoming something altogether new, thanks to the positive influence of her daughter Solandra.

Sheila Spivey is the founder and director of Second Wind Productions. Sheila has performed in a variety of stage plays including *Haley: The Life of Mahalia Jackson, For Colored Girls, You're Going to Make It, Final Witness, Grandma Mistletoe, Our Time Has Come*, and *In the Church*. She's a ten-year veteran as Big Mama in the Urban *Nutcracker* with Ballethnic Dance Company. Sheila received her education from Alabama A&M University and her speaking/acting abilities from God. Her son graduated from Kell High in Marietta, GA, in May 2011. She identifies as a "MOM": Maniac on a Mission to guide a boy seed to manhood.

Karen Su is a clinical assistant professor in Asian American Studies at the University of Illinois at Chicago (UIC), where she directs the Asian American and Native American Pacific Islander Serving Institutions (AANAPISI) Initiative. She has served as the founding director of two student centers: the Asian American Resource and Cultural Center at UIC and the Pan-Asian American Community House at the University of Pennsylvania. She lives in Oak Park, IL, with her two children who are now fifteen and eleven, where she helped establish a parents' organization called Families and Friends of Asian American Students (FAASt). She is working on a series of children's books that share the life stories of everyday Asian American girls and women.

Sumayyah Talibah: Wife. Poet. Mother. Dreamer. Teacher. These are a few words to describe Sumayyah Talibah. In her free time, she reads large stacks of books and dreams impossible dreams. She currently lives in Michigan with her husband and children. Her work can be found on the web at http://sumayyahsaidso.com.

tk karakashian tunchez: Artist, organizer, single m/other, multi-media maker, truth-teller, personal and organizational capacity builder, and transformative justice worker.

Tara Villalba is a queer Filipina ecofeminist mama. She practices growing healthy soil, life-sustaining movements, healing relationships, and learning our stories. She exercises cooperative muscles so we can build another economy that heals the planet and respects every worker's dignity. With the support of biological and chosen family, she is raising four young people, learning with each other that our love is so much bigger than anything that separates us. If you want to build together, you can reach her at katunggan@icloud.com.

Acknowledgments

China:
With gratitude to my co-editors for their trust and love, to all the contributors without whom there would be no book; to the stories yet unwritten or written but not yet published; and to the writing yet to do. And to my chess friend Andrew Manuel Bresko.

I would like to thank, in no particular order and a non-inclusive list of Baltimore greats: Billie Holiday, Harriet Tubman, Great Blacks In Wax Museum, Everyone's Place African Cultural Center, Black Classics Press, Marshall "Eddie" Conway, Poetry for the People Baltimore, Olu Butterfly, HABESHA, Park Heights Community Health Alliance, Marissa Alexander Freedom School, Orita's Cross Freedom School, Baltimore United for Change, Angela B., Baltimore Bloc, and the unstoppable Tawanda Jones and the family of Tyrone West who continues to seek justice every single Wednesday since her brother was killed by police in a traffic stop on July 18, 2013, for their family and all families affected by police violence.

Lex:
Unforgivable debt to my co-editors, co-contributors, the folks at PM Press, and everyone who supported this book with feedback and an endorsement. Special thanks to Loretta Ross for her moving preface.

Gratitude to my mothers: Catherine, Augusta, Edith, Lydia, Georgianna, Rebecca, Eugenia, Joyce and Pauline McKenzie, the revolutionary.

Affirmation to everyone in my motherful community in Durham, North Carolina, especially Afiya Carter, Courtney Ried-Eaton, Dannette Sharpley, Emily Chavez, Kai Lumumba Barrow, Kifu Faruq, Michelle Gonzalez-Green, Michelle Lanier, Nadeen, Bir, Nia Wilson, Osunfunke Omisade Burney-Scott, Rachael Derello, Serena Sebring, Shorlette Ammons, and Zelda Lockhart. Sweetness to all my sister-comrades online, especially the SPEAK familia. Joy eternal to my sisters Ariana Good, Kyla Day-Fletcher, and Faye Thompson, and all revolutionary mothers on the move and in the making. And reciprocal bliss to Sangodare/Julia Roxanne Wallace who brings out the revolutionary mother in me.

Mai'a:

Muchas gracias a mi madre, who has become even more inspiring and radical the older she gets.

To my daughter, Theresa, who teaches me every day what it means to be a mother.

To Essie Mae Lowery, who taught me that I was enough just the way I was.

To all of the people who have sheltered my daughter and I against the storm, who babysat Theresa, who made us laugh in the hardest moments, who danced with us, colored with us, believed in us, and made sure that we were okay.

FRIENDS OF

These are indisputably momentous times—the financial system is melting down globally and the Empire is stumbling. Now more than ever there is a vital need for radical ideas.

In the eight years since its founding—and on a mere shoestring—PM Press has risen to the formidable challenge of publishing and distributing knowledge and entertainment for the struggles ahead. With hundreds of releases to date, we have published an impressive and stimulating array of literature, art, music, politics, and culture. Using every available medium, we've succeeded in connecting those hungry for ideas and information to those putting them into practice.

Friends of PM allows you to directly help impact, amplify, and revitalize the discourse and actions of radical writers, filmmakers, and artists. It provides us with a stable foundation from which we can build upon our early successes and provides a much-needed subsidy for the materials that can't necessarily pay their own way. You can help make that happen—and receive every new title automatically delivered to your door once a month—by joining as a Friend of PM Press. And, we'll throw in a free T-shirt when you sign up.

Here are your options:
- $30 a month: Get all books and pamphlets plus 50% discount on all webstore purchases
- $40 a month: Get all PM Press releases (including CDs and DVDs) plus 50% discount on all webstore purchases
- $100 a month: Superstar—Everything plus PM merchandise, free downloads, and 50% discount on all webstore purchases

For those who can't afford $30 or more a month, we're introducing Sustainer Rates at $15, $10, and $5. Sustainers get a free PM Press T-shirt and a 50% discount on all purchases from our website.

Your Visa or Mastercard will be billed once a month, until you tell us to stop. Or until our efforts succeed in bringing the revolution around. Or the financial meltdown of Capital makes plastic redundant. Whichever comes first.

About PM Press

PM Press was founded at the end of 2007 by a small collection of folks with decades of publishing, media, and organizing experience. PM Press co-conspirators have published and distributed hundreds of books, pamphlets, CDs, and DVDs. Members of PM have founded enduring book fairs, spearheaded victorious tenant organizing campaigns, and worked closely with bookstores, academic conferences, and even rock bands to deliver political and challenging ideas to all walks of life. We're old enough to know what we're doing and young enough to know what's at stake.

Contact us for direct ordering and questions about all PM Press releases, as well as manuscript submissions, review copy requests, foreign rights sales, author interviews, to book an author for an event, and to have PM Press attend your bookfair:

PM Press • PO Box 23912 • Oakland, CA 94623
510-658-3906 • info@pmpress.org
Buy books and stay on top of what we are doing at:
www.pmpress.org

About Between the Lines

Founded in 1977, Between the Lines publishes books that support social change and justice. Our goal is not private gain, nor are we owned by a faceless conglomerate. We are cooperatively run by our employees and a small band of volunteers who share a tenacious belief in books, authors, and ideas that break new ground.

Between the Lines books present new ideas and challenge readers to rethink the world around them. Our authors offer analysis of historical events and contemporary issues not often found in the mainstream. We specialize in informative, non-fiction books on politics and public policy, social issues, history, international development, gender and sexuality, critical race issues, culture, adult and popular education, labour and work, environment, technology, and media.

"Who is your leader?"

We create high-quality books that promote equitable social change, and we reflect our mission in the way our organization is structured. BTl has no bosses, no owners. It's the product of what some would likely describe as "sixties idealism"—what we call political principles. Our small office staff and Editorial Committee make decisions—from what to publish to how to run the place—by consensus. Our Editorial Committee includes a number of original and long-time members, as well as several younger academics and community activists eager to carry on the publishing work started by the generation before them.

www.btlbooks.com

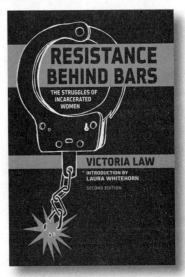

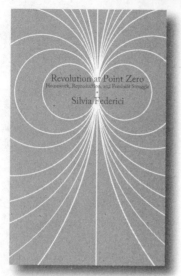
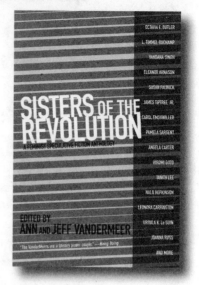
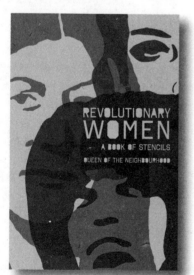